B
Vand   Vanderbilt, Gloria

Once upon a time

C—1

Once Upon a Time

Once Upon a Time

A True Story

Gloria Vanderbilt

Alfred A. Knopf

NEW YORK 1985

THIS IS A BORZOI BOOK
PUBLISHED BY ALFRED A. KNOPF, INC.

Copyright © 1985 by Gloria Vanderbilt
All rights reserved under International and Pan-American Copyright Conventions.
Published in the United States by Alfred A. Knopf, Inc., New York,
and simultaneously in Canada by Random House of Canada Limited, Toronto.
Distributed by Random House, Inc., New York.

Owing to limitations of space, acknowledgements for permission to reprint
previously published material appear on page 307.

Library of Congress Cataloging in Publication Data
Vanderbilt, Gloria, 1924–
Once upon a time.
1. Vanderbilt, Gloria, 1924–
2. Artists—United States—Biography.   I. Title.
N6537.V33A2   1985   700'.92'4 [B]   84-48667
ISBN 0-394-54112-X

Manufactured in the United States of America
First Edition

To
Wyatt Emory Cooper
Forever
and
to
my children,
Carter and Anderson,
Stan and Chris,
and
to
the memory of my Mother
Always

This photograph came to me after the death of Cousin William H. Vanderbilt from his daughter, Anne Hartwell. I had never seen it before. Something about the photograph made me start to write; something about it obsessed me so that I couldn't stop. I wrote on and on, every day, all day, until I came to the end of this part of the story.

Thank you, dearest Anne, for sending me the signal—a signal to write the book I had been writing silently within myself from the beginning.

My Family

In the beginning a child believes that all other children are in the same world that she or he inhabits. That is how a poor child defines all others, and that is how a rich child defines all others. Once upon a time it never occurred to me that my situation was in any way singular or different from that of every other child in the world. To me, family was my Grandmother Morgan, known to me as Naney, and my nurse, known to me as Dodo. No father anywhere reachable, and Mother who was always coming in and then going out — mostly going out. But this did not seem unusual to me, and surrounded by love from Naney and Dodo, I was happy. It was only later . . .

Newport, September 1925

Once upon a time long ago I lay in my crib at Sandy Point Farm while my father lay in the next room dying.

This is what I believe happened—what over and over again I've dreamed happened. The footsteps running in the hallways, the doors opening and closing, the voices signaling to each other come to me at first, before I am really awake, as sounds of jubilation. Seconds later I know that it is night and that something terrible is happening. And that I can stop it from happening if only I can get out of my crib and get to where my father is. Fists tight together, I lie on my back in the darkness unable to do anything at all to help him. The door to my room opens. Noise has stopped. Sharp against the light from the hall is the shadow of my nurse, Dodo, and with her my Grandmother Vanderbilt. They draw closer together as they stand whispering to each other in the silence. Screaming, I pull myself up against the bars of the crib, still believing that if I can get to my father I can save him. Dodo picks me up, rocking me in her arms, while Grandma pats me. But I will not stop screaming. And they do not take me to him. I choke on and on, unable to tell them anything at all . . .

This *must* be what happened, or why would the dream be with me still?

My mother was nineteen years old and in New York City the night my father died. She was at the theatre with Mr. March, described to me later as a friend of the family. I met him a few times. He was giant tall and, yes, he was friendly. My mother also later described her trip from Newport to New York the day before my father died. She had looked out through the train window, remarking that the leaves had been touched by autumn early this year. She said this again three times in the next few hours, until her traveling companion suggested she stop repeating herself. It was then my mother remembered that a fortune teller had predicted this banal, repetitive conversation about autumn leaves as an omen of something about to happen—something that would change her life. I used to wonder what play my mother and Mr. March saw while my father was dying.

According to Norton, my father's devoted valet, my mother, rushing home to Sandy Point Farm, missed my father's death by minutes.

Nurse Dodo took me away. Away from Sandy Point Farm. Away from my father. From death—away. To the Breakers, where my Grandmother Vanderbilt lived. Everyone thought it was for the best until the funeral was over. Then more permanent plans would be made.

Paris, March 1926

Soon after my father died, my mother moved with me to Paris, to a house on avenue Charles Floquet. I still slept in a crib. The shutters on my window made shadows on the ceiling at night when cars passed on the street below. Because of my fear of the dark, Dodo would leave a light on in the bathroom adjoining my room and would sit there until I had surely gone to sleep.

After I was put into the crib, my Grandmother Morgan—Naney—would disappear to another floor, for it was time to draw my mother's bath, which she always did while Maid Marie, dim-faced and silent, descended from her domain on the top floor, bearing the clothes selected for the evening and spreading them out ritually on the chaise longue, waiting for my mother to finish bathing. Marie made all of my mother's dressing gowns, sewing them from velvet or charmeuse, each with the same flowing sleeves, each trimmed in soft grey or white fur. Naney would stand holding a robe, chatting to my mother through the half-opened door as she splashed around in the oil-scented tub, sponging herself. Soon my mother would emerge with arms outstretched for Naney to help her slip into a robe and tie the sash around her waist. Then Naney helped her into pom-pommed mules made especially to go with whatever shade of robe she was wearing. Now she was ready to sit before her dressing table to begin the serious business of bringing face and hair together for the hours ahead.

If I could have looked across this altar of mystery into the mirror at her scrubbed face, it would have been like looking into the face of a stranger.

Spread before her were bottles in shapes of crystal flowers, pomade jars fine as the shells of eggs, a china bluebird fitting the palm with cool surprise, My Sin—the perfume in the black bottle, on it a woman and child, hooded and golden, dancing—or were they tugging at each other? And under them the word Lanvin . . . why did it frighten me?

She would tilt her head back and with an eyedropper squeeze a few drops delicately into each eye . . . blinking. Belladonna, to make her eyes look even bigger. Marie would now advance with tongs heated, tested in advance, ready to stand behind my mother's chair, ready to brush her hair into skeins of silk, tenderly marcelling it into miraculous ridges and valleys before gathering it into the loose chignon at the nape of her neck.

When my mother had finished dressing, Naney would return to me. Or rather to changing places with Dodo in the bathroom off my room. Dodo would move from the lid of the toilet to sit on the bathtub's edge, relinquishing her place to Naney. Still awake, aware of their movements, I lay silent as they whispered on into the night, not knowing what it was they said or what it was I was afraid of. The moving shadows on the ceiling? Naney's sudden, mysterious return, Dodo Elephant silent as Naney Napoleon took charge . . . Was that it? Or was it . . . Lanvin on the black bottle?

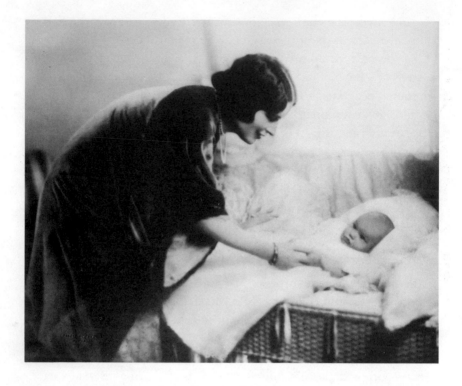

Or the person I was supposed to call Mummy but who remained unidentified . . . was that what it was?

My mother—her face softer than any flower, hair gentle dark and waved as I touched it, the petal of her skin pulling at me with its beauty. How I longed to merge into her, to disappear into her so that no longer would I be separated from her or separate from her. No longer would I exist . . . for to know the mystery of her would be to know the mystery of myself. It was all I hoped for.

A lot of other people lived with us at avenue Charles Floquet, but when Naney Morgan entered a room, space filled with chatter, constant, energetic, swift, and indefatigable. Bronzed hair piled high, lacquered into coquettish swirls above a face of finest, fairest, whitest, rice-powdered skin. Eyebrows plucked away and in their place black rainbows penciled in an arch over eyes of passion, tempering the large nose inherited from her father. Mahogany lipstick, matching nails like castanets—they clicked on windowsills as thin lips hummed Offenbach's "Barcarolle" . . . Time is fly-eeing, Love is dy-eeing, Youth can-not be bought. . . . Diminutive in stature like the adored one, Napoleon, Naney plotted her campaigns with a subtlety and zeal that would have impressed even him.

Outwardly impulsive, she created atmospheres of high drama, unstable, fraught with innuendo, camouflaging the real strategy . . . her plans were long-range, and she had the talent to make each move without impatience. If only I had been born a man! she often said. That she was the daughter of Civil War General Judson Kilpatrick did not go unheralded. Dodo called her the Little Countess and said that she was capable of blowing up subways if things did not go according to her plan. That she had a plan, and that I not only was included in the plan but, in fact, was the heart of the plan, never occurred to me until much, much later.

Butler Fernand, whose name was too much of a tongue twister for Big Dodo Elephant, became Ferno and a great ally. He knew who came and went, and when, reporting back to Naney Morgan so that she would be filled in on anything that might have slipped past her. There was also the silent Marie, who was not so silent when she was with the Little Countess and Big Elephant.

Also with us in the house on avenue Charles Floquet lived Aunt Thelma, known to me as Aunt Toto. Seeing her and my mother together was always a surprise, for they were identical in every way. To look at one and then at the other was like looking into a mirror at Beauty reflected back to Beauty. So identical were the Twins that I couldn't tell which one was my mother— it disturbed me, but I never let anyone know this secret about myself. That was why I loved to go to the top floor and be with Marie while she pressed and sewed my mother's clothes. Given

time, I could learn by heart each and every one of her dresses as they hung on padded hangers in the long closets which lined the room. Then it would be a simple matter to know who was who when my mother and Aunt Toto were together—I could tell by the dress my mother wore. The others who lived there were my Uncle Harry and his friend Angustias, the Marquesa de San

Carlos, but I hardly ever saw either one of them. When I did happen to run into Uncle Harry it was something! It made me feel funny all over, he looked so much like his mother—my Naney Morgan. It was as if Naney had gotten herself dressed up to go to a masquerade party, put on men's clothes, and washed all the makeup off her face. Along with everything else he had Naney Morgan's nose—exactly.

Then on another floor lived my Aunt Consuelo, Naney's oldest daughter. Naney did not get on with her and often remarked how sad it was that Consuelo had inherited this same nose, which fortunately the Twins had been spared.

My mother and Aunt Toto took great delight in admiring each other's hands. The Little Countess admired them too, and everyone else agreed that of all their beautiful features, their hands were probably the most beautiful. Each long, lacquered oval nail was tended by Agnes Horter, who came often to avenue Charles Floquet to manicure and visit—Agnes with her brooding ways, her head, with its neat cap of hair making it look like a little black grape, the sooty eyes sometimes oddly vacant. Naney was not fond of her and often went on and on about how there was no reason to still be so friendly with Agnes just because she had been a friend of the Twins when they had all been schoolgirls together at the Convent of the Sacred Heart in New York. Why did they have to invite her to Paris and include her in all their parties, hoping to help her in her pursuit of a career as a chanteuse, introducing her to Maurice Chevalier and others who might advance her? She stayed on and on, but nothing ever came of it. Naney said it was because Rudolph Valentino, after hearing her sing, had leaned over to Naney and acknowledged that Agnes did have a voice but would never succeed because, as he put it, She Has No Soul.

The Little Countess and Big Elephant thought very little of my mother's friends and never had anything nice to say about any of them. Men especially. There were many men coming to take my mother out for dinner and a cabaret, all of whom seemed to me more or less like Uncle Harry in one way or another. They clicked heels a lot and took Mummy's outstretched hand to kiss, which is what Uncle Harry did when he was there and met one of my mother's women friends. *All* the men did the same to *all* the ladies in Paris, Dodo told me scornfully.

The Doll House

It's fun to make drawings of everybody with my crayons, and I have piles of them—so one thing leads to another and soon I started cutting out my drawings into paper dolls. The two beautiful ones are my Mother—Gloria—that's *my* name too. The other beautiful one is Thelma-Toto. Mother-Gloria and Thelma-Toto are Twin Sisters, so all I had to do was put the drawing of my Mother-Gloria over another piece of paper, cut around it, color, and—presto! There was Thelma-Toto. Then I cut out one with a big big nose. That's Consuelo—she's the Older Sister of Mother-Gloria and Thelma-Toto. Next, I got to work on Harry—he's the Brother of Mother-Gloria, Thelma-Toto, and Consuelo. His nose is big too and he's my Uncle.

Of course the first paper doll I made was of Naney Morgan. It's hard to believe, but Mother-Gloria, Thelma-Toto, Consuelo, and Harry are all Naney Morgan's *children*—even though they're grownups! Naney's my grandmother, but she's more like a mother. My nurse Dodo is more like a mother, too—it all gets very complicated, but with the paper dolls it's easier to sort out. Anyway, for Dodo I made a Big Elephant paper doll instead of a Dodo doll. It's some collection once you see it all together, and I'll make more every time new people come along. I've already added to it by making paper dolls of people who are not here—like my father, who is in Heaven, and someone else called Aunt Gertrude, who is his sister even though she's not in Heaven. She's alive somewhere in a Palace, far away—Naney and Big Elephant say someday I'll get to meet her. Drawing a paper doll of Aunt Gertrude was fun because I had to make her up as I went along, since I don't know what she really looks like. But the best part about all of this is that it's *me* who moves everybody around— putting each one where *I* want him to be. Naney says soon she's going to get me a Doll House, and there'll be doll furniture in every room for me to arrange any way I want. Plans for this go around and around in my head all the time, so when the Doll House finally does arrive I'll be all prepared to move everybody in . . . Mother-Gloria, the Aunts, Harry-Uncle, Naney Morgan, Big Elephant—and most important of all, my father. Then I'll stand outside the Doll House looking in at them—because I'll be the one who's big and they'll be the ones who are tiny. They'll belong to me—all of them—and stay put, right where I want them to be—for ever and ever and ever . . .

Paris

You and I together, Love—
Never mind the weather, Love—

Big Elephant would sing to me as, hand in hand, we took off on jaunts together, leaving the Little Countess behind to hold the fort.

To the Bois to meet Betsy Drake and Peter Salm with their nannies, our *goûter* in a picnic hamper, Pekingese Amber wheezing around us. Betsy said Naney Morgan was a witch, but I pretended I didn't hear her because I still wanted to be Betsy's friend. Big Elephant said I was an Only Child, so, no matter what, she saw to it that we always had a dog of some kind or other. Under trees and sunlight down pathways through the Bois until we came to the Grand Guignol pitched in the shade and surrounded by children, green glimmering, and red, as Judy batted away at Punch. Laughter rolling on grass, Amber grinning as I tried to catch her. This was bliss!

And Dodo, joyous and at ease, the hated French temporarily

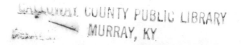

at bay, would be at her best. Suspicious of all foreigners (the fortune hunters, if titled, she called Counts of No Account), she trusted no one—except, of course, Naney, whom she held in highest regard. This would have been confusing to anyone who did not know how connected Big Elephant and the Little Countess were, each to the other; how bonds of fear and hope transcended everything else. For anyone seeing Naney even for the first time could not fail to drop her neatly into the "foreigner" slot. The Little Countess never lost her "foreign Spanish" accent or her "foreign" ways of thinking.

Naney Morgan did not believe in married love, in friendship between women, or that women could ever achieve positions of power except through the men they married. What she did believe in was Power Through Money and that Blood Was Thicker Than Water.

More and more frequently, as in a game of jai alai, the name Prince ricocheted back and forth between the Little Countess and Big Elephant. His Serene Highness Prince Friedel Hohenlohe, nephew of the Queen of Rumania and great-grandson of Queen Victoria. His family were feudal landowners and lived in a turreted castle called Schloss Langenburg in a place Naney said was to be hated and feared—Germany.

Whenever I saw my mother she would be with him, either coming in from somewhere or going out somewhere. The Prince was short, about like Uncle Harry, and must have felt the same way as Uncle Harry about children, since he clammed up whenever I was around. He held a monocle in one eye and carried himself as though a rod had been rammed up his behind. Every time I saw him was scarier than the time before. In the interim I would have been filled in on more details concerning Schloss Langenburg, where he lived when he wasn't staying at avenue Charles Floquet. The castle was as immense as Buckingham Palace, with stone stairs that led nowhere—people, even people who lived there, were always getting lost on them and were sometimes never found. To get to the Schloss you had to cross a moat and drive on and on through a dense forest until you came to another moat with an archway over it with escutcheons of the Hohenlohe arms carved into the stone. But this was only the beginning, for to reach the castle you must drive through two archways under the flag of Germany hanging above, and then on and on for at least an hour until at last you arrived at the door of the castle. The walls of Langenburg were ten feet thick and made of grey stone. Its vast rooms were so enormous they could be heated only by gigantic stoves, with wood carried up the dark stairs by a retinue of dwarfs. Somewhere, kept out of sight far below in the Schloss kitchens, lived other dwarfs whose sole purpose was to taste the food before it touched the lips of any Hohenlohe. Underlings, the Little Countess called them—considered privileged to be chosen for the task of tasting the food first to ensure against poison. Also living in the castle were Friedel's father, Prince Ernst of Hohenlohe-Langenburg, and Friedel's mother. Then there were the two sisters known as Dolly and Baby. There was something odd about the two of them, only Naney never quite told me what. But it hovered about somewhere—as did other unspeakable things about the Prince.

I hardly ever saw Grandpa Morgan, only sometimes when we were visiting one of those places like Biarritz or Monte Carlo. He follows the sun, that's what your Grandpa Morgan does, he follows the sun, Big Elephant would say. He does more than that! Naney Morgan would say and roll her eyes and start to tell Dodo the real reason why he was away all the time—it was because he had done this or that to her. But then all of a sudden she would stop and her eyes would roll around at me, then back again at Dodo, in a most significant way, and she would say in a loud whisper, Not in front of the Little One, not in front of the Little One. . . .

Then one day she got so heated up talking about him that she couldn't stop—she went on and on and put her arms around me. Then she said, Look at your Naney, look at your Naney, Little One, and her eyes rolled up to Heaven. Aie, aie, aie! Listen to me, you listen to your Naney now! And her eyes got all orange as if she were going to kill someone. But I wasn't frightened, because I knew it wasn't me or Big Elephant she wanted to kill, it was Grandpa Morgan and he wasn't here. He was safe somewhere following the sun. Listen now—remember this! And her eyes rolled right into mine and I knew that what she was going to say was something serious and very important. This is what your Naney has had to do, and someday when you're married you'll do it too, ah, yes you will! When your Grandpa Morgan stayed out late with one of those women—she looked over at Big Elephant in a knowing way—oh yes, oh yes—and she nodded her head—I knew what was going on! So listen, listen—someday you'll thank your Naney, oh yes you will, someday when your Naney is in her grave—someday you'll thank her for telling you this, thank her for not letting men make a fool out of you. Because they will, you know, if you let them, oh yes. He'd be out, you understand, your Grandpa would be out with one—she looked over at Big Elephant again—and it would get later and later. But I'd be ready, ah yes! Your little Naney would be ready for him when he got back, ah yes, all ready. There she would be, all dressed in her coat and hat, just as if *she'd* been out too! Your Naney would hide in the bathroom in her coat and hat, waiting for him to walk in. Then, when she'd hear him coming, she'd wait awhile, it didn't have to be too long, then she'd come out all dressed up and laughing just as if *she* were the one who had been out late somewhere having a good time, you understand? Do you, do you, do you? Aie, no—your Naney's no man's fool! You understand, Little One. Do you?

I understood all right. But then I thought about Grandpa, sitting in his chair somewhere in the sun. I kept wishing it weren't true, all those things Naney said about him. He always was nice to me—when I did see him. Maybe I just hadn't been around him enough. Maybe that was why. The more I thought about it, the more it came to me that I really didn't know Grandpa Morgan at all. I just knew he was an old gentleman who walked with a cane and sat on a chair somewhere in the sun.

I run to the door—to the door of my mother's room. It is night. Naney and Dodo are in their beds sleeping. My hair is long and wavy and touches the ground as I reach up and turn the knob. This time the door is not locked and it opens. There on the bed, the long arms and legs of praying mantises battling one with the other. They do not see me as I run to the bed. I do not know what I will do when I reach them; maybe I will kill them, maybe I will jump in the bed with them. I do not know. All I can do is run towards them. . . .

The Caravan

Often we pulled up camp, as it were, setting forth to stay at hotels in Monte Carlo, Deauville, or Biarritz. Later to London and Melton Mowbray. Naney particularly relished these forays with their sudden dramas. Burdened with steamer trunks huge as houses, Ferno would climb the narrow stairs from the basement to my room, while Dodo Elephant lumbered back and forth, to and fro, with froths of tissue paper, emptying drawers and closets. How I wished the room would not be stripped bare when we left. Did it mean that we were never coming back? But maybe it was all right after all—perhaps even better this way.

Even if we did not come back ever to this room with cream-colored walls and shadowed ceilings, perhaps there waited other rooms undreamed of—perhaps even safer. In a Caravan with Big Elephant and the Little Countess—what happiness to travel the earth knowing that no matter how strange the place, we were all together, so it would be home.

A lot of the talk that went back and forth between the walls

of the Caravan was about Money. Money hovered about in one way or another from the beginning. Whatever it meant, it was important and there was a lot of it—not where we were, but somewhere else. In America, to be exact. Extravagantly rash with words, sure that I was still a baby unable to understand, they would go on and on and on about it. About the Little One, as though I would not know the Little One was me. And their voices would lower, circling in and out and around again and again about the Big One . . . my mother, of course. Later, their voices muffled by the half-open door, I strained to hear what they were saying, trying to piece it all together.

Suddenly it was out in the open. Impulsively one day Naney told me that someday I would be very rich. That I would have millions of dollars. So *that* is what they talked about all the time. She told me that once upon a time it had been left to me in trust by my family. Powerful . . . very. Strong and important in

America. Someday I would go across the ocean back to the home where I really belonged and where by rights I should be.

But who were these people I was supposed to belong with, yet who had never been mentioned to me until now?

Dodo and Naney . . . that was Home. And now loss waited across silent oceans. Lost . . . Dodo and Naney . . . forever gone. I could not move or do anything at all. Then into the room came Dodo and I threw myself at her. My force would stop it from happening! Where would Big Elephant be, where would the Little Countess be, when the world grew dark and I was among strangers, living in a place far away? In Dodo's arms while Naney patted me, on and on into the valley I screamed: Don't leave me . . . don't leave me . . . don't leave me. . . . Digging into the soft, sweet mountain of Big Elephant, I sobbed on and on, into valleys deeper and deeper, burrowing so fiercely into her that she never heard.

One Day on the Beach

We are at Monte Carlo. There is a beach, and every day Big Elephant and I go there, and the Little Countess is with us almost every day too. She never goes into the sun because it's fatal to the skin. Never, never go in the sun, darling mine, the Little Countess often says to me. But that's for later, when I grow up; now it's all right, and I fly along on the sand and my toes hardly touch the water. There is a tent on the beach just for us. It is made of red and white stripes, and the Little Countess sits beside it all day long under a parasol, smoking and watching people. It used to be fun but now I'm scared. She has told me I must not go out into the waves with Uncle Harry. He is here too and on the beach almost every day—he and Angustias have their own red and white striped tent a few tents down from ours. Angustias almost never goes into the ocean, but Uncle Harry does, and once or twice he and I happened into it at the same time. And he took me in his arms and bounced me up and down in the waves, and then he took me far out into the water and I knew that if I held on tight to him nothing could happen because it was deep deep where we went and the waves kept coming over us again and again. But he held on tight to me too, and we laughed a lot—his nose is just like Aunt Consuelo's—and then he brought me back and I ran out of the water and Naney was there, standing at the edge of the ocean, and I knew something must have happened for her to be standing there on the hot sand, because the sun came down over everything and it was so bright the sand looked white instead of yellow. She grabbed my hand and pulled me along, and when we got to the tent Big Elephant was there standing, and she had been crying and the skin of her neck and throat was all red like a piece of rare roast beef and I couldn't breathe. Naney took me inside the tent and Big Elephant came in too and pulled the flap door of the tent down and we were all scrunched together there in the heat because the tent wasn't so big after all. There was still some light all around us from outside, and we could touch the red and white stripes of the tent as it closed around us. Listen to me, Little One, listen listen *listen!* You must never never never *never* ever again go in the ocean with Uncle Harry—*never*, Little One, do you understand? Do you? Do you do you do you? Because if you do, something might happen and you might never come back again. Do you know what that means? It means you would never see me again—you would never see Dodo again. *That's* what it means! And I clung to her, and Big Elephant put her arms around me, and we all stood there and I cried and cried. But after a while it got so hot and there were no cries left, and we all moved out back onto the beach, and I looked over at Uncle Harry's tent, but he had disappeared; so had Angustias. Only Aunt Consuelo was there, sitting in a chair. And she looked over at us for a time, but she didn't wave and went back to reading the book she held in her lap, and soon the sun got weak and Big Elephant gathered our things together and I took my pail and shovel and we went on back to the hotel.

Biarritz

One summer my mother found a house in the hills above Biarritz, and staying at the villa were my mother, the Prince, Uncle Harry, friend Angustias, and Aunt Consuelo. After that there were no more rooms left over, so Big Elephant, the Little Countess, and I stayed below at a hotel.

Sometimes the Little Countess, Big Elephant, and I would pile into the huge Hispano-Suiza and be taken up to the villa to see my mother—always in the afternoons, because she liked to sleep late. On the way I kept making wishes to myself over and over again that the others wouldn't be there so that I could see her alone. But they always were. There my mother would be,

stretched out on a chaise longue, the parasol casting a shadow over her face . . . detaching her, somehow removing her from the others who lay stretched out all around her soaking up the sun. For they would all be there—Angustias, Uncle Harry, Aunt Consuelo, Aunt Toto, and, of course, the Prince. When we arrived, some looked up, others just lay there with their eyes closed so as not to disturb the sun-bathing. The Little Countess would say, Come darling mine, we'll sit over here, and I'd go and sit beside her on a bench under the mimosa tree near the pool while Big Elephant would disappear into the villa. Naney Morgan and I would chat away and look out over the treetops, down the hill to the blue blue of the sea until it was time to go into the villa for *goûter*. Then Naney would stay with the grown-ups while I sat with Big Elephant in the cool pantry of the villa having bread and honey with cold milk. Close by, the silver cocktail shaker would go up and down, up and down, as butler Ferno shook the cocktails, the crackle-sound mixing with the laughter drifting to us through the fragrant, dimming light, and soon . . . soon it would be time to go back down the hills, through the pine woods, returning with Naney and Big Elephant to the hotel where the Caravan waited.

Later that same summer the Little Countess, Dodo, and I packed up and moved to another hotel in the mountains near Evian on Lake Leman. Everyone at the villa stayed put. It was while we were at Evian word came that Aunt Toto was going to marry an English viscount and would be called Lady Furness and wear a small but costly coronet. No longer would she be with us when we went back to Paris. And there would be other changes as well. We would no longer be living on avenue Charles Floquet but in another house on rue Alfred Roll. I spent a lot of time wondering what that would be like—not that it really mattered, because Big Elephant and the Little Countess would be there . . . wouldn't they? And that was all I cared about.

But it was not all right. When we moved back to Paris something terrible happened. They were all there waiting for Big Elephant Dodo and me, but most of all they were waiting for Naney—my mother, the Aunts Consuelo and Toto, Uncle Harry, and, yes, even Angustias—all waiting to tell her that there wasn't a place for her in the house on rue Alfred Roll, that she would have to move to a room somewhere else. Not only that, but if she didn't stop her crazed ways, they—yes, all of them—would sign a paper saying she was insane and doctors would put her in the asylum—which was where she belonged anyway, no matter what happened. Aunts Toto and Consuelo, egged on by Uncle Harry, did most of the screaming, while my mother and Angustias stood by without saying anything at all. But when it came to screaming, there was nothing more terrible to hear than the sounds Naney Morgan made as she wrung her hands together and ran around the room hitting her head against the walls like a trapped bird. It was so terrible to see that Dodo Elephant grabbed me and ran out of the room, enfolding me in her big trunk. She rocked me back and forth but all I could do was cry and cry, because now I knew for certain that if this could happen to Naney, it could also happen to Dodo. And that would be the most terrible of all.

Not to an asylum, but to one room in a pension nearby—that's where Naney went. It was a small room. Still, she had managed well enough, fitting her possessions in all around her, even if most of them were piled one on top of the other. Big Elephant was permitted to take me there every morning. We'd go early, because the Little Countess always woke up before dawn. She said she had things to think about and that this was the best time to make plans. But even though she was awake so early, she stayed in bed until late in the day, smoking Chesterfields and drinking cups and cups of *café au lait*. What with all her things around, there was only place for one chair, and I'd sit on the bed drawing pictures of the house we'd all live in someday when I grew up and was able to do what I wanted. In my plans there were only three rooms—one for Naney, one for Big Elephant, and one for me. Dodo would sit on the chair next to us giving the Little Countess the latest news of the goings on at the rue Alfred Roll. I'd catch words here and there, like It's a sin . . . Prince . . . that Agnes woman . . . and, once, Never satisfied, never content, anyone else would have happy to have stayed in America near her only child's family. What child were they talking about? And *who* was never satisfied, never content? Anyway, it had nothing to do with me, and I stopped paying attention. As for content and satisfied—I knew what *that* meant, most definitely indeed, because everything was still the same, wasn't it? Even though Naney didn't live with us any more at the rue Alfred Roll, she *was* close by, and I could see her every morning. Here we all were, in our Caravan, safe as could be, so what else could possibly matter?

England

My mother had a new friend. Her name was Lady Milford Haven, and she had a country house in Maidenhead called Lyndon Manor where she went for weekends. My mother called her Nada, and there was also a Georgie, who the Little Countess said was Prince George of Battenberg. Nada and Prince George were married, and they had two children, David and Tatiana. It sounded like a fairy tale and I couldn't wait to meet them all.

Soon I did, because Big Elephant and I were taken there to visit. Lyndon Manor was enormous. There was even a theatre big as a ballroom, built especially for Prince George's train collection. Each train was an exact tiny replica of a real train—there was a Train Bleu, a Super Chief, and so on, with railroad tracks winding around through tiny villages, past snow-covered mountains and green valleys, past rivers and waterfalls, forever traveling through a vast tiny world. There were also farms with cows grazing and shepherds on hills tending sheep and, here and there, tiny people waving at the trains as they passed by. I made myself small—so small that I went right into the Orient Express, yes I did, and I waved back to the people as I sat looking out from my tiny window as we passed by. It was only a game, of course, but it had endless possibilities.

Meeting Tatiana was kind of a disappointment. She was much older than I was and hefty. The first thing she said to me was Let's see how your face looks if it's on your neck backwards, and she took it in her hands and tried to twist it around as if it were a stopper on a bottle. Stop it, Tatiana, stop it, David shouted, pulling her hands off my neck in the nick of time. But Tatiana only giggled. This David was *not* a disappointment at all. He made me feel weak in the knees. One of his other names was Medina, and I added David Medina to my list of God-Blesses at the end of the prayers every night, not just because he made me feel weak in the knees but because I loved the sound of his name on my lips as I whispered it. Big Elephant kept saying not to pay any attention to Tatiana, she only meant to be friendly. Oh, well.

Prince George wasn't around much, as he spent most of the time in the theatre organizing alternate routes for the trains. They traveled a different schedule each day, and it was hard work, what with planning charts and directing the tiny traffic. Nada hadn't much interest in these pursuits, and she *was* around all the time. Not that I saw that much of her, but Mummy did and it made me happy, because when they were together, the two of them had a party going on all the time. She was very beautiful, Nada, with her masses of maple-sugar hair coiffed into a plump knot on the top of her head, where it was held by jeweled combs. Fabergé, Big Elephant said. Nada had a way of spinning into the room like a top. Other times she'd enter like a dancer, prancing in her shoes with their silver buckles, the chiffon of her scarf trailing, almost catching on the door as she passed. But however it was, light followed her. No wonder my mother adored her. And when they were together, doors might be closed, but it never mattered. I could still hear Nada's voice and the softer answer of my mother's murmuring laughter. Sometimes I would move closer, daring to lean against the door, longing to know the secrets they shared. But I never found out.

As I lay in darkness before I could sleep, I would think about Nada . . . I would think about my mother . . . I would drift into the sunlight of her, into the room where we sat together at a table, lacquering a box made of wood. She liked to do this, brushing coat upon coat of yellow, then pasting cut-out paper fruits and flowers and shellacking over the surface, later giving these boxes to her friends for holding cigarettes on their tables. Once she let me help her. She invited me into her presence, into the sunlight yellow that surrounded her, into the golden yellow of her dress, and together we sat by the window in her room of yellow, close. Sometimes our hands touched.

But then she would go away, down the long corridors of
hotels, down staircases, along avenues in her pale furs, snow-
sprinkled, disappearing into the velvet caverns of waiting cars
and borne away, away, away, away . . . Would I ever see her
again?

Monte Carlo—in gauze yellow, her hair now sprung free,
center-parted, as she walked away towards the beach. Running
past the nasturtiums in patterned gardens outside the Hôtel de

Paris, I leaned down, tearing a flower as I ran . . . the sweet
bitterness as I bit into the stem . . . beach yellow as I looked
for her, toes burning, yellow sand hot, as I tried to catch her,
O shimmering splendor, bird of saffron, my butterfly . . .

Burrough Court, Melton Mowbray

There were always things going on when we stayed at Aunt
Toto's house. Mostly on weekends—during the week my mother
and Aunt Toto were never there, they were in London. But there
was still a lot to do—riding on ponies, watching farmers shear
the sheep, gathering eggs, and so on. My Cousins Sarah and
Caroline Blanford lived nearby, and we saw each other every day.

Everything would be quiet from Monday until Friday, when
the courtyard suddenly filled with cars and out piled Aunt Toto
and Lord Furness along with my mother and their friends. There
was a lot of excitement because one of the cars pulling up at
Burrough Court would always, every weekend, be carrying His
Royal Highness the Prince of Wales. One day he would be the
King of England, so everyone made a big fuss over him. Even
Big Elephant was impressed. As for the Little Countess—she was
ecstatic! The Prince was Aunt Toto's friend and had presented
her with two very yappy cairn terriers called Jazz and Cora. Once
I wandered down the hall into his room, where he sat up very
straight and tiny in a high bed having breakfast on a tray. He
wasn't wearing a crown and he said good morning to me prim
as you please. From Friday to Monday there would be lots of
people laughing all through the house and on the stairs as they
went up and down—it was as if they all belonged to a club with
their own jokes that no one else could understand. They all were
gorgeous! By day, the ladies smiled in their gentle knitted things
and jingled their charm bracelets; the gentlemen were in nubbly
jackets, elbows stitched with patches of leather. At night, changing by magic into long drifting clouds, the ladies would float

Gloria and Prince of Wales & Melton Mowbray

along the corridors down the stairs to the gentlemen waiting in the Great Hall in their black-and-white penguins, for it was here they gathered to have cocktails before going into dinner. Bonfires would be lit in all the fireplaces, and every night of the long weekend a party went on every single minute.

By this time, my Cousin Tony had been born to Aunt Toto. He was a baby and made a great deal of fuss about everything.

His nurse was just awful! She wore a hat all the time and hated
it when Aunt Toto came into the nursery. We had all our meals
there, Big Elephant and I and the Little Countess, only on weekends Naney Morgan played along with the grown-ups and would
be gone for hours. Tony put his fists together a lot—tight.
Holding his breath, he would flay his baby arms up and down
and around like a pinwheel, his face getting redder and redder.
Soon everyone would be really frightened—even Old Witch Nurse.
But he would *not* give in. It was most impressive. Then, just
when you thought he was going to die, his little self would seem
to collapse like a balloon and he'd take a gigantic gulp, another
and another, gulping life back into him. After all this, Old Witch
would get out her broomstick and go to work on him.

I had my own room down the hall from the nursery. It was
there at Burrough Court that Big Elephant lumbered around
waving her trunk very upset about something. After a while she
said Your Naney Morgan wants you to write a letter. Then she
started to cry.

What is it what is it I said.

To her to her, she wants you to write a letter to her.

Yes, yes I said and ran to the desk to make her stop crying
and put paper in front of me and started to write.

DEAR NANEY

Wait, wait Big Elephant said, she's told me exactly what
you must write word for word. And she wrung her hands and
ran into the bathroom and cried so loud I could hear her through
the door even though it was closed.

I banged on the door and screamed Dodo Dodo Dodo.

She came out and her crying had stopped. I went back to the
desk and sat down.

This is what your Naney wants you to write to her. She leaned
over me and said, Under Dear Naney write I miss you.

I MISS YOU, I wrote.

Very good darling, she said. Now under that put My mother
is a rare beast.

Why why why? and I started to cry. So did Big Elephant.

Because, because she said, your Naney says to.

Was my mother going to send Big Elephant away from me? Away, away so that I would never see her again? Is that why Nancy Morgan wanted me to write like that? It was, it was, it was. It must be, it must be. But why did we always have to pretend? Why did I have to keep pretending I did not know when I knew? I knew what they were up to. I might not know what game it was we were playing, the Little Countess, Big Elephant, and I, but I did know the Rules. The Rules were that I was not supposed to know anything—anything at all.

Don't leave me. Don't leave me, Big Elephant. Don't leave me. And I cried and cried as I wrote

MY MOTHER IS A RARE BEASE.

Aunt Gertrude Aunt Gertrude Aunt Gertrude

More and more every day I heard Naney Morgan and Dodo Elephant talking about a place called Good Old New York. It was where we belonged and where soon we would be going. My father's family were all there. Suddenly a lot of names came at me, names I had never heard before. I loved it when Dodo or Naney mentioned my father, but they never said much about him except that he loved horses and had gone to Heaven. Then we would look up at the sky and mull it over. I thought the reason my mother did not speak about him was because it might make her sad. I thought about him a lot and made up stories about him. My favorite was that he had written me a letter, a really long one, and hidden it in some secret place for me to find. Maybe, even, there would be a knock on the door and, standing outside, there would be the postman with a letter, special delivery, addressed to me, from Guess Who.

The name heard most around the Caravan was Aunt Gertrude Aunt Gertrude Aunt Gertrude. Around and around went that name. She was the sister of my father, the one I made the paper doll of, and she lived in New York City in a castle. And was most Important. Soon I would meet her. And soon I started to believe I *had* met her already because they talked about her so much. I could see her standing at the top of a yellow staircase in her castle, which was also yellow, wearing a fluffy-ruffley dress with fluffy pale-yellow hair, just like my paper doll, waving a wand with a gold star at the tip of it while she smiled at me. Big Elephant, the Little Countess, and I would run up the wide stairs, up and up, until we reached her. Close to she'd be even more beautiful (but still not so beautiful as my mother), she would put her arms out to us, beckoning us to follow. . . .

From then on it got blurry. Where was she beckoning us to? Where were we going?

One morning Elephant got a cable from America—her mother was dying. I never believed any of it, because how could Dodo have a mother? *She* was the mother! The Little Countess started wringing her hands and wailing, Aie, aie, aie, don't go, don't go, don't go—it will be an excuse to tell you not to come back! That's what they'll do! Then I knew it was serious. I ran to Elephant and grabbed her legs.

She did not go. And Big Elephant's mother did die. But I still couldn't quite believe any of it.

Old Westbury, 1932

We were on our way. All three of us. On an ocean liner called the *Majestic*. I had a new rabbit fur coat and Naney Morgan gave me an American flag. Soon I would meet my Aunt Gertrude. I kept going over things I wanted to ask her about. What was my father like? Things like that.

We were all on the deck when the boat landed in New York, so I got to wave my American flag at the Statue of Liberty. There was a long grey car waiting for us, waiting to take us to Old

Westbury where Aunt Gertrude lived when she wasn't at her yellow castle in New York.

I kept wishing we would move faster. The chauffeur's name was Freddy. He told us he had worked for the Whitney family all his life, and he looked very old, so it must have been a long time. We were on a highway with lots of other cars until, suddenly, Freddy turned off onto a winding road. Now I knew we were in the country and almost there. We kept passing fences made of wood that was split into narrow shapes and then pieced together side by side. I had never seen fences like this before, and I wondered what sort of gardens and houses they guarded. We're almost there, Freddy said, and around the corner, on the left side of the road, there it was: the entrance that would lead us to Aunt Gertrude.

We drove through, maneuvering the curves, on and on into the forest. There wasn't another car in sight, only trees on either side as Freddy sped the big grey car on and on, with Dodo Elephant and the Little Countess sitting in the back with me between them. Here and there other roads disappeared into the woods, and Freddy would say, that's where Mr. and Mrs. Henry live, or that's the road leading to Mrs. Whitney's stables with meadows around for the horses to frolic in, or that's Mr. C. V. Whitney's driveway, and on the left here, even though we can't see it, is where the carpenter does his work with Mrs. Whitney's farm close by—oh yes, he said proudly, all our own vegetables for the estate are grown on the spot—and this next driveway, that's where Mrs. Whitney's indoor tennis courts are and the indoor swimming pool, and after a while he slowed down and he said, that's Mrs. Miller's driveway, and we moved on past along the winding road going still deeper into the forest. Then Naney Morgan started filling Dodo Elephant in on the details of how and where this information fitted into the map—the map of Old Westbury Capital.

Of course, I already knew that at Old Westbury there were other houses dotted around Mrs. Whitney's where her children and their families lived. Mrs. Henry, Mrs. Miller, and Mr. C. V. were my cousins, and their children were all more or less my age, so we would have lots of fun playing together at Aunt Gertrude's. You might say it was a place separate from any other place. Looking at it on a map, right away you'd spot it—not because of its shape, or its color, but there would be something about it, like a piece from a jigsaw puzzle that did not fit anywhere else, because the piece itself was the puzzle. It was a continent unto itself, with cities named Mr. C. V., Mrs. Miller, Mrs. Henry, and—the Capital of this country—Mrs. Whitney.

Here we are, Freddy said, and we pulled up to the Capital. On either side of the front door stood two animals guarding it, domino dogs, white with black spots, really big, and at first I thought they were real. Then I saw they were just painted statues. Freddy opened the door of the car and helped the Little Countess out. I followed and Big Elephant followed me. While Freddy started taking suitcases out from the back of the car, suddenly the front door opened. There to one side a tall butler stood holding the door open. And coming towards us was another tall, thin person wearing a hat.

It was Aunt Gertrude.

This was not at all the way I thought it was going to be. For one thing, she was wearing pants, and with them high-heeled shoes. Then there was that hat. It just was not at all the way I thought it would be. But nothing ever is. Big Elephant was right behind me and I leaned up against her as if she was a tree. What I really wanted to do was run far away, run back to some place I knew. It didn't matter if it was a hotel or Naney's room in the pension, just as long as it was a place where we had all been together.

Dodo Tree moved forward, taking me along with her. Naney Morgan chirped around on one leg or the other, saying Gertrude this and Gertrude that. All I could do was stare up at Gertrude's hat. I had never seen anything quite like it. Maybe it was swell.

It gave me a whole new idea about things. I mean, until now I had never seen such a hat on anyone—on any woman, that is—or the combination of pants *and* high-heeled shoes. But there she was. Lips of cranberry, hair even more russet than the Little Countess's, long, tapered nails garnet, the jeweled fingers, ropes of white beads—pearls? What more could anyone want?

Mummy Anne and Cousin Bill

We were going to visit, Big Elephant and I. We were going for a whole summer to visit Cousin William H. Vanderbilt. To Newport! I couldn't believe it when they said that was where Cousin Bill lived. It was called Oakland Farm and was right across the road from Sandy Point Farm. Anne Colby Vanderbilt was his wife, the Little Countess said, and they had twin daughters called Anne and Elsie. And there was also another daughter, Emily, called Paddy by everyone, who was about my age. Her mother's name was Emily Davies Vanderbilt and she had divorced Cousin Bill.

There were giant oak trees all along the driveway on each side before you got to Oakland Farm. They were all in a row, each one exactly the same size and as tall as the other. It was amazing! But everything at Oakland Farm was. I had never, ever, seen anyone like Cousin Anne and Cousin Bill. Or like twins Anne and Elsie. Or the way they lived in that house full of squashy flower-covered chairs and sofas with dogs running in and out all the time. The dogs had people names instead of dog names; one was a Saint Bernard, big as a lion, called Tommy, and then there was the cocker spaniel, Peter, with long, tangled hair flopping around as he raced across the lawn after rabbits, and a Newfoundland, Jimmy, and a scottie named Paul. It was the first time I had ever been around a man and a woman who lived together like this. They were happy all the time. And then

there was Paddy with the long ringlets of a doll and the bows of fat silk she and the twins wore at the side of their hair for dress-up. Paddy called Cousin Anne "Mummy Anne," and the first thing Cousin Anne said to me when I met her was, Now, darling, you must call me Mummy Anne too. Yes, those were her exact words!

Cousin Bill was tall and spectacular standing there beside Mummy Anne. It was like something you read about in a book—a book with pictures. He was State Senator of Rhode Island and everyone said he would soon be running for Governor. Mummy Anne was the prettiest lady I had ever seen, but not at all in the mysterious way of my mother. Her black hair surrounded her smiling face in wavy ridges and she wore short snappy skirts belted over checked blouses—shirtwaists, Big Elephant called them. But then there were occasions when she went barefoot and her painted toenails ran over the sand and Cousin Bill would run after her and take her hand and together they would run to the water's edge and soon all you could see were two heads bobbing way out in the ocean. And here I was, part of it all, just as though I had never lived in any other place in the world. Here I was with twin Anne, who had Mummy Anne's black-cherry hair, and twin Elsie with the pale gingery hair of their Grandmother Elsie, whom they called Mamacita. The twins were around a lot, but more in the background, because they were smaller than Paddy and me. It was hard to believe they were twins, but Big Elephant said that was because they were not Identical, like my mother and Aunt Toto.

Almost every day we had lunch with Mummy Anne and Cousin Bill on the flagstone terrace in back of the house, sitting at a glass-top table, eating one grown-up thing or another—sometimes cold poached salmon, or soufflés for dessert made of blackberries and honey. During lunch Mummy Anne talked right to me and really listened to things I said. Then after lunch there would be rides in the Sicilian cart that had orange and blue posies painted on it. It had been found in Italy and shipped to Oakland Farm from far across the sea. And to pull it there was a real donkey, also Sicilian, and the harness was Sicilian too, and with more posies of green and yellow, so everything about the cart was Sicilian and playful as could be. But then everything at Oakland Farm seemed too good to be true. Every day it just got better and better.

The Breakers

We are to go, Paddy, twins Anne and Elsie, and I, to have tea with Grandmother Vanderbilt. But we cannot stay too long as it may tire her. Twins Anne and Elsie wear the same dresses, with blobs of roseate flowers all over and bibs of smocking at the top. The bows of fat silk in their curls are pinky color too. Paddy's dress and my dress also have smocking, only our dresses are not exactly alike. Paddy's ringlets have all been cut off and now she has bangs like mine, so there's no place on our heads for bows, but we look our best anyway.

We drive along past the so tall oak trees, waving good-bye good-bye to Oakland Farm—away away we go singing Merrily merrily all the way. Big Elephant and Paddy's Dumpling Nanny, Deedee, sit squeezed in the back singing along too. After a while we reach gates which are enormous. A giant wearing a tall hat chooses a key from a long chain and opens the gates just for us. We drive through, right up to the doors of the Castle, and by magic they open for us. Twin giants in penguin suits stand by the portals as we enter. They are very solemn and pretend they don't see us. Big Elephant and Dumpling Deedee tell us to run on ahead into the Great Hall to find Grandma. I haven't seen her in a long time, but I remember her because she is a Fairy Queen and loves me a lot. But she is nowhere in sight.

Then we see her far, far away, high up on the long, long staircase of red that reaches right up to the sky. But as she comes closer, Grandma looks even tinier—why, even tinier than the Little Countess. A little soft cloud of dove-grey—is it fur?—rests over the lace of her dress, although the day is hot. Pearls are garlanded around her tiny neck, but they don't weigh her down or jiggle as she walks, for she carries herself so straight I think she is wearing a crown. As we run to her, coming closer, I see that this is not so, yet still I see the crown as if it were there.

We are close close now . . . Grandma sees us and stops. We stop too. She stares at us and we wait for her to speak. But she doesn't, she just keeps looking at us. Why doesn't someone say something? What is the matter? Please, please, someone think of something to say! Grandma, Grandma, I want to call out—I love you, Grandma, I love you. But I am silent. Years go by, hundreds of them, and all the time she looks into our faces, looking into one and then into another, back and forth. And then she says, very curious—

Who are these children?

She does not know Paddy. She does not know twins Anne and Elsie—unknown children, unknown. She does not know me. She is my grandmother, but she doesn't know me, and if she doesn't know me, who am I? who am I? who am I? Someone comes and my Grandma turns and goes back up the long stairs of red, away away away away, back up into the sky.

Come, children, someone else says. It's time to go home. Grandma is tired.

Honeymoon Lane

Sometimes on a Sunday we would all go across the road to Honeymoon Lane, to a house high up on a bluff overlooking the Seaconnet River. This was called Honeymoon Cottage and it was really small. Outside there was a fence painted white and a gate with a painted white archway and lots of pink roses covering it. There were pink shutters on the windows, and window boxes, also pink, and in them pink roses growing and spilling over and waving in the breeze from the ocean. On the door was a knocker in the shape of a seashell. Inside, it was like a dollhouse. There was a bed with a canopy of dotted swiss and on it sheets strewn with pink moss roses. This sounds as if there must have been too much pink around, but there wasn't. It was all just perfect. Mummy Anne and Cousin Bill stayed there overnight whenever they could. It was the most romantic thing I'd ever heard of. They must really have liked me a lot if they asked me to go there along with twins Anne and Elsie and Cousin Paddy.

One night, the night of the eclipse, we were all allowed to stay up late so that we could see it from the bluff outside Honeymoon Cottage. It happened only dozens and dozens of years apart at full moon and was a most important event, because the sky would grow black, and suddenly all the world would be in darkness. We took a picnic of crunchy sandwiches and a big bowl filled with strawberries, and there were also raisin cookies, and we sat and sat on the bluff waiting for it to happen. Finally Mummy Anne and Cousin Bill, hoping to keep us awake for the big event, started to sing: Row, row, row your boat gent-ly down the stream, Mer-ri-ly, mer-ri-ly, mer-ri-ly, mer-ri-ly, Life is but a dream. . . .

Was it? Yes, it was—it is—a dream. A dream! And I was on the edge of capturing it.

A Lunch for Aunt Gertrude

Then, suddenly, all through Oakland Farm—and yes, even to Honeymoon Lane—there spread a quivering around us, a something . . . but what was it? What it was could not be spoken, but it was there and everywhere—in things Mummy Anne said to Cousin Bill, in things we said to each other. Even the animals, Peter and Paul, Jimmy and Tommy, felt it too and shook themselves a lot as though it would shake it all away. But it didn't go away. It was as if something had happened, only no one could say what it was. . . .

Then one day the Little Countess suddenly appeared at Oakland Farm, and there was a lot of whispering between her and Big Elephant, only this time so low I couldn't make out a word of it. It came to me through the doors, only as a hissing, hissing, hissing . . . hissing. . . .

Then the twins were told not to move or do anything at all until Aunt Gertrude had left, for she was coming for lunch and we were all to be quiet and not muss up the dresses we were to put on for this occasion. Anne and Elsie were scrubbed and scrubbed and told not even to touch the dogs for fear of messing themselves up. And Mummy Anne and Cousin Bill marshaled the whole house into action and no dogs were to be allowed inside when Aunt Gertrude was there. It made us all shaky to see Mummy Anne and Cousin Bill behaving in a way so unlike themselves . . . to see that even they couldn't escape the quivering something that seemed to be possessing us all.

The lunch for Aunt Gertrude went off in a la-di-da manner, and it was a relief when it was over and all the grown-ups closeted themselves in the library and told us to go up to our rooms for naps now, the way we always did.

But it was *not* the way we always did, because the something was quivering about still. What was it? By the time naps were over, Aunt Gertrude had left—and someone else had showed up.

Family Doctor Sullivan—there he was, coming from Newport, even though no one was sick. For some reason he had been summoned to Oakland Farm to look us over anyway. After he left we were told that we were in Quarantine as of right now—all of us. And that we could not leave Oakland Farm, not even to go across the road to Honeymoon Lane, and what's more, no one could come in to Oakland Farm or go out of Oakland Farm until the end of summer, when the Quarantine would be over. Were we in Quarantine because of the quivering thing surrounding us? (Was Quarantine the disease that only Doctor Sullivan had been able to put a name to?)

After the Aunt Gertrude lunch and just before Family Doctor's appearance, the Little Countess made ready for a somewhat hasty departure—and this time I heard an earful of the hasty whispering going on between her and Big Elephant.

My mother was going to come to Oakland Farm to see me— yes, for a visit!—those were her plans. But from what I could make out, Aunt Gertrude had other plans in mind, although my mother did not know it yet. Soon she would; and when she did, *her* plans would have to be changed. . . .

And it was true. The Quarantine was upon us and there were no more trips to Honeymoon Lane. And there was no visit from my mother, since there was no more going out of Oakland Farm and no more coming in. . . .

And the Quarantine clung to us, for the worm had crept under the leaf.

Summer Palace, 1932

Aunt Gertrude had forests, lakes, and mountains in the Adirondacks, tended by guides with names like Marvin and Old Bill. It was called Camp Whitney and every summer she moved her Kingdom there. The lakes were joined one to the other, and the houses on each of them had their own names. One was called Camp Kiloquah, another Camp Deerlands, another Camp Togus. Everyone from Old Westbury Capital moved to one or another of these camps until the summer was over.

Aunt Gertrude was at Togus this particular summer, which was why Big Elephant and I were there. As for Aunt Gertrude, sometimes she was there and sometimes she was not. When she was, she would be away all day, on a white boat moored to a tree in a secret place, working at something *very important*, appearing only at dinner time. When seen, she wore the same outfits she wore at Old Westbury—pants with cuffs, usually white, white high-heeled shoes, silky shirts, also white, long lily-white sweaters, lots of pearls—bracelets, too. And then that hat, but every day it would be feathered with a different color. Then the grown-up cousins and the children cousins, and the nannies, and Big Elephant and I would all get to sit with her at a long table while we ate. Won't you sit next to me, Dodo? she sometimes said, bestowing highest favor on Big Elephant, gesturing a jew-

eled hand to the chair beside her. It really annoyed the other
nannies.

Naney Morgan came up sometimes to visit. She now lived
at the Hotel Fourteen in New York City. I missed her a lot, but
every day I would get a letter from her. The cousins did not
know quite what to make of the Little Countess, but there were
other things going on to distract them. We had our own local
dramas. The biggest one was when one cousin was chained to a
tree by her father. Punishment for what? A dog collar around
her neck, a bowl of water beside her. On a most frequented trail.

Eyes downcast for hours, chained to a tree. No one allowed to speak to her. Is that what fathers were like? Is that what it meant to have a father? Maybe Naney Morgan was right after all. Hadn't she warned me about all men?

That summer I was told that my mother was on the Côte d'Azur, at the Villa Croix des Gardes, with Nada and all the others. When summer was over, Big Elephant and I were also told, my mother would be back and we would go to stay with her in New York City, but for how long we did not know. Maybe we would go back to the Capital at Old Westbury, and then again maybe we would not. One thing we did know was that this time we would not be at the Sherry-Netherland Hotel, where we usually stayed with my mother when she was in New York. We would be going to a house on Seventy-second Street.

Every time they brought it up, I walked away. I did not want to talk about my mother. Or I would try to change the subject whenever Naney Morgan or Big Elephant brought it up. *They* still did not know that I *knew*, had known for a long time, ever since I had become, so to speak, a collaborator in the letter-writing sessions that began at Melton Mowbray. I knew they had a plan. Not only a plan but plans within plans. The more aware I became, the further and further away my mother disappeared, as though I could see her only through the wrong end of a telescope. But there would be other times that summer—times when I would faint with longing for the mysterious beauty of her. Fevered, I would run into the woods, hugging a tree, fleetingly fulfilled; it would be as though I had reached her and come to the center of her at last. But I could not sustain it. Tree of oak was not my mother.

How often that summer I wanted to scream at them that I knew—knew what the Little Countess was up to when she had told me to pretend to be sick on those frequent New York visits to the spooky Santa Claus, Doctor St. Lawrence. Ho! ho! ho! he would snort, prodding with icy stethoscope, as on cue I would let out a wail. It was not so hard to do what Naney asked, for there was something about him—what was it? Ever since he had instructed Big Elephant to take a photograph of me naked. With great seriousness she had chosen a suitable setting. Out we went into a field at Aunt Gertrude's Old Westbury farm. Making sure no one was looking, I slipped off all my clothes and hopped up onto a pumpkin. Firmly clutching her Brownie camera, Big Elephant clicked away as I moved around slowly, between takes. Santa Claus said to be sure to get a lot of photographs from all angles, which is exactly what she did. By our next weekly visit they were all ready to give to him. He seemed pleased and, after looking each one over, opened the center drawer of his desk and dropped them in.

Yes, there were times that summer I wanted to scream—at both of them—Stop! But already it was too late. I was in too deep. In on the plan. In with Big Elephant and the Little Countess. What did it matter that I didn't know details of the plan or the nature of the plan? What I did know was that if I went along with it, Dodo Elephant and Naney Morgan would not be sent away. We three would stay together. For without them how could I live? Happiness—Big Elephant. Love. The Little Countess—strength. Without them I would be nothing.

The Visitors

My mother was here. Here, at Camp Whitney. I could not believe it. I *did* not believe it. If she was *here* in this very place, why was I to be taken in the motor launch across the lake of Togus onto the lake of Kiloquah? Why was she not coming here to Togus, to see me here? No, she was at the Carry Landing, far away, waiting for me. There must be a reason.

Big Elephant took my hand and down we went to the edge of the lake. Marvin was driving the boat and I jumped in. Dodo swung one leg over and then Marvin had to give her a hand so the rest of her got up and into the launch. Then he got behind the wheel. The motor putted and putted but would not start. This sound and the smell of gasoline that always came with it frightened me. They never did before, but now they did. It was hard to say why, but it was like a sound you heard before something was about to happen—an explosion or something. But then the motor caught hold, hooked on into a steady hum, and off we went just as though nothing was wrong—nothing was different, that is. Only Big Elephant and I did not sit down the way we usually did. We went up behind Marvin and let the spray fly in snow flurries all around us.

And then, all at once, through these snowflakes, I saw a dark shape away in the distance, coming straight at us. I put my face into Big Elephant, but when I looked out again not only was it there, now it was really getting closer. It was a boat, and in the boat, standing up, were two nuns. There they stood, two nuns, hooded and joined together, and they were staring at our boat and coming closer and closer.

But who were they? And why? Turn around, turn around! I took hold of Marvin's arm and shook it. But we kept on going, moving closer and closer, until the boat was so close I could look right into their black hoods—so close I could see the nose on the face of one of them slicing through the black as she bent towards me, and I could see into the hood of the other as she leaned the beauty of her face away from me. And then I knew who they were and what they had come for—to take me away, away from Big Elephant, far away. They were not nuns at all; they were Aunt Consuelo and my mother come to take me.

Now dearie, now dearie, everything is going to be all right, Dodo kept saying. But it was not. And I kept pounding Marvin.

There they stood, attached together, the One with The Nose and The Beautiful One, side by side, leaning heavily against each other. Don't let them take me please please please! The Beautiful One pulled her hood tighter around her, while The Nose One put her arm out to stop her from falling. Then The Nose nun called something out loud and the boat they stood in turned around and started moving away.

Far and far they went, way away in the distance, far across the lake, until all I could see was two hooded nuns, far far away.

But nothing had changed—nothing. It was all as before, and those nuns seeming to disappear in the distance were not disappearing at all; they were just as close to me, closer even than before. It was as if they were coming towards me—towards me instead of going away.

Cuidado Cuidado Cuidado

When it was time to go to 39 East Seventy-second Street, the summer was over. Big Elephant and I stood for a while looking up at the grey walls from the outside. The house had an empty look about it, as if no one was there. Of course we knew already that the Little Countess would not be there. Ever since the episode on rue Alfred Roll she had finally been banished. But when Big Elephant rang the doorbell and we were inside, it was really nice. There was a hall with big black and white squares like my checkerboard, and a staircase with mossy carpet leading up to the living room on the second floor.

The butler said his name was Zaug and that Mrs. Vanderbilt was upstairs. I couldn't get up fast enough, I was so excited about seeing her. But as I flew up, ahead of Big Elephant, and ran into the living room, it was Aunt Consuelo I saw first. She was standing in front of my mother, and for a moment I thought Aunt Consuelo was the only person in the room. Then she moved slightly to one side and my mother came towards me.

Both of them wore black dresses, but my mother's dress had lace creamily tucked inside the V at her neck, while Aunt Consuelo's was all black. My mother always insisted on greeting me with not one peck on the cheek, but two—one on one side, then one on the other. She said it was the way the French embraced for *bonne chance*. Still, it always put me off—it was as if the first kiss didn't count. Every time I would try getting away with just one peck, but she always caught me up on it, saying in a charming but firm way, No, darling, both cheeks. Kiss Aunt Consuelo, she then said. Only now you must call her Aunt Tamar. She had consulted a Wizard who had advised her to change her name from Consuelo to Tamar . . . things would go better for her if she did. Whatever her name was, I didn't like any of it as I saw her standing beside my mother, not moving or saying anything at all.

Dodo Elephant had stayed behind in the hall, seeing to the luggage that was being taken by elevator to our room on the top floor. Climbing the stairs she now came into the living room where my mother, Aunt Consuelo-Tamar, and I were standing. Hand outstretched, my mother went towards her.

Just as she did—exactly at the same moment—as though pulled by a string, Aunt Consuelo-Tamar moved away. Away from Big Elephant without greeting her, straight to the window, where she stood with her back to us. The blackness of her staring down into the street below.

Looking at my mother's face and then at Consuelo-Tamar, the black mountain of her still standing with her back to us, I kept expecting something to happen. But nothing did. It was as though nothing had happened. Nothing at all.

But It had, It had, It had—It had happened. I knew it, as surely as I knew that nothing would ever be the same again, ever, for as long as I lived.

Zaug had come back and my mother was telling us to follow him to the elevator, to be taken to the top floor.

At the window the dark one stood, her back to us, still silent and unmoving.

As we left the room my mother started to say something, but Consuelo-Tamar turned around and cut her off, hissing
Cuidado . . .
Cuidado . . .
Cuidado . . .

and again

Cuidado. . . .

Big Elephant put her trunk around me as Zaug squeezed us into the elevator.

Press Four, he said.

And up we went.

Our rooms on the top floor were nice too. I had a room all to myself and so did Big Elephant. But I couldn't really look at anything or see anything. *Cuidado . . . Cuidado . . . Cuidado* was all I could think of. It kept hurting me. Not that it was unusual for the Aunts Toto and Consuelo-Tamar to switch to Spanish if I happened to be in the room. I understood none of it, but I did understand *why* they did it. I would try to remember how the words sounded so I could repeat them to Naney Morgan later, so I could ask her what they meant. But I never got the words right. The Little Countess would laugh and shake her head, saying she couldn't make sense out of any of it. But this time I knew I'd got it right. *Cui-da-do.* What does that mean? I asked Big Elephant. I don't know, lovey, she said, and started to unpack.

The next few days were more or less the same. Mornings, Big Elephant and I would walk to Central Park where I would roller skate. My mother and Consuelo-Tamar never appeared until we got back. By then it would be time for lunch. Sometimes they would still be asleep. On those days I never saw them until late afternoon, returning again from the park, when there they would be, sitting in their black dresses, on the second floor, in the living room.

My mother would have a cigarette in her hand or she would be just about to take one from the box on the coffee table. It was silver and had writing on the lid—my father's writing, Big Elephant told me. It had been with us in the house on avenue Charles Floquet and on rue Alfred Roll. I took this as a good sign. There were other familiar things around as well. Cups of giant silver with names on them—Tiger Lily, White Oak Maid, Fortitude. Trophies won by my father for his champion horses. Brought from Paris also were silver knives and forks, on each an *RCV.* Glistening white tureens, white dishes with initials and flowers of gold, inviting the touch. Everything I saw proved that our Caravan was going to stay in this house on Seventy-second Street for quite a long time. Everything was going to be all right.

But when I went into the room where they were sitting, it was not all right. It was all wrong.

Zaug would be coming in and out with drinks on a tray. My mother trying to think of something to say to me. Tamar-Consuelo not saying anything at all. My mother lighting another cigarette and ringing for Zaug to bring another Sidecar please. A phone ringing somewhere. Wann, who had replaced Marie, standing in the arched doorway to say Mr. A. C. Blumenthal was on the phone. It seemed very important. My mother jumped up—thanking God silently for an excuse to leave.

So there we were. Alone at last. Tamar-Consuelo and I. It was on the tip of my tongue to ask her what *Cuidado* meant, but it was too risky. I kept quiet and we both sat there. My mother was away a long time—maybe she was going to be on the phone forever. I better go up and take a bath, I said, casual like. You do that, answered Tamar-Consuelo. I ran up the stairs, past my mother's room on the third floor, and through the door I could see her sitting on the edge of the bed, her back to me, still talking on the telephone. Who was Mr. A. C. Blumenthal? I haven't even heard the Little Countess mention him. Even Big Elephant did not know who Mr. A. C. Blumenthal was. Until days later.

Outside in front of the house on Seventy-second Street there would be a car waiting. Every day. It wasn't that we had never seen cars like it before in England, but this was different. For one thing, it was bigger. Or had I gotten smaller? Dodo said it was a Rolls-Royce, but to me it was a coach. All it needed was prancing horses. Every day, there it would be waiting. Behind the wheel in the front seat sat a man who tipped his cap to us as we passed by.

Then one morning he got out from behind the wheel and came over to us. I'm Beesley, he said. Big Elephant shook his hand and then I did too. Mr. A. C. Blumenthal's car, he said proudly, looking over to it. We all stood taking it in until he asked us if we would like to see the inside. It was something! Seats soft as sponge cake in a color I'd never seen before. On either side a vase, a trumpet of crystal, holding a single flower. Roses—brandywine roses, he said. Mr. A. C. Blumenthal has a standing order—two fresh ones every day. And see, he went on, pressing a panel of silken wood. Presto! It opened. There, on narrow shelves, row upon row, bottles glittery as the ones on my mother's dressing table, some labeled Krug with silver wires around the top, goblets so transparent you almost didn't see the

gold, sparkling swizzle sticks, even a cocktail shaker of
bigger than the jar the Little Countess stored her rice
, and next to it an elfin bucket holding ice. Clinking
the panel gently back in place, Beesley moved back, smartly
shutting the door of the coach. Will Mrs. Vanderbilt be using
the car, do you know, this afternoon? I have no idea, answered
Big Elephant.

So *that* was it. Mr. A. C. Blumenthal must be a great friend
of my mother if his car waited outside all day long just in case
she wanted to go somewhere. Who is Mr. A. C. Blumenthal? I
asked Big Elephant when we got far enough away for Beesley
not to hear. I really don't know, Peach Pie. Just a friend of your
mother's. Just a friend . . . a friend . . .

Things went along more or less like that for quite a while.
Until one day it happened.

Rain all morning, so we hadn't been out. After lunch it
stopped. Big Elephant was getting skates and things together
before taking off for the park. This was a perfect opportunity to
do what I always did whenever I possibly could. Donning invisible
cloak, I moved about the house finding out things. What things
exactly, I didn't really know, but somehow I could not stop doing
this. It became a game. Only no one played the game with me,
because nobody else knew it was being played. It was called
Invisible, this game, and every time I played it, it became more
and more scary. Moving down, up, and around the mossy green
stairs, I would try to see and to hear all that I could without
being caught. It was scary—not because I might get caught but
because of what I might hear or see. This is what made it scary,
so scary that some days I had no courage to play it. But on this
particular day I did.

Cloaked, I stormed silently down the stairs from the Caravan
on the top floor as Big Elephant pottered about. There, on the
floor below, the door to Consuelo-Tamar's room was open. Not
only that, the door to my mother's room was wide open too, and
there was Wann making the bed. What luck! If they hadn't gone

out, they would be on the next floor down, in the living room; and, sure enough, there they were. Halfway down the stairs I could hear them. Balancing on a tightrope, I went on a few steps. Now I could see them. Close together they sat playing their own game. Bezique. They played this a lot when they were not doing jigsaw puzzles. So close—now I was really scared.

The first thing you must do, and the sooner the better, is get rid of the nurse. Consuelo-Tamar said this.

My mother said nothing.

A German Fräulein is what she needs! Consuelo-Tamar sounded angry.

Then my mother said: Maybe Friedel could help. I'm sure he would recommend someone.

Why don't you call him? This quickly from Consuelo-Tamar. Now!

Let's see, my mother said. She looked over at the clock on the mantel.

In Germany it's six hours ahead . . . so now it must be . . .
Must be Must be Must be
Up up up the stairs
they were going to away away send her
Forever Away Forever
Forever Forever Away
What would be left?
Nothing Nothing Nothing
Gone Big Elephant
Gone the Little Countess
Awake—gone
Asleep—gone
Gone Always Forever
Save me save save me drowning
Save me Don't let it happen happen happen happen
Can't breathe can't breathe
The sound of Dodo Elephant—over and over
Listen to me Listen to me Listen to me Listen to me

Save me—over and over—Save me
Listen to me LISTEN LISTEN LISTEN—
This is what we must do . . .
Down we must get
To the Hall
Out the front door
To the park
As if nothing had happened
Nothing nothing nothing
To Mrs. Whitney to Mrs. Whitney
Straight to your Aunt Gertrude
Mrs. Whitney will know what to do
What to do what to do what to do
So loud now I could hear her
Can you do that, darling darling?
Can you Can you Can you, Gloria?
If they stop us on the way out
Pretend nothing has happened at all at all at all
Pretend pretend pretend
Can you, Gloria? Gloria, can you can you?

I put my coat on. And then I put on my knit cap with the
tassel. Outside it looked as if it was going to rain again. Going
over to the mirror, I looked at myself. Dodo was standing beside
me and I looked at the two of us standing there. She put on her
coat. And as though nothing had happened, I picked up my roller
skates, as I always did, and we started on down the stairs.

Slowly down down down we went
You and I
One two three four . . . counting the steps as we went
Together, Love . . .
Five six seven eight nine
Never mind the weather . . .
Past the third floor ten eleven twelve
Love . . .

They were still there, only now no longer at bezique. Close to each other on the sofa.

Where are you going? my mother said.

Just out for a bit to the park. Big Elephant sounded exactly like she always did.

But it's about to rain. . . . Consuelo-Tamar and my mother looked towards the windows.

To rain to rain to rain to rain

Just for a minute to get some air . . .

Gloria hasn't been out all day . . .

See . . . I went over to them, holding open a paper bag of bread crumbs.

To feed the birds

They leaned over and looked inside.

I always do—always. Every day—no matter what, feed the birds.

Oh well, Consuelo-Tamar said.

Have a good time, my mother said.

Somewhere a phone started ringing and ringing.

Big Elephant moved on out into the hall.

Run run run run run—

Slowly one two three four five six—

Nurse! Nurse! Consuelo-Tamar followed us out and stood looking down at us.

Nurse, on your way out tell Beesley we won't be needing him today at all. He can go on home.

Beesley was outside, waiting, as if nothing had happened.

Big Elephant took my hand and we went straight to the coach.

I opened the door and jumped in. Big Elephant pitched in behind me.

Mrs. Vanderbilt's not needing the car this afternoon—Big Elephant spoke really fast—so will you take us for a spin around the park, please.

I didn't dare move or look out the window. If I stayed still enough, the motor would start. If I held my breath, the front door would not open . . . Consuelo-Tamar and my mother would not run out to catch us . . . to stop us from getting to Aunt Gertrude in time, so that she could stop them from sending Big Elephant away. But nothing was moving. I made a bargain with myself not to cry, and then the coach would glide away, away from the grey house where nobody lived, away away away. . . .

Starting, we moved, away from the curb, through the green light, straight into the park, on and on, away away. My stomach started splitting open again. I threw myself at Big Elephant, crying and crying. . . .

Beesley turned around to see what was going on. Take us to Larrimore's drugstore, she said.

But I couldn't stop my stomach from splitting, even when we went into the drugstore, not even pressing with all my might against Dodo Mountain as she stood in the phone booth, with the door open, calling Mrs. Whitney—not even then. My body and my face were coming apart, and everything was exploding—everything except Elephant.

She carried me back into the coach. Very sick, she said to Beesley. Very sick. We're to go down to Mrs. Whitney's studio in Greenwich Village. Hurry, Beesley, hurry hurry . . . very very sick . . .

When we got there Beesley helped Elephant carry me in. Into where Mrs. Whitney was. Into her studio with all her statues standing around. Then up some steps into another room. There was a couch and they tried to put me on it, onto this couch which was in front of a fireplace; they wanted me to lie down in front of the mantel of this fireplace which was all made of polished metals sculpted into the shapes of flames, so that when the fire was lit it reflected the flames as if they had escaped and raged out into the room and climbed up the chimney right up onto the ceiling. . . .

Legs cracking, unable to hold on any longer, Dodo still holding me . . . I faded into her. On and on we went, back and forth in our little boat, swaying back and forth, until over us a curtain dropped—a caul of cheesecloth—a tent covering us, as our Caravan drifted on and on and on, on out into the sea. . . .

Santa Claus?

Much later we landed at an unknown destination. I was on a bed in a room filled with hazy light and shapes, some moving, some just standing around as they spoke to each other in languages I could not understand. The silken warmth of a hand held mine and I knew then that Naney Morgan was there, sitting beside me, and that it was her hand I held. Even the cool of the ring she always wore, three round, perfect diamonds, had become warm from my grasp.

Standing behind her floated that hat. It was all I could see of Aunt Gertrude through the cheesecloth. The unmoving blocks of brown-black came closer and I knew they were pieces of furniture, furniture I had seen before, and it was then I knew that the bed I lay in was a bed in a room somewhere in the castle of Aunt Gertrude on Fifth Avenue and that this was where we had landed, Big Elephant and I. But where was Dodo? Where was she?

I sat up, and just as I did, far away, a door opened at the end of the room. And marching towards me in a row were two persons in black dresses with veils over their white masks— sweeping forward, faster forward, no one to stop them. I started screaming. Where was Big Elephant? Where had they taken her? Stop! one of them shouted. This is your mother! She lifted her hand to slap me, but even if she had, nothing could have stopped me. Grabbing Naney Morgan's hand even tighter, I screamed on, pulling her with me as we sped on and on into a tunnel. All at once, on one side, trying to catch us, Santa Claus appeared, bobbing along almost as fast as we were. How did *he* get here?

It's the Doctor, Gloria! But it *wasn't* the Santa Claus one, and Aunt Gertrude zoomed up next to me as we careened on through the tunnel. She was so close to my face now, all I could see was her mouth with the red of her lipstick running up her face along the lines over her upper lip, tracing tiny pathways leading nowhere. Dodo Dodo Dodo I tried to call out, but no sound came, and now the tiny pathways over her lip wiggled closer to me and Aunt Gertrude was shouting—It's Doctor Craig, Gloria, Doctor Craig's come to see you, Doctor Craig—and I knew I would throw up if she didn't stop. And that's just what I did. All over the pure white I choked and choked, and as I looked down at the sheet, at the white lace, I snapped out of the tunnel. My head whiplashed back and I saw Dodo Elephant right there beside me; sitting where Naney Morgan had sat, squeezing my hand, there sat Big Elephant. The palm of her other hand pulsed against my forehead. My eyes closed. When I opened them maybe the two persons in their veils of black would be gone. But they were not gone; when I opened my eyes, there they were, only now they were far away again, way at the end of the room. And Aunt Gertrude was there too, talking to them; and there, what do you know, standing in the middle, I could see the top of Santa Claus's head. Their red mouths moved open and shut, open and shut, but I couldn't hear one thing they said. Someone had brought sheets to put on the bed, and I climbed up into Big Elephant's lap and went to sleep.

It was morning when I woke up, and Big Elephant was still there in the same chair sitting beside me. All the others had disappeared. The room looked as if it had always been the way it looked now. Just like all of the rooms in Aunt Gertrude's castles. Every place that belonged to her felt as if it had been there from the beginning of the world and nothing could ever shake it or topple it over. Every other place I had been, whether hotel or house, now seemed to me to be made of sand—yes, even Aunt Toto's Burrough Court. But this—this room with its shapes of burnished wood, the floors of intricate design, the ceilings going up into the sky—no wave could ever reach it.

I put my arms around Big Elephant. Good morning, Peach Pie, she said, and leaned over to press a button in the center of a green stone that was on the table next to the bed. Soon the door opened and in came Hortense. She was Mrs. Whitney's very own private maid, just like my mother's Wann, and she never lifted a finger except to do what Aunt Gertrude bid. She never even had to carry things. In the morning when Aunt Gertrude summoned her breakfast in bed, Hortense would wait outside for the butler bearing the tray to totter up the long stairs until he reached Aunt Gertrude's room, where Hortense stood barricading the door. Before taking the tray from him she would lift every lid and examine every dish, hoping to catch him up on having forgotten something. Then she would take the tray and sniff her nose in the air for him to open the door. Proudly bearing it aloft, Hortense would sail into the room with Aunt Gertrude's breakfast. But this time it was to sail in and say, I'll tell Mrs. Whitney that Miss Gloria is awake.

What was going to happen now? We waited and waited, Big Elephant and I, for whatever was going to happen to happen.

Years went by until finally the door opened again. It was Naney Morgan and behind her was a very tall Aunt Gertrude. Big Elephant stood up. I could not move or do anything at all. They came over and sat down at the foot of the bed, Aunt Gertrude on one side and the Little Countess on the other. Dodo sat down again too. There we were, all sitting.

You are going to drive out to Westbury, Gloria, Aunt Gertrude said, smiling at me. I looked at Big Elephant. Oh, Dodo is going with you, she said, and smiled on.

Yes, Little One (now Naney Morgan was smiling too), isn't that lovely—you'll be with your Aunt Gertrude in the country. Naney sounded sincere. Big Elephant sat listening. But you'll have to see your mother before you go, Naney said, kind of laughing it off. I wanted to take Big Elephant's hand and run with her, run down the marble stairs of the Castle, run and run.

Do I have to? Do I really have to? Do I?

Oh, only for a minute, Gloria, Aunt Gertrude said, still smiling. Now everybody, even Big Elephant, was smiling—everyone, that is, except me.

Yes, Little One, only for a minute, and when you do—remember to . . . well, you know . . . you don't have to say much . . . just pretend nothing happened . . . you know what I mean. . . .

I knew what the Little Countess meant all right!

Now, get dressed, darling mine. The sooner you are, the sooner we all will be on our way.

All—that is what Naney said. All meant the Little Countess, me, *and* Big Elephant—oh, and I guess Aunt Gertrude, because it was her house we were going to.

I jumped up and felt like singing. Then Aunt Gertrude and the Little Countess went out of the room and Dodo started getting us together to make the great escape. But almost as soon as the door closed, it opened again. Naney came back into the room, this time without Aunt Gertrude. Was anything wrong? She put her wings around me without saying anything and I could feel the love spreading through me. I could feel love from me spreading back into her.

Listen to me, Little One, she said. You must show your Aunt Gertrude how much you love her. You must hug her more and kiss her a lot—you must show your Aunt Gertrude—

But how can I love her when I don't know her? I don't know her yet—

Hush, hush, Little One, what kind of talk is that? You do know her, you *do*, and if you don't know her yet, you will know her soon, very soon. So you see, darling—show her, hug her a lot and kiss her a lot and tell her how much you love her.

I want to—I want to love her! I'll try, I'll try, really I will, really and truly. . . . Tighter and tighter I kept holding onto

Naney, hugging her. I want to—really and truly I do—I do . . .

I looked up at Big Elephant standing behind us. I looked high up, trying to get into the grey mountain of her. Trying to steady myself, trying to hold on to the anchor of her face . . .

I was all dressed and as ready as I ever would be—which wasn't saying much. My stomach had started that squirming thing again, but I still didn't dawdle getting myself dressed, because I knew the sooner I saw my mother and got through that, the sooner Big Elephant and I would be sitting in Aunt Gertrude's big grey car with Freddy driving us along and away.

Soon there was a knock on the door.

Come in, said Big Elephant. And in came Hortense.

Mrs. Vanderbilt is here now, she said, looking at Big Elephant. She did not look at me at all. You are to go down, Mrs. Whitney said, and wait in the car with Mrs. Morgan. Miss Gloria will meet you in the car quite soon.

Quite soon Quite soon . . .

Go on, lovey, Big Elephant said, I'll see you soon.

Soon Soon Soon . . .

So I followed Hortense out the door and down the long marble corridor, on and on, down the wide slabs of white marble stairs, until we arrived at the place they called the drawing room. The door was already open when we reached it. Hortense stood back and said, You can go right in.

It was so huge, this room with the wide windows looking out on Fifth Avenue and the park, so big that everything in it had to be enormous. And it was. There would be a sofa with chairs on either side and tables, and then there would be another grouping just like this, only it would be placed in another part of the room. There were so many of these dotted around that each one became its own island. There could have been dozens of people in this room, each group gathered on a different island, having their own party, without getting mixed up with any other party going on in the same room.

The party that *was* going on when I walked in was taking

place on a big sofa in front of the fireplace. The fire was burning, as usual, and the walls of watery green with the crystals every-where glimmered as usual, and everything was as it always was—except *there*, sitting on this particular island, in front of the fireplace, still wearing veils over their white faces, sat the Two in their black dresses. When they saw me they unglued them-selves from each other and moved apart, and one of them patted at the space between them. Aunt Gertrude had gotten up from her chair and come towards me. I knew everyone expected me to go and sit on the sofa in the space between my mother and Aunt Consuelo-Tamar. It was not easy for me to do this, but I did.

Aunt Tamar-Consuelo said nothing at all, and if she had not moved to make room for me on the sofa I would have thought she was blind and deaf. Her face never had any light in it when she looked at me or spoke to me—ever. And now it was as if I was not even in the room at all. There we sat in front of the fireplace as it burnt on and on, and I got more and more frightened.

Then Aunt Gertrude said something in her graceful way, and—to my horror—my mother reached out to take my hand. I was torn apart not knowing what it meant or what exactly was going on or what I was supposed to do. No one had ever said this might happen—no one ever said that my mother might reach over and take my hand into the beauty of hers. I left my hand there, dumped on the cushion, as if it were a dead thing. I kept staring at Aunt Gertrude's hat, holding my eyes onto it, as if something about it would tell me something and give me a clue as to what I should do and what to expect next. But no answer came. So there we all sat—Aunt Gertrude going on as if nothing was happening . . . Consuelo-Tamar, on one side, with her veiled nose and her angry, blind eyes unblinking at the fire . . . my mother, on the other side, her veiled beauty now turned from me. I sat in the middle, half wanting to throw myself into her arms, half wanting to yank my hand away from hers so fast and hard that it would tear her soft fingers off into mine—for then she would belong to me forever!

Then I could not stand it another second. May I be excused? I said, not looking at anyone.

Of course, said Aunt Gertrude. My mother turned her head away.

Over the carpet, towards the door I walked, over the sweet soft roses nestled in the pale green of their leaves, treading lightly, not too fast, not too slow, looking down until I reached the border of vines, vines of woodbine—for I knew then that I was almost at the door, and all I had to do now was step across, through the high arch, and out into the marble of the great hall.

As I did, a shadow came forward. It was Hortense. Follow me, she said in her French voice. This time we went down the halls until we came to the cage of the lacy iron elevator. With both hands she pulled at the ton of its door and held it open for me to enter. Down down down it crept, so slowly that I thought I would scream.

But I did not; and soon, all at once, I was there—there in the car between Big Elephant and the Little Countess—yes, there we all were! Freddy at the wheel in front of us in the grey uniform that matched the grey car. The grey hair on the back of his head under the grey of his cap looked like it always did. Yes, everything was just like it always was.

No one said much of anything as we drove on and on towards Old Westbury. Even Naney Morgan was silent most of the time. I guess we were all exhausted; and, anyway, what was there to say? What could be said, really, about any of it? And if the Little Countess couldn't think of anything, how could anyone else be expected to?

My room at Aunt Gertrude's in Old Westbury was on the second floor on the right when you came to the top of the stairs. My room had a big closet, and through the wall next to it was another closet that was Aunt Gertrude's. This huge closet of Aunt Gertrude's was connected to her room, so we were quite connected, Aunt Gertrude and I, even though we could only get to each other's rooms by going along the hallway. The room that was my room was as large as Aunt Gertrude's. The reason for this was that it had been the room of Mr. Harry Payne Whitney, the husband of Aunt Gertrude. He had been dead for quite a while, but his room was left exactly as it was when he wasn't dead. The pictures on the walls of horses doing one thing or another hung just as they had then. The same brown carpet, the curtains with brown blobs on them, the two brown blob chairs in front of the fireplace—everything in place, just as if he was expected back any day now. But I was told that this room now belonged to me. It was My Room. And that the smaller room across the hall from me was where Big Elephant would be. Naney, when she wasn't at the Hotel Fourteen, would stay in a guest room way around a curve at the other end of the long hallway. So this is how we were all placed and where we settled back in, when finally we arrived at Aunt Gertrude's Capital.

Of all Aunt Gertrude's palaces, the one in Old Westbury was the one I liked the most. The curve of the stairs seemed to glide up and down. Even the space between each of the twenty steps was placed so you felt buoyed up or wafted down, without being aware that you were making yourself move at all—as though it were really someone else who was doing it for you. Even Big Elephant drifted down and up those stairs like a baby blimp.

At the foot of the stairs to the right was the dining room, where Aunt Gertrude would sit at the head of the long chestnutty table, so shiny you could see yourself reflected in it. Always, tall butler William, in swallowtail and striped vest, stood behind her chair throughout the meal, as though he were a silent guest. They had signals known only to each other. Without even turning, Aunt Gertrude would lift her finger so slightly no one else would notice, and butler William would know, without her having uttered a word, what she meant—Pass the Brussels sprouts again, or More pheasant, please.

Out the dining room on through the hall, on into the living

room, into its honeycomb of paneled wood, its tall windows that started at the ceiling and ended at the floor, curtained by flowers of all colors, butterflies of emerald, bees of black and yellow stripe. In front of the fireplace more flowers strewn on chairs and sofas as squashy as the ones at Mummy Anne's in Newport. In another corner, a piano, with Steinway in letters of gold centered over the licorice and icing-white of the keyboard. Always flowers, lots of them, everywhere in vases piled high. Others in low bowls next to other shallow bowls, holding the dried buds of tea roses, cinnamon, and other leaves and blossoms I had never seen before. Potpourri, Miss Gloria, butler William said as he caught me with my nose in the dried petals.

Everywhere there was . . . what was it? Something . . . but whatever it was, I did not know a name for it. Was it order? Maybe that's what it was— order. The more I thought about it, the more I was sure that was what it must be. Like when Big Elephant straightened out our bureau drawers. Everywhere order, and it was perfect. And it lived with such ease. Is that what luxury meant? So effortless! What made it so smooth, everything so perfect, as though some magic person directed it all, made it all happen? But who? The flowers in their vessels of gold and silver were never allowed to die. Overnight they would be re-placed, massed into new shapes and colors, by unknown hands, each group different and lovelier than the one before. Other bouquets—these of mint, speckled with powdery sugar—placed, also by unseen hands, on top of iced tea, served in columns of ice crystal, arriving on trays of filigree; in each a shell-like spoon, tapering upwards into a straw of silver.

Across from the living room there was a small room called the telephone room: in it, a little sofa just big enough for two, and next to the sofa, on a table, a telephone. Now this telephone was no different from other telephones I had seen, but somehow it *was* different. It stood tall, and quite like a black flower—a daffodil, perhaps? Yes, a black daffodil that you spoke into as you held another flower—a black tulip, maybe—cupped to your ear as you listened. Next to it rested a neat little pad of paper and a pencil of elegant slimness, for doodling.

Leading away from this room on and on was a hall, with more pictures of horses hanging on either side, on and on down this long hall which had been added to the main house after it was built. And at the end of the hall you arrived at another house, much smaller than the main house, but still a house.

This was called the Cottage. It had a staircase going up to cozy rooms with slanting ceilings and fireplaces. And downstairs, other rooms, even its very own living room. A whole other life could have gone on there and no one living in the main house would ever even know it, unless they followed the long hallway to the Cottage. But no one lived there, and it was only used sometimes when guests came to visit.

Going in the opposite direction back through the dining room you came to the huge pantry, and next to that the enormous kitchen, with its larders storing bounty from Aunt Gertrude's farm, and spreading up and out from that, lots of cubbies where Cook lived, butlers William and Charles, and Bridie, and others whose names I did not know yet.

So that is what it was like Inside. But when I was Inside and looking Outside, through the wide windows of my bedroom I saw a green hill sweeping down to the green of meadows far away. And looking to the left, I could see part of the garden, its flowers contained in patchwork squares with pathways so narrow there was only room for one person at a time to walk on them. These pathways led around and about but finally arrived at a little house placed right in the center of the edge of the garden. Outside it was painted all white and inside there was only one room—a perfect little room with just enough in it for two people to sit and have a tea party. And if they turned around, they would see a tiny lace-curtained window looking down onto another hill, on down into meadows of green as far as you could see.

So after the endless fear in the enormous room of Aunt Ger-

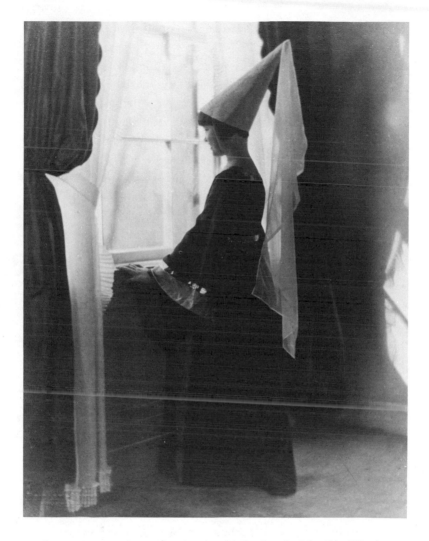

trude's Winter Palace, this is where it had ended for Big Elephant,
the Little Countess, and me when we arrived at the perfect order
of Aunt Gertrude's Country Capital.

Ever since we left the Castle in the city, around and around
in my head and all through me I kept trying to imagine what
was going on and what had happened in that enormous room
after I said Excuse me please and walked across the roses and

woodbine, through the archway of the door on out into the hall, never to go back. How long did they sit there still thinking I *would* come back? What did Aunt Gertrude say? And did Consuelo-Tamar glue herself back onto my mother? What would have happened if Hortense had not been waiting for me in the hall? Would I have dared go back and do what I really wanted to do—to dive between the two black dresses on the sofa and have my mother throw her arms around me?

But it was too late. Already my mother had become a person of terror. She loomed over me inseparable from Consuelo-Tamar, whom I feared more than anyone else. But what had been said, and what had been done, when Aunt Gertrude decided the moment had come to break the news of my . . . departure, so to speak? And more than anything, I wondered if Big Elephant and I were really out of danger.

The next day Aunt Gertrude had still not appeared, but there was a lot of telephoning back and forth between her and the Little Countess, and just as much back-and-forth talk between Dodo and Naney. They even told me some of it. The most amazing thing they said was that my mother was accusing Aunt Gertrude of kidnapping me and that she was having a banner stating this nailed onto the giant gates of bronze that guarded Aunt Gertrude's castle on Fifth Avenue. This banner was a proclamation, said the Little Countess, rolling her eyes as wide as they would go, showing the world what a terrible person my mother was. But try as I would, I could not figure out what she meant. What *do* you mean? I wanted to ask her. What does she mean? I wanted to ask Big Elephant. But I kept my mouth shut. Already things were too unsteady in our little Caravan. And it was just as well. Just as well I did not know then what was to come, because I was to start going to school right away, here in Old Westbury. It was called the Green Vale School and I would be driven there every morning by Freddy in the grey car. So I had things on my mind.

And what's more, the school had started and classes begun

weeks before, so I felt funny walking in late like that. Also, I had never been to school before, and all I knew was what Dodo and Naney had taught me, here and there, about writing and reading and so on. It did not add up to all that much, and I felt panicky as Big Elephant and I drove up to the square grey-and-brick buildings of the Green Vale School and walked through the halls that smelled of wet linoleum, right into Mr. Jenkins's office. He was the headmaster of the school, and he sure was a dead ringer for the father who had chained my cousin to the tree in the Adirondacks. Right away he made you feel that he knew what it was you had done even though you did not know what it was yourself. After looking me over, he told Big Elephant to come back for me at three o'clock.

Then he took me back through the linoleum halls and into a classroom filled with girls and boys. Everybody stopped when we walked in and turned their heads around. The teacher stopped writing and turned from the blackboard that covered the wall in back of his desk. I was told to sit in back of the class until it was over. Everyone had his own desk of taffy-colored wood— row on row, each one exactly the same as the other, with a well for ink and trenches just the right size for pencils. The top of each desk lifted up and there was space inside to keep books and papers. Every desk even had its own chair attached right to it. I really liked the smell of the chalk when it scratched against the blackboard. And on another wall, on top of a shelf, there was a jar of water, and in it, held by toothpicks, a ball with vines coming out of the top, traipsing high up onto the windows as if they were going to creep right out and teach the sky. It was hard to believe that so many vines could grow out of that little ball, but they did. There was also, on another shelf, a long bowl with fishes swimming in and out through forests of wavy grasses and lazily drifting through doorless castles.

The teacher was called Mr. Breen and he wore a jacket of black and brown tweed, somewhat like the jackets Aunt Toto's friends wore on those Burrough Court weekends, with leather patches at the elbows. Everybody kept very quiet while he talked and scribbled on and on over the blackboard. What he scribbled was all numbers, all of it; and the more of it there was, the less and less I liked it, because Big Elephant and I had never taken much time over the numbers thing, other than two and two is four—along those lines. And so it was really hard for me to concentrate on what he was saying and talking about.

Soon a bell clanged—it was really something—so loud it might have been a fire. Everybody except Mr. Breen made a lot of noise and crowded out through the door. They were all running out to the playground for recess. I sat there not knowing what I was supposed to do until Mr. Breen came over and said, Come with me. We went into another room and he said, Now I'm going to give you some tests. He put some papers in front of me. I could hear the sounds coming from the playground, shouts and laughter and now and then the sound of a ball bouncing from a wall. I looked up at the clock stuck high above us. It was as white and big as a full moon. The angry black arrows pointed at two-thirty. Well, soon it would be three o'clock and Big Elephant would be back. I looked down at the tests. It seemed hopeless, but I did the best I could.

Mr. Jenkins called later that day. He said to bring me to school tomorrow, that I could start then. I would not be in the class I had visited but in the class below that. What a relief! I had expected him to call and say that there was no place at the Green Vale School for me at all.

The Three Wise Men

It was more or less about this time that I started seeing a lot of the Three Wise Men. One was fat and tall, one was short and fat, and the third one was tall and different from the other two. These other two I called Tweedledum and Tweedledee—but only

to myself, of course. Tweedledum was a Mr. Crocker. Tweedledee
was a Mr. Dunnington. And the tall one was Mr. Gilchrist, only
I called him Gilly or Fish-Face, depending on the way the wind
was blowing. They were all lawyers. And the more I saw of them,
the less I liked it. Oh, there was also another one—Mr. Smyth,
the Ever-Smiling One, only he was not in and out the way the
others were until later.

Big Elephant and the Little Countess thought all these lawyers
were Great Gentlemen, and whenever they could, they would
work into the conversation just how great they really were, and
why I must listen to them and remember everything they said.
They told me that the reason Tweedle Crocker was great was
because he was smart, very smart, and because he was a great
friend of Aunt Gertrude's and always looked after her best interests.
Tweedle Dunnington was great because—here Naney and Dodo
would look at each other, each expecting the other to fill in what
it was he was so great about. Then they would flounder about,
muttering to each other in a vague way, until finally Naney said
positively, You'll just have to take our word for it, Little One.

But when it came to Gilly they had a lot to say. What a
wonderful father he was to daughter Giselle and so on, why,
when you thought about it—and then they would leap into lots
of details about Giselle's problems. It was not hard to gather that
when it came to problems, Giselle's problems sounded very much
the same as Tatiana's. Why couldn't people with names like
Giselle and Tatiana be the way they were in fairy tales?

Sometimes, although I never let on, I was even jealous of
Giselle when they went on and on about her. What problems
did *she* have—she had a *Father*, didn't she? Then I would imagine
what it would be like if Gilly were *my* father. Once I even got
up enough nerve to ask him if he would be, but he got all flustery
and patted my hand in a blustery insincere way while saying in
a sincere way, Now now, no, no—that would never do, that
would never do . . . never, never!

I wish he would stop going on about it. I heard you the first time, Fish-Face.

After the banner proclamation was nailed up onto the bronze gate of Aunt Gertrude's castle, everything started to move fast.

Although I hardly saw Aunt Gertrude at all, I did see a lot of the Three Wise Lawyers. Naney Morgan would be along too, and not often, but sometimes, Big Elephant. From what I could gather, my Mother and Consuelo-Tamar wanted me to live with them and not at Aunt Gertrude's. But no matter what any of them said, to me it meant only one thing. It meant that our Caravan would be blown up. It meant that never again would I see Big Elephant. Never again, for in her place would be Friedel's Fräulein. And in the place of the Little Countess, who would there be? The same Friedel's Fräulein with the ever-present Consuelo-Tamar, urging my mother to pack our things and go to the Schloss Langenburg, where we would stay forever, along with Prince Ernst and Friedel's mother and the two unknowns, Dolly and Baby. It was all I could do to stop from jumping out the window. But I was determined not to. I kept holding on—onto a thread that I could feel being dangled out to me by the Three Wise Lawyers. And yes, Naney Morgan was in on it too. The more they talked, the more I could tell that if I did this and that, and said this and that, nothing would happen. Big Elephant would stay. The Little Countess would stay. Nothing would blow up. The Caravan would settle in forever at Aunt Gertrude's. Yes, all their heads nodded up and down, up and down, until, finally, they said it over and over again. *Forever!* Now I knew that it was up to me. Up to me not to jump out the window. Up to me to listen to every single thing each and every one of them said, every word they uttered. Because it was up to me—*I* could save us. I could save Dodo and Naney and myself from being ripped away from each other. Nothing was going to happen to our Caravan, nothing at all, because I would not let it. I caught on to this thread they had given me, and soon it became a string, and soon the string became a rope, and when it did—I knew we were almost home free.

There was going to be a battle, I was told. A Custody Trial. What was that? It would be like a War between Aunt Gertrude and my mother. And I might have to go into the battlefield myself and fight for what was right. But I would not be alone. The Gladiators would all be there to help—Tweedle Crocker, Tweedle Dunnington, Gilly, and the Ever-Smiling Smyth. All of us together, to fight against, I was now told, the hated Mr. Burkan. This was the first time I had heard of him, but I caught on quickly. He was my mother's lawyer, they all said, while the Little Countess rolled her eyes and said I'd have to look out for him because he was Jewish and so he was really *conniving* and very smart. It was the first time I had ever heard the word Jewish and the first time I had ever heard the word conniving. What is Jewish? I asked Big Elephant later. Oh, you know, lovey—like Mr. A. C. Blumenthal. Well, I did not know. And conniving? I asked the Little Countess. She rolled her eyes again. Never mind, Little One, never mind. You'll find out, you'll find out soon enough. . . . So I didn't ask any more questions. It was going to take everything I had to be ready to fight with Mr Burkan when the time came.

It came soon enough. For a few days later I was taken out of school by the Wise Men and driven from Old Westbury Capital to the Courthouse in New York where I would meet Judge Carew.

But first we drove to pick up Aunt Gertrude at her castle on Fifth Avenue. We waited in the car for her to come out, and finally when she did, she was smiling. Not only smiling, but wearing a dress! And over this dress, around her shoulders, an animal was draped, a smiling animal with a little brown face and two beady eyes and little smiling reaching paws. Not only that, but because of that dress it was the first time I had ever seen the legs of Aunt Gertrude. Long, they were, and at the bottom of them long tapering feet, and on these feet were long tapering shoes made of something green—lizard maybe—with a green T holding them together. Then to top it all came the hat, that hat which seemed to match and go with everything. All in all it was quite an effect. Most interesting—so interesting I could not stop gazing at her. Especially at that animal. It looked so real. What was it? Dare I ask? No, I did not.

It was strange to me, but my mother's name never came up when Aunt Gertrude was around; I never heard her mention her at all, ever. It was as if she did not know what was going on, although of course I knew she did. We all did. I guess whatever had to be said the lawyers said for her; that's what it must have meant when Naney said that Tweedle Crocker looked after Aunt Gertrude's best interests. On this particular trip, I had been told, nothing would happen and I did not have to say or do anything. So as we drove along, my mother's name never came up. All I had to do was be there. The really big fight would come later. And they all told me that when the time came, I would know what to do. I thought about that a lot.

They all said Judge Carew was most friendly and loved children because he had children of his own. But that did not impress me the way they thought it would, having already seen some examples such as the tree episode in the Adirondacks. However, I let it slip by. Maybe he would be someone related to Sara Crewe in *The Little Princess*, a book I had been reading. But then I found out his name was spelled Carew, so already I knew he would not be any relation to my Sara at all.

Aunt Gertrude spoke gracious words all during the ride down. Now we are near Wall Street, she said, and we drove along through canyons on either side—until suddenly everyone, even Aunt Gertrude, stopped talking. We had turned a corner, but we could not move. The street was filled with hundreds and hundreds of people, hundreds of people waiting for something. And the something they were waiting for was—Us! Then there were policemen, dozens and dozens, all trying to keep them back

so our grey car could get through. Hundreds peered at us through
the car windows, all trying to get closer, shouting to get our
attention by calling out to us, shouting and trying to tap on the
windows, whenever they could slip by one of the policemen. But
Aunt Gertrude stared straight ahead as if none of this were happening; so did the lawyers. I do not know how she did it, but
she did. You would have thought she was a Queen in a coach of

gold, going along a country lane in springtime with no one in sight. I tried to act just like her, though it was all so unlike anything that had ever happened to me. But it was worse, much worse, when at last the policemen cleared a pathway through and the car edged up to the long grey steps that led up to the Courthouse where Judge Carew waited for us. Much worse when we got out of the car, for there, on the steps, were even more people, only these had cameras, and they were fighting among themselves and yelling at each other, all trying to get ahead of each other, some even tripping each other up and falling, all trying to get pictures of Aunt Gertrude and me. It must have been just as awful for her as it was for me, but she was amazing! In all that pushing and shouting, in all that hullaballoo, she took each step, on her thin long legs in their elegant green shoes, up and up, just as if she did not have a care in the world. If she can do it, so can I, I kept saying to myself over and over, but it did not work, and finally I made myself think about Big Elephant and of the sunlight and of the times we had been happy together in the Bois, and how safe I felt when we were all together, Big Elephant, the Little Countess and I, and how if I could get through this, I would get through to that—to that other place, of happiness, where we would be together always, Dodo and I, always and always. . . . I hung on to that as I went on and on up the steps.

And all at once we had reached the top. We were inside an elevator, up and out, going down hallways until we came to a door which opened to us and we went in.

I could feel *her* close, so close; my dress almost touched the beauty of her, but it did not. I was afraid that if I even looked at her the spell would be broken and I would be pulled out of the place it had taken me such effort to reach. I did not even know anymore what it was I clung to, but whatever it was, it had made possible my climbing up the steps and through the crowds and into this room where my mother and Judge Carew sat waiting for us.

So what happened that first day at the Court was, I was told later, just a formality. The really big stuff had not started yet— except in the newspapers. Custody Trial—lurid headlines, I heard some of the teachers at Green Vale say, and I knew they were talking about me and my mother and Aunt Gertrude. But I did everything I could to prevent myself from seeing what it was they meant, and whenever anyone in school started in on it, I would look those persons straight in the eye and say, I Do Not Want To Hear About It! Then, if that didn't shut them up, well, I'd turn my back and just saunter away out of reach, casual-like. I knew that if I let myself, it would be easy to get sucked in and drowned. So I kept holding on and thinking about that place where I could hide and be safe—that secret place that no one knew about except me—that place in the Caravan filled with sunlight where I could go, as if by magic, whenever I wished to. All I had to do was close my eyes tight, and soon, presto! a door would open, and from darkness I would step into light. I never dared tell anyone about this, because I knew if I did, the spell would be broken and it would be taken away from me, and then all would be lost.

Things happened every day now. More on some days than on others. Weekends, Aunt Gertrude would drive out from the castle in the city to the Old Westbury Capital. On Sunday afternoon she would drive back in again and be gone all week. In between the weekends Naney stayed with Big Elephant and me. To keep the pot boiling, you might say. All of my cousins who lived at Old Westbury Capital were my Aunt Gertrude's grandchildren and called her Gamoo. But there were other cousins, I soon found out, who belonged to my father's other sister, my Aunt Gladys. They were in the same boat as I was regarding how they were related to Aunt Gertrude. I had not met them yet, as they lived in Washington, but the Little Countess told me that they all called Aunt Gertrude Auntie Ger, and that I should too, because it would show the world, including Aunt Gertrude, how close we were and how much I loved her. Well—why not? I thought.

Also, the Little Countess went on to say, show more excitement—
a lot more, Little One—a lot more excitement when your Auntie
Ger arrives here on Fridays. Keep looking out the window waiting
to see her car come in the driveway, then run down the stairs as
fast as you can and throw yourself into her arms the second she
comes in the front door. You know what I mean, Little One.
You know what your Naney means. Do it next time—show your
little Naney. Well, when the next Friday came around, I really
did show her. I got myself all keyed up looking out that window
onto the circle of the driveway, and when finally the car came in
sight, I was raring to go. Down the stairs I went lickety-split,
just like a racehorse at the sound of the bell. I almost knocked
Aunt Gertrude—I mean Auntie Ger—over. Don't overdo it,
Little One, Naney Morgan said to me privately later—don't
overdo it. But I could tell she was pleased. As for Aunt Gertrude,
well, I really did not have a clue as to what she thought. She
was a hard person to figure out.

Then one Friday Tweedle Crocker came to Old Westbury to
tell me that Aunt Gertrude would not be coming out until late,
very late, on Saturday. He told me that Judge Carew had decided
my mother should come out to Old Westbury to see me—*here*
in this house. I was flabbergasted; I could not believe it. I did
not want her to come here and take me away, away from Big
Elephant. She will *not* take you away from your Aunt Gertrude,
he said over and over again. But I did not believe him. The judge
just wants to give your mother a chance—a chance to see you,
just to make sure everyone is doing the right thing. The right
thing! What did any of them know about the right thing? I
hardly knew myself anymore. So you see your Aunt Gertrude
will not be here when your mother is here but will come back
after your mother has left. I begged him not to let this happen—
not to let my mother come and take me away—away from Big
Elephant. Only I could not ever say this out loud, because I knew
that I had to pretend it was Aunt Gertrude I was afraid of being
taken away from. Now now—he was getting more and more

ruffled—Now now—he was really angry. Stop this, this minute. You have nothing to be afraid of. And, he went on, guess what? What? what? what? I begged him. Your Cousin Bean will take you riding in the morning—isn't that nice of him? He'll take you around for a nice ride and stay with you until it's time for your mother to arrive. Then he'll bring you back to see her. Cousin Bean! Cousin Bean! *He* was the one who had chained my cousin to the tree. Please no, please no! But I knew I had to pretend. Please yes, please yes! I could not think of one single thing to say in answer to all this. Huge, silent, grim Cousin Bean with a pipe rooted in his mouth, who never had anything to say to me at all—why had *he* been asked to do this? Where would we go on that long silent ride? Before it was time to come back to meet my mother, where would we go and what would be said? And—oh—he went on—Dodo will be sent away. *Away!* I screamed. Oh, just for the day away, so she won't be here for the few hours your mother's here. Well—that's about it for now anyway. You be a good little girl now and have a good time, have a nice ride with Cousin Bean tomorrow.

Freddy came early the next morning and took Dodo away somewhere. She swore to me that she would be coming back. She promised me. Then she put on her hat with the fur trim and her coat with the shawl collar and she got into the car and drove away.

It was not long before Bozo Bean arrived on a big horse with Walter, the groom from Whitney Stables, leading a smaller horse. From where I was, I could look up and see Bozo Bean looking me over from where he sat high up on his horse. Come on now, Gloria, he said, let's go for a ride. It was the first time I had ever laid eyes on him without the pipe in his mouth. Maybe it would be like a whole new person.

But it wasn't. Walter helped me up onto the horse I was to ride and I followed Bozo Bean down the hill, away from the house and on into the meadow. He did not say one word the whole time and I could not think of one myself. So we rode on

and on. Cat got your tongue? he finally said, and we turned off on to one of the roads leading around Old Westbury Capital. There were a lot of policemen there, as if the place was being guarded—which was exactly what was going on. Guards were at every turn, it seemed, but Bozo Bean still did not say anything and stayed hidden in his silent unbending self, and we trotted on and on. It was endless. Why were police guards around?

I thought maybe it was to stop my mother from taking me away from Big Elephant—I mean from Aunt Gertrude. Of course that was it! Maybe it was going to be all right after all. Bozo Bean kept looking at his watch, and at last he said, Well, it's time. Now come on. And he clicked at his horse to go faster and my horse clicked on behind as we both galloped back across the meadows. But again I became frightened. When my mother saw me, what would she do? . . . And Mr. Burkan—would he be with her? And if he was, what would *he* do?

I jumped off my horse and ran away, away from Bozo Bean, ran away, in through the door, along the halls, up the stairs, so fast he could not keep up with me. I made it to my room and I slammed the door shut. I turned the key in the lock just in time before they all got there and started banging on the door.

Your mother's here—here—here, pounded Bozo Bean on my door. Open up, open up! Come on, Gloria, open that door! Open that door or—I'll huff and I'll puff and I'll blow your house in!

Oh no you won't, Bozo! And I ran to the fireplace and took a match and soon it was roaring up into the chimney. Now there were others outside the door banging on it. I was trapped. There was no place else I could go. I started to throw the key into the fire, but instead I ran into the bathroom and took off the lid of a big round box of bath powder. Under the downy puff, way down, until the key hit the bottom, I pushed the key down down until it hit the bottom—yes, that is what I did. And when it did—when it hit the bottom—I shook the box so that the sweet-smelling powderliness of it settled down smooth, so smooth it was as though it had never been touched. Then I put the puff back in place and over that the lid. Now I was safe. Only, of course, it was a lie, and I knew it—a lie that I told myself, kept telling myself, as they banged on and on, pounding on the door.

If you don't open up, we'll have to call the doctor! The doctor—the doctor—the doctor! Then a lot of scrambly loud talk and more banging. Then it was quiet. I ran to the door and tried to hear what they were saying.

Take her into the other room, she can lie down there—that was Bozo talking.

Outrageous! Outrageous what that child is doing to her mother! Consuelo-Tamar, of course.

Let *me* get at her! Now it was Aunt Toto. So they were all here! And Mr. Burkan—had he come too? Listen, Aunt Toto

said, you listen here to me. Nobody is going to hurt you—can
you hear me?

I could hear, all right. But I still did not believe her.

Listen to me now—her voice had softened. Just open the door
to me—will you do that now?—just to me. Your mother isn't
even here now, she's not feeling well—she's lying down in the
other room. Your Aunt Tamar is with her.

My Aunt Tamar indeed! And Bozo—what about him? But I
kept quiet.

No one's here now except me. Please let me in.

Maybe he had gone away with the others . . . maybe . . .
maybe. . . .

Listen, Gloria—we are going to be leaving soon. Won't you
see me for just a minute? Your mother drove out all this way
just to see you.

Open up, Gloria. It was Bozo—he was back again. Open up
or we will have to break the door down! Do you hear me, Gloria?
Your mother has a court order to see you—a court order—so
make it easy on yourself, do you hear me? Make it easy on yourself
and open up—she has an order from the court! Otherwise I'll
have to get one of those policemen you saw to come and I'll have
to ask one of those policemen—listen to me now—I'll have to
ask those policemen to break this door down—down—down—
this door down—

Well—go on—go ahead! I won't care—care—care—no, never
never never. Let them do that, let them! See if I care—care—
care—

I ran into the bathroom and slammed the door. But there
was no key to that. Then I sat down on the floor with my back
against it because there was no place else to go.

Soon—it was not long—soon they huffed and they puffed
and they blew my house in. Bozo lifted me up from the floor
and took me into my room and put me down on the bed. I looked
up at Aunt Toto and Consuelo-Tamar—there they were.

But my mother was not anywhere in sight, and I turned over and screamed into the pillow.

You have to see—to see her—you *have* to see her! Do you understand, Gloria? Do you? Do you understand? Do you? Do you?

Bozo Bean was tap-tap-tapping me on my back tap-tap-tap right on through me tap-tap-tap until he almost tapped right through me to the other side as I lay face down on the pillow.

A court order—your mother cannot leave this house without seeing you, do you understand? Your mother cannot set foot out of this house until she sees you. Now it was Aunt Toto, and, in between, Consuelo-Tamar saying, Outrageous! Outrageous!

Look Gloria—now Bozo Bean busting in—if you don't stop this I'll have to call Doctor Jessup. Do you hear me? Do you?

Doctor Jessup Doctor Jessup I didn't need a doctor—why didn't they leave Doctors out of this. Why were Doctors always being brought in? What I needed was simple—what I needed was Big Elephant.

Listen to me tap-tap-tap, Gloria—you listen now!

I could not stand it another minute, so I whirled around and threw the pillow right into Bozo's face and ran past the two aunts, straight through the door right across the hall I ran, into the room that was supposed to be Dodo's room, straight over to the bed that was said to be Elephant's bed—and there, sure enough, there lay my mother stretched out on it with her hand lifted up over her face to cover it from view.

Someone had put a blanket over her and she lay there so quiet and still I thought she might be dead and I reached out to touch her. For a second she did not move at all and I felt cold and as though I would melt away into the death of her. But then her fingers moved just a little bit and then her hand moved and then she took it right off from her face and looked at me.

Hello, Mummy, I said.

But she closed her eyes again as if she were so tired she just could not keep them open, and as she did Aunt Consuelo-Tamar and Aunt Toto came into the room and behind them there was Bozo Bean.

I turned around and walked through them, out the door, across the hall and back into my room. I sat down on a chair and looked into the fireplace at the burning shapes and tried to think about nothing at all. . . .

Soon it started to get dark outside and out of the corner of my eye I could see a clump of black dresses all stuck together move past the open door and out of sight. They never stopped to glance in the door or look around at all. Well, what else could they have done? There was no need to say good-bye. Down the stairs drifted the clump of the black dress of Consuelo-Tamar, and down the stairs drifted the clump of the black dress of Aunt Toto, and somewhere sandwiched in the middle was my mother, although their arms were so tightly pressed around her I could hardly see her, only one side of her head as it bowed against the shoulder of Consuelo-Tamar, so sharp in profile it was like a silhouette cut out of paper.

Dinner as Usual

Big Elephant did come back that same day just as she promised. And as she came in the door, Bozo Bean went out the door. Boy, was I glad to get rid of him!

I went into Dodo's room with her and watched her while she took off her coat and put her hat back on the top shelf. Where did you go to? I asked her.

Oh, just for a drive, just for a drive—Freddy just drove me around.

But where? I wanted to know.

Nowhere in particular—we just drove around.

Well, you must have driven *somewhere!*

Well, we really didn't, dear—we just had a nice drive around.

What places did you see?

Oh . . . Green Vale, we drove past there, and around and around, here and there.

Oh, I see, I said.

And now I'm back again.

Yes, I said. And now you're back. I went over and hugged her. And just as I did, who should come in the door but Aunt Gertrude, and with her there was Naney Morgan. I was so glad she was back too. Dinner will be ready soon, said Aunt Gertrude, and we all went down the stairs to sit in the living room the way we always did every evening before dinner.

Butler William came in with a silver tray and on it the glass of vermouth Aunt Gertrude always had before dinner was served. Then Aunt Gertrude said to the Little Countess, just as she always did, Sure you won't change your mind, Laura? And the Little Countess answered, just as she always did, No no, Gertrude, no thank you, nothing for me. Then butler William passed the tray to Big Elephant and over to me, the way he always did, and we each took a glass of tomato juice. It was thick and shaken up and frothy on the top. The goblets had juicy red tomatoes painted on, and I always closed my eyes for a minute to trace a finger over the cool glass, outlining each shape so that I could remember it later. There was also a little plate of biscuits, thin as communion wafers, with melted cheese bubbling on top, and Dodo and I each took one.

I wondered if Aunt Gertrude was going to say to me, as she always did when she first arrived for these weekends, Well now, Gloria, what did you do today? But she didn't. Instead, she encouraged the conversation to trip back and forth between Naney and herself about mutual friends who lived in Europe and were all titled personages. It was always very boring. But Naney got even more lively when this kind of gossip came up and she never failed to bring up this one or that one when she had Aunt Gertrude captive, so to speak, not only before dinner but continuing on through dinner and even after if possible. It was exhausting to listen to her, and I often felt that by the time dessert arrived, Aunt Gertrude had taken all she could stand and was at her wit's end. A glaze would drift over her and she would nod and nod just as if she were really hearing Naney's every word. But this particular evening Aunt Gertrude was all ears and even added her own two cents here and there to the chatter. She even made a point of bringing the prized Infanta Eulalia into the conversation to get Naney off on that. This Infanta was not only the Twins' godmother but, according to Naney Morgan, her closest friend, and it was part of life's destiny that distance always separated these best friends from seeing each other. For the Infanta lived, of course, in Spain, and Naney never got a chance to go there. How could she when she had to—her eyes would shoot over to me and then back to Aunt Gertrude, and then she would say, But you know, Gertrude, blood is thicker than water. Then her eyes would close and her head would tilt in my direction and she would whisper so I would not be able to hear her—needs me, needs me, the Little One she needs me! So along those lines we all, in one way or another, got through the dinner that night.

Only this time when dinner was over I did not go up to do my homework as I usually did, because Naney said she had to talk to me. Had to talk to me? What about? All I really wanted to do was go to sleep. She's tired, said Dodo. And Aunt Gertrude looked at me, then at Naney Morgan. Why don't you wait until tomorrow, Laura? Naney rat-tat-tatted the long red castanets of her nails on the table for a while, thinking hard, then she said, Yes, darling, yes, Little One—now you run upstairs and your Auntie Ger and your Naney will be up soon to tuck you in, tuck you in in in. . . .

All during the time I was taking my bath, all during the time I was getting ready for bed, and all during the time Naney and Aunt Gertrude were tuck-tuck-tucking me in, and all during the time they turned the lights out out out, and all during the time Dodo sat sat sat in the bathroom with the light on waiting for me to go to sleep, there was only one thing going around and around in my head—Wait until tomorrow tomorrow tomorrow. . . .

Wait until tomorrow for what for what for what? What was going to happen then?

Tomorrow

I hadn't been able to sleep thinking about all this, but sometime I must have, because the next day was Sunday and my eyes opened and here it was tomorrow and I did not have to wait another minute.

It was a quarter to eleven and I knew Aunt Gertrude would be well into breakfast in bed behind her closed door. No one but Hortense ever saw her until she emerged from her room fully hatted much later in the day.

Dodo was probably back in her room.

Running along the curve of the hall, jumping over the one step, I ran into Naney's room on the left. She was propped up on a lot of pillows stretched out under the canopy of the high fourposter bed. There she sat without her eyebrows drawn on, wearing the reddish-amber sweater she always wore as a bed jacket over her nightgown, smoking, drinking café au lait, and skimming through the newspapers. Only she wasn't alone. Dodo wasn't in her room—she was here, sitting right in the chair next to Naney Morgan's bed. Quickly, as soon as I came in, quickly Naney swooped up the newspapers and pushed them down to the foot of the bed and yanked the puffy coverlet over them. They made a big hump at the foot of the bed and I could not stop my eyes from going back to it over and over again. I knew that under that soft mound of palest blue silk there would be photographs; some would be good and some would be bad, but they would be of us—Dodo and Naney, Aunt Gertrude and my mother and me—depicted in one way or another. And there would be angry black letters in tall capitals forming words in a shorthand I could not read for fear of understanding what they meant.

How are you feeling, darling, today? Naney Morgan said.

Oh, fine, I feel fine fine.

Precious One, are you sure?

Oh—so that was it. *That* was all it was.

But then she went on. How can you feel fine after what happened when They were here, when They all came here? How can you?

I picked it all up right away and sailed right on and out with it—but how far did I have to go? Did your stomach pains come back? You know, those pains you get in your stomach when something upsets you? *They* came here, didn't they? she said, rolling her eyes. Right to this house. So why wouldn't you be upset, terribly terribly upset, seeing the three of them here, right on this spot, trying to take you away from your Auntie Ger, away from me, and—where do you think *Dodo* will be when the Fräulein appears? You don't think Dodo will be around then, do you? You'll never see either one of us, when they take you back to Europe or who knows where—forever. Do you know what that means—forever?

I knew all right!

Pains, yes—I had terrible terrible pains all through the night—I couldn't sleep sleep sleep. Pain pain yes that's what it was, that's what was keeping me awake—pain.

She better go back to bed, Nurse, Naney said to Dodo, the Little One better lie down, and then you better call Doctor Jessup.

Doctor Jessup Doctor Jessup—but suppose he doesn't believe me? Suppose he *doesn't*?

He will, he will, said Naney Morgan loudly, and so surely that suddenly I found myself, I found myself—yes, yes, it *was* true, it *was*—it would be, it *would!*

Naney put her little legs over the side of the high fourposter bed. Her little toes were painted red mahogany just like her fingernails, only they were clipped so short there was hardly enough room to brush the color. They dangled there valiantly at the edge of her nightgown. Without her face on she had no eyebrows, and without lipstick she had no mouth, and without a mouth everything about her had shrunk small so small. Maybe she was not as powerful as I thought, as we all thought—why, maybe she was not powerful at all, as she dangled there no bigger than a marionette. I grieved for her, longing for her to come back to me, with her face together and her lips on and her eyebrows back where they belonged. I put my arms around her to help her down off the bed, but I felt so sad about her I wanted to cry.

What the Little Countess Had to Tell Me

Dodo and I went back along the hall and into my room. The bed was just as I had left it, and I got back in as though I had just awakened in my pajamas and had never gone down along the hall to Naney's room at all. I lay there with my hand on my stomach wondering how long it would take for Doctor Jessup to show up.

How about some milk toast? Dodo asked me. That ought to slip down easily.

That would be swell, I said, I'm really hungry.

She straightened out the covers and said, I'll be back in a minute.

Then she went out the door and closed it behind her. I thought about her gliding down those stairs, through the dining room and on into the kitchen for the conference with Cook, to tell her exactly how to make milk toast. I hoped it was not going to take too long. That back-in-a-minute thing didn't mean anything. It could even mean I'll be back in an hour. . . .

Just when I was starting to get worried, the door opened and in came Naney.

Her eyebrows were in place and her mouth was in place too. There she was in high-heeled shoes, and on her the usual skirt and blouse of crêpe de chine with its V of flat ruffles, and over this blouse was the sweater that doubled as a bed jacket. Naney had few changes of clothes because clothes cost money and Naney liked to save. There, as usual, on the lapel of her sweater was the diamond arrow pin which I knew would be mine someday, even though I did not want it, because whenever Naney told me This will be yours someday, darling, she always went on to say When your Naney is in her grave. It made me die every time she said it. The arrow looked really pretty pinned against the knit of black and orange wool of her jacket which was just the right scramble of color to go with Naney's hair. So now when she came towards me through the door I could see that everything about her was right back in place where it belonged and I knew that my Naney had come back to me.

She came over and sat in front of me on the edge of the bed and took my hand. Listen, my Precious One. Listen carefully. One day next week you are going to have to drive into New York to see someone—just for a visit, a little visit to see the Judge again—just for a half hour or so.

I stared at Naney's hand holding mine. I stared at her gold wedding ring and at the ring above it, at the three round diamonds all in a row, each exactly the same size as the other. Grandpa Morgan had given this ring to her, and each diamond heralded an event of earthshaking importance. The first one presented to Naney celebrated the birth of Consuelo. And later, with lots of things happening in between, two perfectly round glittering matching diamonds had found their place nestled in beside the first, for not one but two births had taken place in the world—the Twins had been born, and Grandpa Morgan had presented Naney with two glittering round diamonds even more perfect than the first. But it was the way Naney told it, like a fairy tale always, and I never tired of hearing it over and over again.

You remember the Judge, darling, you remember when you went in to see him? Well, it's the same one, but this time he will see you in his private chambers, the Judge's Private Chambers—isn't that nice? The same Judge Carew. So when you go there, the day you go—it won't be for long, Precious One, but it's a very very important thing you will be doing, and what you do there and what you say will decide the Judge on whether he will let you stay here with Aunt Gertrude or whether he will send you back to your mother who will take you to Germany and we will never see each other again—never never again. Never! Dodo and I will never set eyes on you again. The Prince has a Fräulein waiting for you, all ready and waiting at the Schloss, just for you to arrive—aie, aie—yes he has! And *that's* where they will take you, do you hear me, darling? Are you listening to your Naney?

I kept looking at the ring and nodding my head up and down fast fast.

Now Doctor Jessup is coming—he is on his way here right this minute, and when he gets here you must tell him how much your stomach hurts and how you couldn't sleep last night because it hurt so much, and then when he starts poking around here and there on your little tummy, you can go like this—Oooo-ouch, um-um-um, ooooo-eeeEEEEE—and her eyes careened around while her voice skidded up and up into the wailing sound of a creature possessed.

If you do this right, then he will be able to tell the Judge how sick it has made you knowing you may have to leave Auntie Ger and go back to your mother who will take you to Germany.

But suppose he *knows* I'm making it up, making it up, making it up that my stomach hurts hurts hurts?

He won't know, if you do it right.

But suppose he *does*?

None of them have known so far, have they? have they? St. Lawrence doesn't know when you say you feel sick. Doctor Craig doesn't either. None of them know what's going on, so why will Doctor Jessup?

Maybe she was right . . . maybe I *could* do it.

Right then the door opened and in came Dodo with a tray and on the tray a big bowl of steaming hot buttery milk toast.

Naney looked at her watch. Sit up, Precious One, sit up now quickly! Sit up and eat the nice milk toast Nurse has brought. Hurry up, hurry up—we don't want Doctor Jessup to walk in until after you've finished eating, do we, do we!

Dodo came over and put the tray on my lap. I looked down into the floating whiteness of it, but I could not bring myself to pick up the spoon.

Already the cheesecloth had started to descend around me. The tray and everything on it—the sheets, the bed, and, yes, everything in the room, everything I looked at—I could only dimly see through this wall of cheesecloth. Naney dim and far away, and Dodo, yes, even Dodo, the soft mountain of her blurred and dimmed as the cheesecloth descended. All around it fell down and down, everywhere I looked, with its sheet of silent snow, down and down. . . . I tried to lift my hand up to catch Dodo before she disappeared. But it was too late—the cheesecloth had turned to frozen glass, and try as I would, I could not reach through to her.

Doctor Jessup's Sunday House Call

Doctor Jessup was tall, very tall, and I liked him, so it made it easier for me to get through the cheesecloth when he walked through the door of my room and came over to the bed where I lay. I liked him, but the only one I *really* liked was Doctor Craig. But he was only for noses and throats, and in the game we were playing, well—it was much easier to play make-believe about tummy pains than it was to make-believe about runny noses and sore throats. Doctor Jessup's daughter, Joanie, was in my class at Green Vale School, which made a difference, too—quite why I don't know, but it did.

Well, here he was, and I would not keep him long. I wanted to get through this as fast as I could.

He put down his bag and took out old friend stethoscope. Then he pulled the covers back and gently explored my tummy and listened around here and there. From time to time I made the oooo-eeEEE-ouch sounds and I got quite carried away by my own performance. But Naney came closer to me and I could sense that even she thought I might be overdoing it—and if *she* thought that, I better tone it down a bit. It was a relief to be sincere, so I told him about the cheesecloth. How everything I looked at I could only see through this veiled wall of cheesecloth. But he did not get that at all at all at all. It made me angry, because *that* was true and the stomach ache was *not* true, and yet he believed me about these terrible pains in my tummy. Not only did he not understand about the cheesecloth, it was clear to me that he did not want to hear any more mention of it, because he turned around to Naney and Dodo and said, Maybe she needs glasses—better get her eyes checked next week. Isn't that something?

Then he packed the stethoscope back in his bag, and Dodo took the wooden stick he had pressed my tongue down with and threw it in the wastebasket. He wrote something on a pad and gave it to Dodo. She can start two of these as soon as possible and then two every four hours. Call me if she's not feeling better by tonight.

Thank you, Doctor, thank you. Naney lit another Chesterfield and chirped around, Nurse, have the chauffeur take the prescription to get it filled immediately—yes, and close the curtains, she needs rest. . . .

Naney went out the door with Doctor Jessup and Dodo went over to the windows to pull the curtains. I'll get this to Freddy, dear, she said, then I'll be right back. I closed my eyes and waited.

Getting to Know Mr. Smyth

Do you feel well enough to see Mr. Gilchrist? Naney asked me later that day.

I guess so, I said.

What about Mr. Crocker and Mr. Dunnington?

You mean all at once?

Well, Precious, maybe not all at once, maybe just Mr. Smyth, how about him? You do feel well enough to see him, don't you don't you don't you?

Yes Yes Yes I answered quickly. So *he* was going to be the one who would take me to see the Judge. Well, the sooner I got to know him, the better it would be. I feel fine, fine, yes fine, but not too fine, just fine enough to see him.

Well, darling, guess what? He is here *now!* Yes, right here in this house, in the living room, talking to Auntie Ger. He is going to do everything he can so that the Judge will decide not to send you away to Germany. Auntie Ger is downstairs right now talking to him and making plans—only these plans won't come true unless you understand certain things—that's why it's important, very important, you feel well enough to see him today right now. So you do, Precious One, don't you—don't you?

Oh, I do, I do, Naney, I do I do! I would have to chance it that the cheesecloth would go away when I did see him. No fuzzy edges at this meeting—it was too important.

Mr. Smyth bounded into the room so quickly it was hard to believe he had not been outside the door, listening and waiting for some secret signal from Naney, instead of where Naney had said he was, downstairs in the living room making plans with Aunt Gertrude.

But here he was, bounding in, his smooth-faced, ever-smiling and unlikeable Self. I really did not like him at all. No, not even a little bit. But I would have to. I would have to make myself

like him no matter what. I tried to think of some
him I could like, but I could not think of a thing—
smirk I couldn't get past. Each road led back to tha
I thought about all these reasons why I *couldn't* s
would be something to hold on to, something to get me through,
until it was all over and Dodo and Naney and I would be safe.
Any one of the others would have been better than this—yes,
even Tweedle Crocker or Tweedle Dunnington would have been
far better. Fish-Face would have been best of all, even if he did
not want to be my father—at least I knew him a little better
than the others. But Naney and Dodo both said that Mr. Smyth
was brilliant—not only brilliant but *the* Brilliant, far, far superior
to all the other superior Brilliants mixed up in this mess. So here
I was stuck with him, and I was determined to do the best I
could.

As he sat there talking to me, every word coming out of that
smiling pie face was a lie—a lie—a lie. No one would be there
except the Kindly Judge who already was a friend of mine and
who would receive us in his Private Chambers. What *were* these
Private Chambers they all went on and on about? No one else
would be present, he went on, except me and him and The
Judge—oh, and the stenographer, he would be there too, just
so he could write down everything we talked about, so the Judge
could go over it later in case he needed to refresh his memory.
Not that he would—when it came to memory, Judge Carew had
no problem—but it was the custom to write down everything
that was said. The Judge was kind, very kind, and wanted to be
fair to all concerned and come to the right decision. So there was
really nothing much to it. We were going to pay a little call,
Mr. Smyth and I, and it was in that spirit I should prepare for
it, a little visit to Judge Carew to have a nice cozy chat with an
old friend in his Private Chambers.

But what about the crowds of faces in the streets outside the
Private Chambers—the crowds of tumblers from the circus with
their hands and their cameras shouting as they piled over each

other, shouting at us and at each other as we huddled up the grey steps leading to the Courthouse—what of them? I wanted to ask him, What of them? Were they part of the cozy visit too? Or maybe they would not be there this time? Well, we both knew the answer to that.

You see, it's very simple really, the Judge wants to hear it directly from you—your feelings about your mother, about your Aunt Gertrude, and why you want to live with Aunt Gertrude here at Old Westbury instead of living in hotels here and there traipsing around all over Europe, and then maybe even having to settle somewhere—Germany, for example. Have you thought of that ever? Settling somewhere in Germany? Your mother has always been interested in marrying a Title, so who knows what could happen in the future? Has that ever occurred to you? How would you feel about that?

I wanted to spit in his face—that's how I felt about that!

So, he went on, we have certain problems here, nothing that cannot be solved, providing you can make the Judge aware of how it is you really feel about being taken away from Old Westbury and from Aunt Gertrude. You have to be very adamant . . . do you know what that means? It means that you must not be afraid of overstating how you feel. You must put it in strong words, you must not hold back your true feelings. The Judge is there to help you, and he cannot do this unless he understands, and he will not fully understand unless you can communicate it to him by expressing your true feelings. I cannot stress this strongly enough.

You have you have you have. Let's get on with it, on with it, on, on with it—but instead the scream exploded inside my chest and he never heard. I sat there, listening quietly, as quietly as I could bring myself to do without fidgeting, until I sensed the time had come, the time when I could open my mouth without the shout. And when it arrived, I could hear a voice coming as from a great distance and it was my voice saying to him,

Mr. Smyth, help me, will you, will you will you, help me so I can know what to do?

And the cheesecloth—what of that? It was strange, really weird, because in the week ahead I forgot all about it.

Homework

So a few days later the time had come. The day and the time had come, and I was to be taken to the place I remembered so well, to have that chat with my friend Judge Carew. I kept going over and over all the things Mr. Smyth had said during the hours we had spent together the past few days. All the things and all the hours added up to quite a lot of hours and quite a lot of things. When I thought about it, there really had not been time to do much of anything else. Everything had come to a stop, so to speak, and I did not have to think about school or homework or anything else. I just prayed I could keep it all straight in my mind so I would not make a slip about anything. I kept trying to picture Judge Carew in his robe the way he had looked that only time I met him. He impressed me the way a religious card does, like the ones in the prayer book Dodo had given me. Saint Theresa was on the cover, smiling and holding a cross draped with roses. Inside were the small loose cards I collected that fit between the pages: on one side would be a watercolor of a saint, and on the other side there was a prayer. Yes, decidedly so— that was the way the Judge impressed me. There was one of Saint Joseph in particular, one arm outstretched and the other pointing to a big heart with something on it written in Latin and rays all around it—only, of course, Saint Joseph's robe was long and red and Judge Carew's was long and black. Come to think of it, maybe it was not Saint Joseph at all. Saint Joseph would not be sporting a red robe, would he? No, if it was red, it must be Jesus Himself. . . . Then I kept trying to remember what the face looked like on the card, but it was a faceless face, just like the face of Judge Carew, as I tried to pin it down. And anyway, Judge Carew's long robe was black, so what did he have to do with Jesus Himself as colored on the card in my prayer book? None of this made sense or mattered anyway. It just gave me something to hang on to other than the things going around and around in my brain like mice in a cage.

Then other times would come when I burst with hope, because maybe what Mr. Smyth said would turn out to be true. Maybe it would not be a circus after all. Perhaps when we turned that corner we would turn onto an everyday street, with everyday city things moving here and there, to and fro, up the steps and on the sidewalks. Maybe we would even get by with no one noticing us at all . . . at all . . . at all.

Mr. Smyth and I Drive to the City

Well, here we were, Mr. Smyth and I, at last together in Aunt Gertrude's car and just about to turn a corner—so we would find out soon enough.

And there we were, right smack in the middle of it, or rather right smack against it. Even before we turned the corner, lining the street on every side were the same hundreds and hundreds of people, only this time there were even more. And there were even more policemen trying to hold them back behind barricades that had been placed all along the street on either side right up to the steps of the Courthouse. Out of nowhere, shrieking through all this, so suddenly it made even Mr. Smyth jump, came a motorcycle. It grazed in front of the car we were in, making that sound which split right through you. The crowds jumped too and pulled back; but then they surged forward again, trying to get even closer, while they shouted things out to us, none of which we could hear as the windows were closed tight as tight could be. I wanted to die right there. Everything kept getting crazier and crazier, the people lining the streets, but most of all

the ones with the cameras—even the policemen got nuttier and
nuttier, trying to keep the crowds and the men with the cameras
back as they shouted at each other.

When we got out of the car we stepped out into an ocean of
seaweed, into the noise and into the center of a mighty ocean of
seaweed swelling around us. But even through the seaweed and
the waves I could hear them shouting—

You treat your ma good, Little Gloria!

Stick to your ma, Little Gloria! A mom's love, Little Gloria! You be nice to your ma! Nothing like a mother's love! Nothing—nothing—nothing—

What did they mean? Why were they yelling those things? What did they mean? I felt myself tumbled over and over, far far out into waves, down down into the seaweed and the sand, where I struggled for breath and could not swim. And between the struggle not to drown, between the sand and the seaweed and the roar of waves in my head, I could hear them shouting—

Down with Gertrude! Down with her millions! Down with the aunt, up with the mom! Down down down, Gertrude!

Then the police pushed more and more at the men with the cameras, urging them to let us through so we could start the long climb up the steps. Enough now, boys. Come on, give us a break! Move it, move it. They kept shouting things like that, but the boys paid no attention and did not even hear them. They kept pushing with their cameras and yelling at me. Over here, Little Gloria—smile, Little Gloria, over here—just one more— smile smile smile—Little Gloria, smile—

Then the policemen got more and more angry, and more and more serious, until they ganged up together and formed a wedge, and with this wedge they made a pathway, and up this pathway we climbed, up and up, through the thunder of the seaweed, through the wet of churning sand, on and on until we were outside a door, and Mr. Smyth said, Here we are—here we are— here we are at The Judge Carew's Chambers.

The Private Chambers

Mr. Smyth guided me in front of him and in we went, into a room with a long brown hard table and chairs on either side. At another small table there was a machine, something like a typewriter, and a man sitting in front of it paying no attention to us at all. The door closed behind us and another door opened. It was The Judge Carew in his long black robes, and he strode into the room as though he had come from somewhere very important which was why he was a bit late.

He shook my hand and said, Come and sit down here next to me, Gloria, so we can have a little visit.

Would you like to take off your coat? Mr. Smyth said. Yes? And your hat too if you like.

Make yourself right at home, right at home, said Judge Carew, and he sat down at one end of the long table.

So I took off my coat, but not my hat, and the Judge said, Come and sit down here next to me, and he leaned over and patted the chair in the place of honor on his right. Mr. Smyth slid himself in next to the Judge opposite the table from me. So here we all were, at the long dining room table, gathered together to ask the Lord's blessing.

Well now, the Judge said to me, doing his best not to be stern, well now. He looked over at Mr. Smyth in another smiling way, as though he were waiting for *him* to start saying whatever it was that had to be said.

I sat there going over and over all the answers I had to the questions he would be sure to ask me. All week I had told myself that maybe this would be no worse than taking a test in school, and I did not dread that, did I, if I was well prepared in advance? Mr. Smyth was The Teacher, so to speak, helping me to cram for this particular Test. Only, of course, now that we were actually here in the Judge's Private Chambers, it was not at all like being at the Green Vale School, and the Judge was certainly nothing like Mr. Breen. Come to think of it, he was a lot like Mr. Jenkins.

Already I could tell it was going to be much more like the games Naney and Dodo and I had played with each other for as far back as I could remember. But then again, that was not fair either, because we did not always play games. And even if sometimes we did, why, the games were only a small part, were they not? a tiny part of what went on in the Caravan, and had nothing at all to do with what the Caravan was really about.

You and I together, Love, never mind the weather, Love! was what the Caravan was about—and *that* was not a game!

But this was, for sure. I sat there silent, waiting to see what move they would make next.

Finally Judge Carew spoke out.

Tell me, Gloria, how do you like the Green Vale School?

Oh, I love it, I love it I love it, and I love being there with Auntie Ger.

Do you have many nice playmates to play with?

Oh—playmates—I love my playmates. There's Gerta and Patsy and—and—numbness was coming over me, and I looked over at Mr. Smyth, who smiled back at me and nodded.

What about things to do? Do you have a lot of things to do at your Aunt Gertrude's?

Oh yes, I do I do—lots of things to do—like my own horse called Black Beauty and lots of riding around in the woods!

And what about playmates at the Green Vale School? What about them?

Oh, tons of them! There's Gerta and Patsy and Cammy and Cammy and Patsy and Gerta.

Are there any other animals at your Aunt Gertrude's?

Oh, yes. A dog—lots of dogs—and I love Auntie Ger too.

Was I doing it right? I did not want to keep looking over at Mr. Smyth, but out of the corner of my eye I could tell by his slight nod and unchanging flat pieface that I must not be doing too badly.

Well now . . . The Judge Carew shifted his long black robe into another position. We sat there for a while and nobody said anything. The stenographer stopped tapping on the machine and looked out the window. The Judge looked out the window too, as if there might be something going on out there that demanded his attention.

Was it over? Was this all there was going to be? I held my breath. The Judge Carew turned and looked at me, but he said nothing. Then he looked across the table and said, Mr. Smyth, would you like to help me?

Would he! The very thing he had been waiting for—charmed, I'm sure—and he waltzed right in.

You have a nurse, don't you? Mr. Smyth said. A nurse whose name is Miss Keislich, but whom you call—Dodo, is it?

Yes. . . .

Has Dodo ever told you to say things or do things that—?

Never, never, no, she never told me not to . . . nothing, never. . . .

Now tell me about your mother, said The Judge Carew.

Mother mother mother—be good to your mom—there's nothing like a mother's love—nothing—nothing—

I hate her. That was the word Mr. Smyth had said, wasn't it?

You hate your mother? Why do you hate your mother?

Afraid . . . That word is mine. That word belongs to me, not to Mr. Smyth.

Why are you afraid? The Judge seemed interested.

Afraid because I don't want her to take me away. I don't want her to take me away, I am afraid that she will take me away. . . .

Who—who are you afraid of being taken away from?

If only I could struggle from the seaweed, up onto him, into his body, climb so he would feel my heart banging against his. He would know then, then he would know that it was not Aunt Gertrude I was afraid of being taken from—it was Dodo! Dodo! Dodo!

But I did not hurl into the dark rock of him—hold on hold on pull pull pull up up, through the wet sand, up up through the jelly of seaweed, through and up and out until I reached the Caravan, someday in sunlight, no matter where, with Dodo—

and yes, Naney would be waiting there too—you and I together, Love—never mind the weather, Love!

Yes yes yes, from *Aunt Gertrude*, don't let them take me away from Aunt Gertrude, don't let my mother take me away from Aunt Gertrude, please please please, I beg you, I beg you, beg beg—

Now, now, there's no need for that, no need for that at all. The Judge looked out the window again. But not Mr. Smyth; eellike, he oozed his way over between us.

Someone was holding my coat for me to put on, and The Judge Carew was bumbling around in the background, and Mr. Smyth was saying, Gloria, you can go home now—home now.

So out the door of the Private Chambers we went, Mr. Smyth and I, back down the long hallways, into the elevator, back down the steps of the Courthouse, making our way through the circus and the merry clowns, until we reached Aunt Gertrude's car. It was not the Caravan, to be sure, but it would take me there.

And the wet sand still churning on the streets around us, and the seaweed roar—what of that?

None of it made any difference anymore, for I was on my way home. I was, wasn't I?

Mr. Smyth was in a good mood when we drove away from the Courthouse. He stretched his legs out and said to no one in particular, Now all we have to do is wait. All we have to do is wait for the Judge to hand down his decision.

I thought about the days that had passed leading up to this day. About the others who had, as Naney said, taken the stand. They passed before me in procession, as they made their way up the steps through the seaweed, to give their testimony in court. My mother, the Aunts Toto and Consuelo-Tamar in their veils and black dresses, Aunt Gertrude—had she worn her green shoes again, I wondered? Naney Morgan and her three perfect round diamonds curled around her pearl rosary beads, and—Dodo. And

the many others who had journeyed by ship from places across the sea. Had Nada come? and Uncle Harry, and Angustias— what of Angustias? had she taken the stand too?

So there would be much for The Judge Carew to ponder before he handed down his decision. How did he ponder, I wondered? Did he lie down in the dark of his Private Chambers? on that hard brown table in his long dark robes, closing his eyes and thinking over all the things I had said to him mixed in with all those other things that had been said to him. Or did he ponder best by taking off his robes and putting on another disguise to walk about unrecognized here and there, like everyone else?

Waiting for the Judge to Hand
Down His Decision

I went back to Green Vale just as though nothing had happened, as though we were not waiting for the decision that would
be handed down by the Judge. This waiting part was terrible. I
could not think of anything else. It was not so hot at school
either, because although up until now there had been things,
lots of things, in the newspapers about my mother and Aunt
Gertrude and all of us, it was nothing to what it was like now.
When I walked into school after that day visiting the Judge in
his Private Chambers, it was like walking into an arena with no
clothes on. I tormented myself by imagining that the only clothes
I wore were made of newspapers, and on each would be words
in those black thick spider letters spelling out what I could no
longer pretend not to read. Not that I actually saw them, the
spiders with their messages of black, but they juggled about over
and under and around the sides of everything.

But what came through more terribly than anything else was
one something. It was about my mother. One something had
been discovered about her, one something discovered during what
they all called the Custody Trial, but what it was was so terrible
I could not know about it because I was too little to understand.
What was it? What was it? If it was so terrible and she was my
mother, it must mean I was in some way terrible too. I must
know, must find out *what* it was. And I was torn apart wanting
to find out and not wanting to know. Because if I did know, it
might be a thing so terrible that I would no longer be able to
live. I would be struck dead.

Then I would go back to thinking of the beauty of my mother
in Paris as we sat together in the crystal sunlight of her room.
Closing my eyes, I leaned against her, melting into the skin of
her, into the flower of her, deep deep until I reached the center

of her, and then I could feel myself slipping away, becoming part of her, more and more into the heaven of her—deeper and deeper until there would be no more of me left, because I would have become her. If that oblivion were death, I would gladly die.

But then terror would come into my heart, and the memory of her turned into the way it had been in the Adirondacks as she came towards me in the boat, the nun of her leaning against the nun of Consuelo-Tamar.

And in horror I would turn away, not wanting to know what the terrible thing about my mother was. But then back around again, around, the *wanting* to know would come—then the *not* wanting to know, around and around, so that I did not know what to do or where to go.

The Decision Handed Down

Tweedle Crocker was coming in to see me later that day. I was told this before I got into the car to be driven to school. He would be waiting for me when I got back. Big Elephant told me this and I said, What about? What is he coming to see me about? I have no idea, dear, she said. No idea, dear—no idea, dear—no idea, dear. It ran around in my head all day and I could not think of much else.

Even the sight of Peter Haddon, seen from a distance in assembly, didn't make me melt the way it always did. He was this boy I had a big crush on and he left me limp and speechless every time I set eyes on him. I even set No idea, dear—no idea, dear—to the music that was always played as we marched on saddle-shoed feet into the assembly each morning at Green Vale to pledge our allegiance to the flag before classes started. Usually to this music I put the words Peter Haddon Peter Haddon I like you best of all the boys, but today I forgot all about Peter Haddon and everything else except No idea, dear—no idea, dear—no idea, dear. . . .

When I got back from school, No idea, dear was already there. He was in the living room waiting for me. Big Elephant looked funny. Her face was all blotchy and kind of shredded as if maybe she had been crying. It was awful. Tweedle Crocker was in the living room all alone, not sitting but walking around, as if he had someplace else to go. Big Elephant did not come into the living room with me even though I wanted her to. I did not like the idea of seeing Tweedle Crocker all alone by myself. The fatness of him always put me off, not to mention the big thing about him that really put me off—that his showing up always meant some message from Aunt Gertrude. Why couldn't she tell me things herself? Instead it was Tweedle Crocker who always showed up as a podgy messenger. And here he was again. Yes, and with a message at last, a message.

Well, he said, well, well, well—this is your lucky day, Gloria. Sit down—sit down.

I went and sat on the sofa to the right of the fireplace and examined the lilacs on the chintz as if I had never seen them before.

He ambled his roly-polyness over to the piano and plucked at a few of the keys with piggy fingers.

Yes indeed, Gloria, this is your lucky day! The Judge has handed down his decision, *and*—he came over and sat down beside me—*and* he has decided in favor of allowing you to remain here with your Aunt Gertrude!

For how long? I asked.

Well, for a long time. Unless, of course, your mother decides to appeal the case, which would be most unwise of her, in my opinion, but who knows what goes on in her head, and she may be ill advised and do it—appeal the Custody Trial—and that would mean—

Custody Trial? I interrupted.

Yes, Custody Trial Custody Trial, he said peevishly. That's what it's called—Custody Trial—this business between your mother and Mrs. Whitney.

Would it mean having to go see the Judge again?

No, I don't think it would come to that. It would go to a higher court, that's all—the Supreme Court, to be exact, which would simply mean the judges—

Judges?

Yes, why yes—judges.

More than one judge?

I got up, but he took hold of my arm and said, Sit down, just for a minute, there's one other thing I forgot to mention.

I wished he would take the pudginess of his fingers off my arm.

Nurse Keislich is going to be leaving soon. Yes, The Judge Carew decided that would be in your best interests, so soon she'll be on her way. But not immediately—probably just before Christmas. Yes, we all concur that just before the New Year would be the best time—start the New Year off on the right foot, so to say, and that will give you ample time to adjust, adjust to this little change—yes, ample time before the new nurse takes charge.

Run run. Down the hall. Run run upstairs. I ran into the soft mountain of Big Elephant. My heart broke and the blood of it gushed from me into the soft sweet love of her, the torrent of it sped and sped on and away, spreading on into her. . . . And from that moment to this—nothing has ever been the same again.

What Can Be Said?

What can be said of Love? What of hope can be said, or for that matter what can be said about anything, when it is no longer there? When all is lost and taken away. Big Elephant was to be sent away, forever away, and in the days that followed, death descended with its finality, and I was told I would not be allowed to see her or write to her or even know the place she was being sent to. So each day would be a day in which I would awake to find her gone.

And Naney, what of her? Naney Napoleon with the multitudes of armies behind her. Surely the power of her could prevent this terrible thing from happening? But no. There is nothing nothing I can do, Little One, was all she kept saying over and over again. There is nothing anyone can do, not even Auntie Ger. No, even if she did want to do something about it, there's nothing she or anyone else can do because this is what the Judge wants done and what he wants done has to be done. So it won't do any good to bother Aunt Gertrude about this—nothing, nothing, nothing can be done—it's all in God's hands now.

I saw this hand of God brushing across the sky and sweeping the blue of it into night's darkness. And in this bowl of darkness rushing around us, the hand of God filled the sky, and in the center of this hand of God we all stood, Dodo, Naney, and I, with the tininess of our hands welded together in the hardness of chain. Only something bigger than all this was happening, or rather something smaller. For as we waited there, Big Elephant had grown smaller, yes, much much smaller . . . why, I could see the top of her head where the grey hairs sprung like grass, and she had become no taller than me. And the Little Countess— the top of her head, I could see that, too. And there we were all standing, holding on, one tight hand each in the other, side by side, no one taller than anyone else . . . all gazing up into the sky of night trying to find the face of God, the eyes of God, to plead with him to listen to us and intercede with Justice Carew on our behalf.

But why had the Judge done this? There must be a reason. Was it something I had said to him or not said to him on that day in his Private Chambers? I had to piece things together here and there, but it was difficult because no one wanted to talk about it. I kept trying to get Naney to tell me something, but all I could wheedle out of her were snatches here and there— influence—Judge says Nurse influences you against—*you* know!

Then she turned away and started to hum, and I knew, of course, *whom* she meant. Then she jumped onto something else having nothing at all to do with anything, as if already she had said too much.

Big Elephant went around and around and around, saying things like If only Mrs. Whitney would let me stay on to take care of the linen closets, no one would even know I was here— things like that, which I grabbed onto although I knew all along that Mrs. Whitney would do no such thing. But I knew there was nothing to be said—nothing, ever since Tweedle Crocker had put his fat hand around the trusty giant sledgehammer of Justice Carew and aimed it with all his fat force at my head, and then once more at the head of Big Elephant. For ever since that day we had walked around struck dumb, and there was nothing at all to say, or that could be said, or that any one of us could do, to change this terrible thing that had come down upon our Caravan.

Big Elephant gathered her things together and they were carried down the curving staircase into the hall to wait for Freddy. There they were, a little island, all her possessions huddled in suitcases, one on top of the other, waiting there in the hall by the front door. Waiting for Freddy to drive me to school and then come back to take her away. That was the plan.

There were still moments when I did not believe what was happening. But then I would know it was true and that I had been drawn without knowing it, led on into a strange country, a country that knew no boundaries and was called Pain. And I thought back over all the days leading to this day, to this place where I now lived, and I wondered if we had been part of a trick, a gigantic trick none of us had been aware of, and now here we were and it was all a mistake, a terrible blunder, because nothing had turned out the way it was supposed to. And try as I would, there was no way out, no path leading back to our Caravan, no way to return, and I knew if I was to keep breathing I would have to find another way of saying Good-bye. Because how do you say Good-bye to someone you can never say Good-bye to?

I came back from school that day and the hall was empty. The suitcases had disappeared and Big Elephant was gone. In her room was a Mademoiselle Ruel. She was hard, fat, with hair in a fisted bun and bangs frizzed low above her eyes in a ridiculous fringe. I hated her.

They

The days followed one after the other as days do until it was almost Christmas. Justice Carew had said I had to be with my mother all that day, and so Aunt Gertrude was arranging that we would have Christmas at Old Westbury Capital on Christmas Eve and open presents at that time. The Little Countess would be there and also the cousins who lived at the Capital. Behind closed doors Hortense supervised the elaborate plans of decorating the Christmas tree.

And behind other closed doors I was doing my own elaborate planning with Naney on the telephone, pleading with her to tell me where Big Elephant had gone. Every night, just before I was put to bed at seven o'clock, I always called her at Volunteer 5-6000 which was the number of the Hotel Fourteen. This put-to-bed came round every evening at seven o'clock although I was wide awake and far from ready to put on pajamas and bed down for the night. Doctor Santa St. Lawrence had this idea, as he said I was a very high-strung child (whatever that meant) and so I needed a lot of rest. He also believed that the dark was most conducive to rest, so no more door left open in the bathroom, if you please, and no more was any light left on there or anywhere else. And as for the Mademoiselle Ruel sitting there waiting for me to go to sleep—well, that is what had contributed to my high-strungedness in the first place. But now with that Keislich gone and this new routine, all these problems, high-strung or otherwise, would disappear.

So every day after school I would go to my room and try to finish homework with the Mademoiselle Ruel before dinner. Then if there is time, Doctor St. Lawrence said, she can listen, yes, certainly, why not, let her listen to her Uncle Don on the radio if that's what she wants. So after listening to my Uncle Don with his Hello, Nieces, Nephews mine, I'm glad to see you lookin' fine—how's Mama? how's Papa?—I would make my good-night call to the Little Countess at Volunteer 5-6000.

This lights-out at seven popped into my mind frequently during the day at school when I would try not to waste time anticipating the dreaded evening ahead. I even asked around at Green Vale what time some of my friends went to sleep, but not one went to bed at seven and they all seemed to me as high-strung, in one way or another, as I was. So it was often still light outside the drawn curtains as I waited for the Mademoiselle Ruel to stand by the door of my bedroom and simper, Dormez bien, Petite, in that cruel way of hers, before she switched off the light and shut the door firmly and forever. For Mademoiselle was strict in following Santa St. Lawrence's instructions, and no matter how often I asked for just a crack of door with its crack of light, she would say, Bébé, stop, stop being Bébé, no light because with light this high-strung habit of yours will never be broken.

It would darken as flat on my back I lay rigid, turning neither left nor right. It was my strategy to prevent *Them* from getting me. Who were these *They* who had no name but who waited until night to claim me? I had no answer but to know that *They* were always there and would try to find a way to get at me. Either *They* would come in through the window or, if by accident my foot ventured out over the edge of the mattress as I lay there, the unseen hands of *Them* would dart out and up from under the bed to grab my foot, and all would be lost. But I had power to outwit *Them* if only I could keep lying still on my back without moving even a toe.

Hours later, still there in the same position, I would ache with strain. But it was nothing to the ache of missing Big Elephant. Nothing to the feeling of dread knowing that soon it would be Christmas Day and I would be taken to see my mother. What would she do to me? Worse still, what would Consuelo-Tamar do? But more terrible than all this was panic, knowing I had no present to give to her. The box I had tried to make for her in school, somehow I could never bring myself to finish, and now it was too late. And I lay on my back in the dark trying to think of something, knowing it was not *Them* that I feared but *Her*, and the agony of what might happen in the day ahead— the day everybody said was Christmas.

The Christmas Present

It was some tree Hortense had put together. I hadn't seen anything like it since the Christmas at Melton Mowbray with Aunt Toto. It was in the living room in front of the long window, and when I first saw it, it was of such beauty that I forgot Big Elephant was not here to see it too.

By then I knew the secret of where Dodo had gone. The Little Countess had told me. Not only that, but she also said she would get any letters of mine sent right to Big Elephant—only no one else must know about it. Well, certainly no one would get it out of me, no matter what. But it helped some to know that she was not too far away from Old Westbury Capital, in a place called Freeport, staying with a Mr. and Mrs. Ambrose Schiller, and that she would stay there and not go anyplace else. Maybe I could find a way to see her, but it was hard to figure out exactly how. Maybe Freddy could help me—drive me there someday? But plans along those lines were unlikely, and for now at least I knew where she was and could write to her. Dare I try

to call her? I would have risked it, only I knew that once I heard
her voice I would start to cry, and I had enough of that already.
Who were Mr. and Mrs. Ambrose Schiller? I had never heard of
them before, and if they were such good friends of Big Elephant,
I puzzled over why I hadn't. The Little Countess said she would
tell me all about it later. For now, just to know she had not
dropped off the face of the earth was fine enough for me.

I still had no idea on Christmas morning what I was going
to do about a present for my mother. As any mention of her was
discouraged, it was something I hesitated to bring up; but something had to be done, didn't it? It seemed funny to walk in
without something, and most of the night after the Christmas
Eve party, I was unable to sleep thinking about it and wondering
what I could do.

Mademoiselle Ruel was cheerful as we drove in, and so was
Naney. We would be leaving the Little Countess off at the Hotel
Fourteen before going on to my mother at 39 East Seventy-second
Street. So by the time Freddy got to the Fifty-ninth Street Bridge,
everyone was in a good mood except me. I was worried sick about
the Christmas present situation. Finally I made myself say out
loud, What am I going to give my mother for Christmas? Why,
nothing, Little One, don't give it a thought, Naney said, stuffing
out her cigarette and lighting another one. Mademoiselle Ruel
said nothing. But I have to give something! No, you don't, Naney
said. She'll have enough presents from Blumie. (This is what
they now all called Mr. A. C. Blumenthal.) Well, I want to I
want to I want to give her something—it's Christmas, isn't it?
Well, all right then, give her something, give her something,
give her whatever you want. But it's so late now, we're almost
there and I don't have anything, I have nothing at all to give
her. Nobody said another word until suddenly the Mademoiselle
came to life. Look, she said, pointing, we are in luck today—
look there, a place that sells the flowers is open. How about the
pretty plant of *poinsettie* for Madame Vanderbilt?

That was not a present! and I wanted to reach over and yank

the frizz of her silly hair. But she kept on about it. Slow down, Fred-die, slow down—there, see, in the window, there is one, a perfect *cadeau* for Gloria to take to Madame Vanderbilt, so apropos for the season festive. Now I really wanted to hit her. But Freddy parked the car and I followed the Mademoiselle into the florist, leaving the Little Countess humming in the car. The plants all looked pretty ratty and left over to me, even the one in the window—even the red bows tacked on here and there looked more like pin-the-tail-on-the-donkey instead of proper bows. If you looked closely they had all been pre-tied. But what else was there? All the shops were closed, and maybe it was better than nothing. So I stood by while Mademoiselle Ruel hurriedly said, We will take this one—no, that one—and now write on the card, Gloria, hurry now, we are late, write the card. There were miserable little squares of paper on a high table with messages already written on. I took one saying Seasons Greetings and wrote under it, To Mummy with love from Gloria. The man in the shop took it from me and clipped it onto the bow.

Merry Christmas, he said, and put a lot of thick brown paper around the plant and around the pot as well so the effect was like a package of sorts. Then the Mademoiselle beckoned to Freddy who carried it out to the car. It would not be long now. I kept wishing and wishing I did not have to be there when my mother opened the package. Maybe we would be in an accident before we got there. . . .

Instead, something else happened.

Apples

The Mademoiselle Ruel moved onto the front seat alongside Freddy, balancing the poinsettia plant on her lap so it would not get crushed. Soon we drove up to the Hotel Fourteen. The Little Countess and I hugged and kissed each other a lot. Then Freddy assisted her out of the car and on up the steps and in through the door of the hotel until she disappeared. I always hated saying good-bye to her, although I knew I would always be seeing her again. They could send Big Elephant away because we were not related, but they could not make the Little Countess just disappear the way Dodo had, because she was my grandmother. None of it made sense, but I knew that was the way it was.

Well, it would not be long now. Soon, there I would be, watching my mother unwrapping that hideous brown paper, listening to her saying something like Oh, a poinsettia plant, just what I've always wanted. . . .

The car stopped for a red light. The big grey door swung open all at once—but who had opened it? It was a little furry person who kneeled on the steps of the car, leaning in towards me, almost coming in but not daring to. She was grey all over from the matty fur of her squirrely coat to her hair falling out under the grey scarf on her head, right down to the grey wool socks falling down over her grey heelless shoes. The only thing about her that was not grey was the apple she held out to me in her mittened paw. She leaned in closer on her knees and shoved the apple under my face.

Little Gloria, help help me please, Little Gloria, please! She lunged closer. Only you, Little Gloria, you can help me help me help me please please.

It was a most awful thing to watch as she pressed on, now almost stretched out face down in front of me, ardently praying and calling out, Little Gloria, Little Gloria, help me! Help me!

Freddy turned around and so did the French one, but it was all happening so fast we froze there, paralyzed and speechless. Then Mademoiselle let out a shriek—*Qu'est-ce que se passe, dit donc, qu'est-ce que se passe ici?* and Freddy jumped out of the car and pulled the trembling mole person off the floor, making the apple leap out of her paw onto the pavement. He banged the door shut, and the red apple rolled under the car out of sight. Then he huddled her over to the side of a building next to a brown carton filled with apples all in neat rows. She kept signaling to me and trying to call out again and again, pleading with Freddy to let her come back to me. But Freddy disentangled himself and ran back to jump behind the wheel, and we sped away.

How could I help her? What could *I* do? What? What was it about? What was any of it about? The grey bundle of her, stretching towards me with that apple, and on the pavement those other apples in their neat rows. What?

When we got to the house on Seventy-second Street Mummy was there waiting. The tree looked as if it had been put up in a hurry. Merry Christmas, Mummy, I said, trying to pretend it wasn't a poinsettia. How lovely, darling, she said. But I couldn't tell by the sound of her voice if she meant it or not. I would have known if I'd looked at her face—but I couldn't I couldn't I couldn't. . . .

The Hotel Fourteen

The Little Countess lived on the tenth floor of the Hotel Fourteen. Her two rooms were really one small room, alcoved into two rooms by an archway. They were on the back side of the hotel, and from the windows you looked out to see the elevator shaft. It was always dark, and even by day at least one of the lamps had to be lit. Two would be better, but Naney was very careful about not wasting electricity, even though the hotel was paying for it. She kept milk in a bottle outside on a windowsill, along with lemons, one to be squeezed into a glass of hot water every morning. This was her breakfast, and she had nothing else all day until three o'clock, when she dressed and sallied forth to walk around a bit, here and there, before ending up at Schrafft's or Caruso's, restaurants all within a few blocks of the Hotel Fourteen. The Little Countess was well known throughout the hotel and around the neighborhood, and she in turn made herself a network of cohorts, from the telephone operator at the Hotel Fourteen right through to the blind man at the newsstand on the corner of Sixtieth and Fifth Avenue, where she went every evening after her dinner to pick up the *Journal-American*.

So although our Caravan appeared to have disbanded since Big Elephant had gone, to my view it had only partly disbanded and temporarily moved camp to 14 East Sixtieth Street. And every chance I got, I would go to our Caravan on the tenth floor to be with Naney Morgan.

And although the room was hotel furnished, when you opened the door from the putty-walled dreariness of the hall, it was to walk into a room transformed by the Little Countess into a gypsy Caravan of secrets and treasures. The narrow bed with its head-board of brass was placed beyond the archway facing one of the three windows; over it hung the familiar crucifix of wood with the ivory Jesus nailed to it. Naney always hung it over her bed, no matter where she landed—even on the ship *Majestic*, as we traveled from Europe, it had hung over the bed in her cabin. It was not all that big, this crucifix, but it was very real and had blood spurts painted where the nails pierced, which made it seem bigger than it really was. There were other crucifixes around here and there as well, and a rosary which always hung on the brass headboard above her pillow when she was not praying. Pictures were sitting on the bureau and table tops—mostly of me. But there were others as well. One, in a frame of swirling silver roses, a creature in tiny-waisted dress, beautiful and young, leaning on feather-boaed arms, gazing out with passionate awareness, and centered in her wondrous hair, a star of diamonds. In one corner Laura Kilpatrick Morgan had been written in a writing I knew by heart, and New York, and under that a date, only that part had been inked over. Then there were other pictures put away in a drawer. One was, I knew, of Jacqueline Archer Stewart. She was my godmother and had been a friend of my father. She was very rich, everyone said, and lived in a castle in Easton, Maryland, when she wasn't traveling here and there. This castle of hers was an exact replica of the Alhambra in Spain, right down to a button you could press which would make the floor of one room slowly

drop down into another room below. The Little Countess said that someday Godmother Stewart was going to present me with a blue diamond ring. But none of this had taken place yet, so it was something to look forward to. Naney had a big photograph of her face in a leather frame. A turban of satin covered all her hair, and at the top of this turban, held by a pin of carved jade and diamonds, a feather fluffed straight up. She was splendid in the way of an opera diva. But this photograph always stayed in the drawer unless Godmother Stewart was coming to visit Naney Morgan. Then it would be pulled out and placed on the table near the door so it would be the first thing she would see upon entering the Little Countess's room.

Hanging on another wall near the bed was a calendar that filled up most of the wall. It had no pictures on it, just the year and the month in block letters at the top and, underneath, row on row of squares, with the number of each day plunk in the middle. Every day the Little Countess took a thick black crayon and made a big cross from one end of the square to the other and then back again, so by the end of the month each date on it had been crossed out. I wondered when in the day Naney did this. When was the day considered to be over? Some mornings I would be there and already that day would be crossed out. Then other times I would be there in the afternoon, late, but the square remained untouched.

Under the Little Countess's bed was a long wide chest. Every time we slid it out from under, I never thought it would fit back again, but by some magic it always did. In this chest was a cape. It was of ermine, with extra tails of the ermine, black tipped, delicately sewn here and there over the rippling soft of its whiteness. This Queen's Cape had been given to Naney Morgan the summer of Aunt Toto's lucky streak, for it was a summer when Aunt Toto had Broken the Bank at Monte Carlo, and the very next day she had gone out and bought presents for my mother and for Naney and for herself. What a nifty thing to do! I knew that when I grew up and if I was lucky enough to Break the Bank at Monte Carlo, I would do exactly what Aunt Toto had done and go out the next day to spend it all on presents for Big Elephant and Naney Morgan and myself. But Naney only looked at her ermine cape now and then and had never worn it outside anywhere, ever. She kept waiting for that special occasion. But the years went by and no occasion special enough had come to be, and it came in view only when we pulled the long wide chest from under her bed. Then I would put it around her shoulders to admire, and she would stand looking into the mirror at herself in Aunt Toto's cape, then at me standing there beside her. And I knew she was going to say those dreaded words about being in her grave. Then that calendar, looming behind us on the wall, with its black crosses. I wanted to tear that away too, and never ever again hear When your Naney is in her grave grave grave! Please *please* don't say that! Please! But she would only laugh and gaily shake the cape from her shoulders and put it around mine. See, darling, see, see . . . see how pretty you look!

Every time I went to the Hotel Fourteen there would be something to do or see that was different from the time before. And although it was hotel furniture, it did not seem so. The faded mole carpet, from wall to wall, did not seem thin to the tread, and the French-style chair with the Little Countess's shawl embroidered with poppies of purple draped over it seemed to have traveled here with us in our Caravan from across the sea. Even the walls of painted dullness transformed themselves into lacquered brilliance by the lacquered red castanets of the Little Countess's nails as she opened drawers and pulled out things to show me.

· Handkerchiefs cornered with lace . . . letters tied together, each pile held in place by a different color ribbon, neatly bow tied . . . here and there, a comb of tortoiseshell and a pair of white kid gloves—unworn. And then! her jewel box of alligator with silver capping each corner, and in the center a medallion of silver, and on this medallion of silver a crown was engraved. Inside, the jewel box was lined in chestnut satin so soft that at the touch, your fingers melted into it. A tray, also of satin and holding jewels, resting on the top, and under this a pillow, poached into puffiness, cushioning Naney Morgan's tiara of emeralds. This tiara, so delicately strung together by invisible cobwebs, could be transformed into necklace and bracelets—that is, if you knew the magic spot to pull apart unseen clasps holding it together—and these secret places were known only to Naney and now to me. On my visits to the Hotel Fourteen, opening Naney's jewel box would always be the event saved for the last, not only because of the magic tiara but because under the cushion bearing it there would sometimes be hidden among Naney's rings and brooches—a surprise! And it would be for me. It might be a cherry covered in chocolate or a Kewpie doll charm of Celluloid. And once, a walnut painted gold, and inside, a scene with a tree and a tiny person standing under it—imagine!

Naney also always had crayons and pads of paper for me to draw on, and my most favorite thing to do was to cover these pads with different versions of the house Naney Morgan and Big Elephant and I would live in when I was grown up and could buy a house for the three of us to live in. We each had our own room, but other rooms as well, to spread out in. It would be the Caravan, but it would never move because it would be a house built so solid that even volcanoes couldn't budge it. It was *so* fun planning all this, and getting it down on paper made it all seem like it might happen tomorrow.

But it didn't. What happened tomorrow was that I was back at Old Westbury Capital. Now if I only had patience, who knows? tomorrow might come even sooner than I could imagine. And until then, I had my drawings, didn't I?

By now there was quite a collection. Some of them were at the Hotel Fourteen and some I took away with me back to Aunt Gertrude's. Naney Naney, may I have one of your handkerchiefs, I said, to take back with me? The linen one she gave me was tucked away between my drawings. Sometimes, aching with the missing of her, I would bury my face into its coolness. I would close my eyes . . . and with the scent of her surrounding me, the Caravan would be mine once again. It was something to hold on to until the next time we would be together.

Tootsie Eleanor

Tootsie Eleanor was a trained nurse called Miss Walsh, Miss Eleanor Walsh, and she had been brought in especially to go with me for the weekend visits to my mother. She was really nice and looked sort of like Madge Evans, one of my favorite movie stars, and even though she wore her hair in a severer way than Madge Evans, she was not what you would call severe at all—just the opposite. I longed for her to stay on all the time, but this was not to be, and it was the French one who stayed on at Old Westbury Capital and who would be waiting for me when Sunday came around and I left my mother's to return to Aunt Gertrude's. Whenever I asked Tootsie Eleanor why she could be with me only on the weekends, she would say, Don't ask me, I just work here. There were a lot of reasons why I hated to hear her say this, but the main one was that it somehow suggested that she was being paid to be where she was and doing what she was—all of which was true, if you wanted to put it that way, which I did not. The feeling I had for Tootsie Eleanor had nothing at all to do with being paid. Don't ask me, I just work here also conveyed to me the nature of her permanence, or rather the truth of how long she would be around or not around. On top of this, there was also the problem of Tootsie Eleanor's heart, which was weak, so she had to lie down from time to time and rest. This was another reason why she was unable to be with me all the time. Well, at least I had her for those weekends and not the Mademoiselle Ruel.

The best thing about weekends at my mother's was that she let me go to the movies. Not only that, but most of the time the movies were double features, so I knew that every weekend I could count on seeing at least four movies. But even four was nowhere near enough for me. If I had had my way I would have spent all my time looking up at those dancing feet or at those faces spread across the screen with their dazzling beauty. Oh! to be Ruby Keeler tap-dancing her way to fame and fortune, or Dolores del Rio with beauty that rivaled my mother's. Then the blond singing glory of Grace Moore as she appeared in *One Night of Love* overwhelmed me and I longed to grow up to be her. Or how about a combination of all three! Yes, all was possible sitting there next to Tootsie Eleanor in the thrilling dark of the movie theatre.

It was Tootsie Eleanor who sat beside me on weekend jaunts to the movies and not my mother because, always at the last minute, my mother was too exhausted to go with us. One thing we *had* to do together was go to Mass on Sundays, so I guess she was saving her energy to get through that. And it took some getting through. We *had* to go to church every Sunday because of another one of the decisions handed down by Justice Carew. I was now to be raised as a Catholic. Apparently, early on I had been baptized in the Catholic Church for my mother's side of the family and in the Episcopalian Church for my father's side of the family, but this sudden raised-as-a-Catholic was news to me, as I thought I already was a Catholic, what with Nancy and Dodo and all the Hail Marys floating around. But now it turned out I was not really a Catholic, because I had not received Holy Communion or been confirmed, and none of that could take place until I had Religious Instruction. This was being given to me by Father Feeley at the parish close to Old Westbury Capital, and I always looked forward to going there to talk to him. There would be a little bowl of sugar-loaf mints on the table in front of the sofa where we sat for the Religious Instruction, and next to it another little bowl of cashew nuts. To taste one and then the other was a delicious combination. But what I really looked forward to on these Religious Instruction visits was Father Feeley himself, for he not only looked like Pat O'Brien in the movies, but he had the same gentle way about him, making me feel happy

to be in his presence, and even when he got to the Hellfire part of the Religious Instruction—the way he made it sound, it did not frighten me one bit.

So every Sunday my mother would pull herself together for the twelve o'clock Mass at St. Francis of Assisi and we would take off in Mr. A. C. Blumenthal's car following the sirens of a police escort. This ride never failed to release in me a fit of giggles so uncontrollable that it took all of my will to hold myself together and not make a fool of myself by collapsing into waves of laughter that I would never be able to stop. And what made it worse was that I felt that if I caught Tootsie Eleanor's eye, she would get the giggles too, and all would be lost. Losing all control, we would drown in a fit of giggling laughter, taking my poor beautiful little unsuspecting mother down with us.

So this was a stagy drive, to say the least, but even more stagy was the moment of arrival at the church. Crowds would already have gathered, as they did every Sunday, to wait for our entrance. This sight of crowds stopped my fit of giggles ice cold, so there was no need to worry anymore about drowning my mother or about Tootsie Eleanor's heart attack. Some just stood standing respectfully back and staring at us, while others shouted out encouraging things at my mother. Others, also rooting for her, had written cards and letters, which she had placed on the mantel in the living room at 39 East Seventy-second Street just as some people did with their Christmas cards. It was quite a collection, and I always wanted to read what was said, but I only got a chance to glimpse phrases here and there, as I did not want to be a Nosey Parker reading other people's mail.

My mother often felt faint at Mass on these Sundays. We would be escorted through the crowds of oglers up to the balcony where we would be seated in the front row with the choir behind us. This was supposed to put us in a less conspicuous position, but it never turned out that way, as there were no other worshipers seated up there with us. The congregation sitting in the pews below would turn around from time to time to get a good look at us—or two, or three, or four—as we sat there, my mother with me on one side and Tootsie Eleanor on the other. All during the ceremony my mother would remain kneeling, even when it was time to stand up or sit down, bending far over with her hands holding on to the wood of the balcony in front of us. She did this so the blood could rush to her head, hoping to prevent herself from fainting. It was a shock to see the paleness of her face, eyes closed, behind the mesh of black veil as she bent there in profile beside me. Who would catch her as she fell? Would I be strong enough? Or would strange hands come forward to lift and carry her down to the car, to Mr. A. C. Blumenthal's car parked in the street, waiting with the crowds below, waiting to take us back to 39 East Seventy-second Street when Mass was over. But it never came to that, and each time we got through the Mass without mishap.

Once back at the house we would have lunch, Tootsie Eleanor and I, with my mother, sitting up straight in the dining room. Every Sunday there would be Le Sueur French peas, the taste of which I never tired of, along with the roast beef or whatever, and right after that Tootsie Eleanor and I would usually be free to hotfoot it to the movies.

But sometimes it did not work out that way. Sometimes, if she felt up to it, after Church we would all go to have lunch at the Sherry-Netherland Hotel. This usually meant no movies afterwards, for my mother really dawdled over those lunches. They started out fun. There was a dish on the menu made of lobster which had been diced up with hard-boiled eggs and celery, all folded together with lightly curried mayonnaise and piled high in the boatlike shell of the lobster. My mother and I ordered it just about every time we went there for lunch. Tootsie Eleanor did too, and finally one Sunday when we got there—I couldn't believe it, right on the menu, there it was, only now it was called Lobster à la Gloria Vanderbilt! Of course, I knew they meant my mother, but it made me feel famous too.

Then it came time for dessert, and I knew my mother would just have a demitasse. She would ceremoniously take a lump of sugar and unwrap it as though it were a tiny present, then hold it suspended, tentatively, in her long nails of red over the steaming coffee. Slowly the sugar lump would be infused and its color changed from white to a delicate pale shade of café au lait; and when this color reached the top of the cube, my mother would give it to me to crunch into. She called this a petit canard, which was French for little duck. And if only we could have gotten up from the table then, it would have been fun. But this never happened, because after the canard, my mother wanted another demitasse along with another cognac, and along with the demi-

tasse and the cognac would be Camel upon Camel. And so it went, on and on, until I was the one exhausted and fidgety—and then, at last, I would hear her say to the waiter those blessed words *L'addition, s'il vous plaît* and, mercifully, it would be time to go. But not to the double-feature movies. More like time to drive back to Old Westbury Capital.

Every weekend I would wonder if maybe this was the one in which I would be introduced to Mr. A. C. Blumenthal, but so far I had only caught a glimpse of his back as he went down the stairs on his way out to his car. It was curious to me that I had not met him, especially when he gave me lavish presents. He even wanted to give me a car, a small version of a real car to get around, here and there, on the roads of Old Westbury Capital. But of course Aunt Gertrude put her foot down and said it was much too dangerous and out of the question. So that was that, but anyway it was a swell idea, to put it mildly, and I thought about him a lot, and wondered if my mother was maybe going to marry him. He gave her lots of presents too: a platinum case encrusted with sapphires to carry her Camels in, and so on. Going away from me, from behind he looked awfully short, and I kept imagining how he would look coming from the front towards me. Well, there was always another weekend coming up, and perhaps that would be the one in which I would get to meet him.

Getting Close to Aunt Gertrude

Meanwhile some things had changed at Old Westbury Capital. For one thing, Auntie Ger now came down during the week for a few days instead of on the weekends. But as the weeks went by, I felt I knew her no better than at the beginning when I had first met her that day in the hall as she came towards me in her hat, wearing pants and those shoes with their haunting high heels.

It was true that a few weeks ago she had invited me to sit beside her on the sofa in the living room, and together we had leafed through a magazine of fashion, and she had made various observations to me as pages were turned. But that had been it as far as any confidences between us went, and I kept waiting, hoping that some other such move would come from her in my direction. Not only *that* move but the other move—the Big Move—the move when she would start talking to me about my father—what he was like, his voice, whether he laughed a lot. Things like that. After all, my father had been Aunt Gertrude's brother, hadn't he? And she does have a sculptured head of him in her bedroom. But when I asked her who it was she only said, Oh, Joe Davidson did that, it's of your father. This was a riveting piece of news to me, and I closed my eyes and touched each feature with my fingers, trying to get a sense of him. But it was cold and told me nothing. Aunt Gertrude told me nothing, either. So many hours were spent thinking about this, wondering about my father and about Aunt Gertrude . . . what was she like—*really?*

Whenever the opportunity came to us, my cousin Gerta and I would spook around Aunt Gertrude's studio hoping to find some clues. Gerta and I were sworn best friends and we kept no secrets from each other. This studio was way in the woods of Old Westbury Capital, and although Aunt Gertrude no longer worked her sculpture, it was filled with examples of it—not only with gigantic examples but with smaller examples as well, some on pedestals, and one in particular with a cloth mysteriously draped over it. This was the one that I could not stop thinking about, and finally I got my courage together and drove myself to look and see what was underneath.

I could not believe what I saw. It was a head of someone . . . of a girl . . . and this girl had hair in bangs just the way mine was. All the other sculptures around were metal and hard, all except this one, high on its pedestal. There it was, and it was soft, all soft clay, as though someone was still at work on it, and soon, quite soon, it would be finished. Could it be that Aunt Gertrude came here secretly just for this one reason—was it possible that this head of a girl with bangs was soon to emerge and turn out to be . . . me? Why did I not know of this—or was this to be a surprise? And if this was so, it must mean that she really liked me a lot. Not only liked me but, yes! *loved* me. And for days I was obsessed with only this, going back there over and over again, through the woods, back to her studio to lift, with pounding heart, that cloth so casually hung over its armature of clay.

Lightly, hardly touching the surface, I would trace over each plane on this face of clay, again, over and over, searching for signs of identity . . . *my* identity . . . searching for proof of a closeness, searching for some sign that would direct me towards not only what I was but what I could become and what I could make of myself. For if this was true, and this head of a girl was indeed me, a direction would be pointed, and I could follow it out of darkness, be led into light, and it would be in this way that I could come to, and find, the truth of myself.

After this discovery, every time I would see Aunt Gertrude I was sure that by then I would dare to ask her about this. But coming face to face with her, my courage would vanish and I was unable to utter a word. And that was just as well, for in the not knowing, each day came to me with hope.

Finally, I did find out—that clay head of a girl was not meant to be me at all. No one seemed to know who it was supposed to be. It was just a head of some unknown girl Aunt Gertrude had worked on long ago, even before I existed, and she had left it there on the pedestal—for one reason or another—unfinished.

Soon after this, two events took place. The first had to do with Fred Eberstadt and the second had to do with stuttering. Mine. Now these two events, although they occurred at the same time, had nothing to do with each other—or did they?

The stuttering had come to me in recent times, ever since the Custody Trial, come to think of it, and it made complications for me in classes at Green Vale when my turn came to speak. But that was only the half of it. For it pursued me no matter where I went, and every day I woke up with the same two choices available to me—either keep silent or attempt conversation, for it was a hurdle to complete even one word, much less a sentence. My mother said that I had inherited this stutter from her, which she thought was a cute idea. Could she be serious? For one thing, her stutter, as she called it, wasn't a stutter at all. Her stutter had a hesitant way about it that was shy and devastatingly appealing, whereas mine was a nightmare, and no one, myself most of all, knew where to look when I got stuck on a word, desperately hooked, trying to spit it out, trying to finish the sentence. The dreaded English class hit me most of all as I sat holding my breath waiting for my turn to come around, my turn to stand up in class and recite a treasured poem. Prayers for the ceiling to fall upon me were of no avail, and inevitably my turn would inch around, and I would find myself standing before the class, the struggle only just beginning.

Now at this precise time there was another fear, but this fear was not singular to me, because it hung over the school like a miasma. It concerned not only Mr. Jenkins, the giant Principal of Green Vale, but Mrs. Jenkins. This Mrs. Jenkins was not Mr. Jenkins's wife but his mother. Yes, his mother. Which was impossible to believe, for to set eyes on Mr. Jenkins, so far along in years, so ancient, it would be inconceivable to think he ever could have had a mother, much less a living one. But he did, and we were all made uneasy by her snooping ways, for she roamed through the halls of the Green Vale School searching to catch one of us in a misdemeanor, sending the culprit straight up to Mr. Jenkins's office, where a harrowing interrogation awaited us. But then something occurred to change all this.

For one day Mrs. Jenkins was caught in a most unseemly position by Fred Eberstadt, one of the boys in school. He had excused himself momentarily from class and had blithely skipped out into the hall and on down to the lavatory. Brightly swinging open the door, he came upon Mrs. Jenkins sitting on the toilet seat right there in front of him. Each screaming at the sight of the other, Mrs. Jenkins had leaped up, brandishing her little fists at him, while Freddy backed out into the hall, not knowing where to turn or what to do. When speech did return to him, he told everybody about it, and it spread through the school like wildfire and was discussed for days, months. Even years later it was remembered and repeated.

For sitting there on the toilet seat, with her skirts spread around her, Mrs. Jenkins looked no smaller or less gnomelike than when seen standing up to her full height, prowling around the halls of Green Vale. In fact, she might just as well have been standing up on the toilet seat instead of squatting down, for all the difference it made. And knowing this, don't ask why, made *all* the difference to us who had been spooked by her for so long.

Luckily, there was nothing Mr. Jenkins or Mrs. Jenkins or anyone else could do to reprimand Fred Eberstadt, because, after all, it was just one of those things. But what a bitter blow, not only to the giant Mr. but to the gnome Mrs. as well, because from then on Mrs. Jenkins became as ineffectual as an effigy of wax and faded away into the folklore of Green Vale, and not one single person at school ever feared her again, and we all felt that Fred Eberstadt had done a most heroic thing.

Now the very next morning after this happened, I discovered something amazing. That there were two words, and if I put these two words in front of whatever it was I was trying to say, speech flowed from me without any stammer at all at all at all. And these two words were I Say! Yes, when I said I Say, words followed after, flowing along without mishap. It was astonishing that such a small thing, two words, made all the difference, but they did. And although it might make me sound British, saying I Say this and I Say that, none of it would matter, because now I would be able to put sentences together the way everyone else did. And the first thing I said was I Say, hooray for Mr. Jenkins, hooray for Mrs. Jenkins, but most of all, hooray for Fred Eberstadt! And you know what? It came out smooth as cream.

The Start of the First Unfortunate July

My mother rented a house near Nissequogue on Long Island which was not all that far away from Old Westbury Capital. It seemed strange to be going there because it was as though I was going away on a trip, only not really, as it was more like moving next door.

Tootsie Eleanor arrived at Old Westbury Capital on the dot, the first day of July, and off we went. The rented house was on a hill overlooking Smithtown Bay and from the outside it looked really big, which it had to be to have room enough for my mother's friends as well as Tootsie Eleanor and me. Who these friends would be, this turn, I had no idea. All I knew was that Consuelo-Tamar would *not* be among them, and this made me feel much better about what this July was going to be like.

Everything was quiet all around us as we waited to go inside. This was because they were all still asleep. My mother and her friends always slept late in the morning and showed up only by lunch time, which also took place late in the day—late, that is, for me, but not late for them. Wann opened the door and Tootsie Eleanor and I followed her up the stairs to our rooms. We all whispered and were as quiet as could be so as not to wake my mother and her friends. My room was a corner one with windows looking out onto a lawn sweeping down a hill, and beyond it I could see the bay. On the walls hung prints from *Godey's Lady's Book* of women in summer dresses of white and sky blue, and right across the hall from my room was the room of Tootsie Eleanor. Who is in the room next to me? I whispered to Wann. Mrs. Meredith, she whispered back. Oh, I said. You'll meet her later, said Wann, at lunch time. I wanted to ask her where my mother's room was, but she was in a rush to go back downstairs— to see to the lunch, I guess.

It was hot, and I went over to the window and pressed my face against the scratchiness of the screen. Outside, everything was green and silent, and far beyond lay the strip of thin-spun water, quivering, suspended by the heat. I wondered if Mr. A. C. Blumenthal was here, and if he was, which room he was in. If he was staying here, I would *have* to meet him, wouldn't I? We couldn't just play a game, trying to avoid each other in the halls or going up and down the stairs, could we?

There was a knock on the door and I turned around. It was my mother. At first I thought she was alone—but no such luck. Reflected behind her stood Aunt Toto. Hair unbound, they both had on summer versions of the robes I knew so well—the robes Marie had made for my mother in Paris. Who sewed them for her now? I wondered. Probably Wann. The robe my mother wore was of a color she called eau-de-Nil, and the robe Aunt Toto

wore was also in this same eau-de-Nil, only with her robe Aunt
Toto wore her necklace of pearls, black pearls strung each on the
other, large as the eggs of a plover. In the heat, my mother's
hair hung around her shoulders in a shimmering haze. The tendrils around her forehead were slightly damp, and I longed to
press my lips against them.

Hello, darling, they both said at once, and we all moved
towards each other for the customary pecks on all cheeks. Lunch
will be ready soon, darling, said Aunt Toto. Come on down and
join us when you're ready. Oh, I'm ready now, I said. And Miss
Walsh, is Miss Walsh ready too? Oh yes, yes, I'm sure she is.
And just then, as though she had been listening at the door, out
came Tootsie Eleanor into the hall, and we followed Aunt Toto
and my mother downstairs.

We went past the living room, out onto a porch which had
wide steps going down to a hill of grass beyond. On these steps
a lot of people were sitting. Some I knew and others I didn't
know. Tony was there, and I hadn't seen him in a long time,
not since Melton Mowbray, and I wondered if he had perfected
his breath-holding technique or if he was onto something else.
His Awful Nanny was nowhere in sight, but I found out later
that she was here all right, only she didn't mingle with the rest
of us and had her meals on a tray upstairs. Then there were two
others considered children by everyone. A girl, Diane Meredith,
was one, and a boy, Melsing Meredith, was the other. They were
more or less my age—mostly more, in fact definitely more, because I was ten and Diane was perhaps thirteen and Melsing was
maybe eleven. Tony was five. So there we were, the children,
grouped on the steps at Nissequogue, trying to scramble in with
each other along with the grown-ups as well.

These so-called grown-ups, also sitting on the front steps of
the porch, were Mrs. Meredith and her guitar and Miss La Branche,
known as Wee Bell because of her teeny-weeniness; then there
was Mr. Gardner, the handsome Oliver, but called Ollie by
everyone—he looked much like a movie star, only not at all like

the Ollie in the Laurel and Hardy movies we saw. As for Mr. A. C. Blumenthal—not a sign of him. All the grown-ups talked to each other and drank orange blossoms while we children sat around drinking Coca-Colas and said nothing at all. On Mrs. Meredith's mouth there was lipstick shiny as red patent leather. She smiled a lot, and the many colored bangles she wore clicked together as she strummed from time to time on her guitar and hummed bits of tunes in unknown tongues. Sitting there, all of us gathered as we were on the porch steps with the freshness of the lawn before us, there was something about it that was lovely— as if everything were all right after all. As if none of what had happened had happened—as if there were no such person as Justice Carew. And I kept hoping Mrs. Meredith would go on and sing a song all the way through to the end, but Wann came out and said lunch was ready, and we all got up and went into the dining room across the hall from the living room and ate fresh corn on the cob with lots of butter.

After lunch all of us went to our rooms for naps. I still didn't know which room my mother was in, or anyone else for that matter, except Mrs. Meredith. I knew she was in the room right next to mine, because through the walls I could hear a soft strumming and that voice of throaty beauty over and over again—

Hello, all my friends out there in Radioland—this is *your* friend Melba Melsing, here to sing melodious melodies from faraway Lands just for you. . . .

And then, in a voice so personal and warm I believed it was just for me, out came the most wondrous song, in a language I knew this time to be Spanish. Think of it! She was a star on the radio, with her own fifteen-minute program every day, called "Melba Melsing Brings You Melodious Melodies." And here she was, in the room right next to mine! Sometimes, although it sounded perfect to me, she would pause in the middle to go back over it all again, right straight from the beginning. But I never tired of hearing her, no matter how often she stopped to begin rehearsing all over again. Everything about her fascinated me, and I longed to hear more of her songs and to know everything there was to know about her. Then there was the Wee Bell, blond and quite fascinating too, in her own twiggy way. Something about her—the voice and the overall effect—not unlike Jean Arthur, which was certainly intriguing enough for me.

I just hoped *I* would be intriguing enough for *them*, the grown-ups . . . my mother included, of course.

The Middle of the First Unfortunate July

After naps every day we would troop down the hill until we came to the stony strip of beach far below. Tootsie Eleanor and Awful Nanny in her felt hat would trudge behind, following us down through the staggering heat in their slow way. Tootsie Eleanor's heart bothered her that summer, but she always said for me not to worry, that all she had to do to make it all right was to lie down for a bit. She was always calm about her heart and calm about everything else, so when she said, Don't you worry, that is just what I did, I didn't worry. . . . Yet somewhere I did worry about her—worry about what I would do if her heart did attack. Awful Nanny and Tootsie Eleanor were the only grown-ups with us on our afternoon parades down the hill to the beach. All the other grown-ups were usually in their rooms, sleeping or whatever, and the house was as silent as though empty when every afternoon we tiptoed down the stairs to meet on the lawn before making our descent to the stony beach below.

There were no waves in the Smithtown Bay and the sand was sharp and jaggedy with broken clam shells, continuing on as far out as feet touched the ground, so for swimming it was not so nice. But it was nice for something else—airplanes! Not only nice—it was perfect. What more perfect spot for an airplane to land? First, there was talk about it, a lot of talk about it. Wouldn't it be fun to fly in an airplane, oh yes, fun, fun, fun, wouldn't it? And maybe it could be arranged. Why, Aunt Toto and my mother even knew someone, a friend, who had a small perfect little airplane big enough to fly yet small enough to land right here by our beach so we could all take a ride.

Now when I first heard about it, this sounded swell. But then they went on and on about it—the grown-ups went on and on and on, until it seemed they went on and on about that airplane much too much. There was something fishy going on. And I was determined to find out what.

Then, sure enough, one afternoon an airplane did show up, high in the sky. The tiny dot of it circled around and around, closer and closer, until it landed far out on Long Island Sound and putt-putt-putted towards us until it nosed itself right up in the shallow water of our beach.

All the grown-ups were there, standing around in their dry bathing suits (none of them ever went swimming), waving at the pilot who waved back as if he were an old friend before he quickly jumped out into the shallow water and pulled the airplane further up onto the sand. We all clamored around him and after a while he said, Well, who wants to go for the first ride? There was room in the airplane for four people, including the pilot, so we all could have turns before the afternoon was over.

From up in the sky looking down, everything appeared as a land of toys. The house we lived in was a toy house with toy trees around it, and the path leading down the hill was a toy path leading down to a toy beach. And there they were below us, all the little toy people in a cluster, the dots of their white faces craning up to us, and their little toy arms waving frantically at us as though they might never see us again. Far out we circled, far far out, until we could no longer see them at all and I wondered how I would feel if we just flew on and on and out over the water, on and on, out into the nowhere, and never did come back. Later, I almost had a chance to find out.

How about that! Aunt Toto said, laughing, as Tony and I and Tootsie Eleanor got out of the airplane. I like that a lot, I said. Well, there'll be lots of other chances to fly around. Next time, your mummy and I will go up with you for a ride. How about that! I thought it was funny that they hadn't this first time. But except for Tootsie Eleanor, none of the grown-ups went up in the airplane at all. Diane and Melsing had a ride, and when they got back the handsome Ollie said, It's getting too late now, we'll go up for a ride next time. Next time. Next time . . .

It was all getting fishier and fishier. Especially coming from Mr. Gardner, who showed up for lunches and dinners on weekends, but after each dinner went on the three-hour drive back to the city, returning the next day in time for lunch. At least that is what the grown-ups said he did, when all along everybody knew that he kept his things in the guest room over the garage and spent the nights in Aunt Toto's room. So what? It was the pretend business that got to me. And getting to me now was another feeling of pretend business—a feeling of pretend business having to do with this airplane and the handsome Ollie saying We'll go up for a ride next time. Next time. When would next time be?

Well, there was no next time. Tweedle Crocker got in touch with Tootsie Eleanor in one of the tom-tom ways they had of communicating with each other. And he had a message: No more airplane rides—no matter what! because these airplane trips in the sky were all only rehearsals for the really long Big Ride that was to take place later. It was all part of a plot cooked up between my mother and Mr. William Randolph Hearst. I had heard a lot about him from the Little Countess. Not only did he own Naney Morgan's favorite newspaper, the *Journal-American*, he was powerful in other ways—almost as powerful as Aunt Gertrude. And he had offered to pay for an airplane that would take my mother and me across the border into Canada, where we would live together happily ever after. Oh, Tweedle Crocker did not put it that way, but I knew that is what Mr. Hearst intended. Kidnapping! is the way Tweedle Crocker put it. Kidnapping by my mother and Mr. Hearst so he could use it for publicity in his tabloids. Fortunately, Tweedle Crocker told Tootsie Eleanor, he had lines of contact with the press (I bet he did), which is how he had come to hear, in the nick of time, of this dastardly plot.

I could tell Tootsie Eleanor was embarrassed as she tried to put Tweedle Crocker's message into words, but after all, as she so often said—Don't ask me, I just work here.

Airplane rides were never mentioned again that July. But there would be nights when moonlight came onto my bed and onto the wall near me, and I would drift into the gauziness of it, going over and over again the Big Plan Mr. Hearst had in mind. On the walls there was something centering about the Godey Ladies of Fashion as they hung there in their precise frames. In the pearliness of the moonlight, each curve and line of their bodies and the colors of their dresses came into my mind's eye as clear as by day. I would make up stories about one or the other of them, imagining one to be my mother, another to be myself. But we would never be able to fit into Mr. Hearst's little airplane in those petticoats and bustles, and I would be drawn on, into the strange moonlight of the hot night, straining to hear the sounds of laughter coming from the steps on the porch below.

In the half-light, I dreamed back into the time when we were gathering on the porch steps before bedtime . . . dozed into the outdoors, where everything was different and there was nothing to fear. Or so it seemed, in the sweet dusk, as Melba Melsing paused for a moment, throwing back her head, before bending it down close over the guitar, as she laughed her beautiful poppy-red laugh and plunged into song and then on into another, lovelier than the one before. . . .

> Tin tin tin tin
> Esta noche va a llover
> Tin tin tin tin
> Hasta el amanecer

Sometimes, tearing myself away from where we all sat on the porch steps, I would slip across the darkening grass to stand in the tree shadow far at the edge of the lawn. Invisible to her, I would gaze at my mother as she whispered something to Aunt Toto which made her laugh and pile her long hair up on top of her head, to cool her neck in this heat of moonlight. Ollie leaned over and grazed his lips, fleetingly, across the back of her neck, before her hair fell back around her shoulders. And Wee Bell, sitting off to one side, looking across the grass to the moon on the dark water beyond, the dry papery timbre of her voice a beat behind the others . . .

Tin-tin-tin-tin- . . .

. . . Melsing and Diane, leaning forward adoringly, unmoving . . . listening in the gossamery light . . .

How I longed for it to be forever so.

Then, not bearing to be separated another second, running to reach the steps before the darkness claimed them from me— run, run, run over wet sprinkled grass, back to the steps, back to my place . . . soaring . . . soaring . . . *Tin-tin-tin-tin, esta noche va a llover* . . .

But now it was over, the Children tucked in and put to bed. Nothing of it was left but a song I tried to remember, a song that came from somewhere, drifting up through an open window and soon even that would be gone, for July was almost over and I would never be in this place again.

I lay there and tried to put us all within a frame—a portrait, it would be, painted as we had been this night—so that it would remain like a frieze on my brain forever. But it kept slipping away from me . . . and nothing was real except the moonlight on my bed . . . and the Godey Ladies hanging on the wall in their fine summer dresses. . . .

The End of the First Unfortunate July

Then I got poison ivy. Rambling around, up and down, on the walk to the beach. First it was an itch here and an itch there, but when the itches got to be something fierce, it was impossible not to itch all the time. And this itching all the time made the poison ivy spread, until soon it had crept all over my body and really drove me nuts. My head swelled up and had to be supported on pillows every time I lay down. Then there was the calamine lotion, with its ickiness, that had to be whitewashy patted on oh so gently every few hours but which really didn't help much at all. Of my ballooned flour-face all that was recognizable were two little eyes embedded like raisins in a puffed cake.

The only thing that did help me forget all this was a trip to the movies. I pestered and pestered until every single day, in the high of noon, Tootsie Eleanor and I were driven about Long Island to one hamlet or another to see a double feature. There, from the blaze of sun, I would slink with my swollen chalky whiteness into the cool dark of the almost empty movie theatre, while Tootsie Eleanor stocked up on Baby Ruths and soda pop. This was swell for a while, but soon we started running out of double features, because the show changed only once a week. So we had to resort to going farther and farther afield. Sometimes we even had to sit through movies which had no appeal whatsoever—Our Gang movies and even a few with Patsy Kelly. But still it was better than not going at all. So by the time we had gone through the hamlets nearby, we found ourselves driving such distances that we might as well have driven into New York City and seen something really good. But often we were lucky and there would be a movie playing, one we had already seen months ago—a Ruby or Ginger one—which was even better the second time, even if we knew what was going to happen next.

It was a funny sensation coming back out into the glare of

summer after those hours enthralled within the musty dimness of those local movie theatres. For one thing, the seats inside never felt really clean, not to mention the crumpled waxy papers thrown under the seats with their vague hovering smells of stale chocolate and—what was it?—licorice. But no licorice could dispel the glamour of that screen of silver suspended like a magic carpet before us. Only when Tootsie Eleanor had just about had it, suggesting we take a day off and do something else, did I relent in my pursuit of Beauty.

It was inconceivable to me that she might not herself feel the same passion about the movies I did. But then it came to me. It was *different* for her, because she was already a grown-up—she was already . . . there. For surely what happened up there on the silver screen was a harbinger of things to come—*that* was what it would be like. And *that* is why I longed to go to the Movies, why I never tired of sitting there, watching the movements of those gorgeous people as they went about in their grown-up gorgeous ways showing me what I had to look forward to. Tootsie Eleanor was a grown-up, so none of what happened up there on the screen was news to her—whereas all of it was news to me. Ginger dancing with Fred—that was the way it was going to be. And of course Tootsie Eleanor already knew all about that.

Let's drive around and see if we can find some new movie magazines, I said. She thought that was a nifty idea and so instead of going to a movie we drove to Patchogue and fooled around and ended up with strawberry ice cream cones.

One day I woke up and the itchiness didn't itch so much. I looked in the mirror and my head no longer looked as if it were encased in a white diver's helmet. July was almost over and soon I would be going to the Adirondacks. The moments on the steps of the porch would never come again. . . .

Unfortunate—wasn't that the word Tweedle Crocker had used about this July? Yes, unfortunate. Well, it hadn't been so unfortunate, really. True, I hadn't seen that much of my mother—but I did get to see a lot of movies.

August

It was really strange arriving at Camp Whitney after having been at Nissequogue with my mother. For one thing, everyone was settled in and had been throughout July, so it was like going into a movie in the middle of it. Also settled in were the little intrigues between the cousins, each at a different camp, so the summer was well on its way. But Gerta was there, and I fitted right in with her as I always did, and although she was across the lake once again at Camp Kiloquah and I was at Camp Togus, we were in constant communication every day.

Also on the lake in their usual places at Camp Squirrel Point, across from Camp Kiloquah, was the family of Bergaminis. This group always stayed in the same camp, year after year, for the father Bergamini was a doctor, and as Whitney Camp was in so remote a place, far from the places of doctors, there had to be a doctor on call all the time, day and night, in case anyone got sick. In the Bergamini group, besides the Doctor father Berga-mini, there was a Mrs. Bergamini and a lot of boy Bergaminis. Gerta and I didn't see much of them, as they were uninterested in our activities, and so when we did see them, it was usually from a distance, across the lake, when they drew attention to themselves with their noisy ways.

Auntie Ger's first daughter was Mrs. Miller, whom I was to call Auntie Flora although she was my cousin and not my aunt. It seemed to happen that way. She was married to Mr. G. Mac-culloch Miller, and I was to call him Uncle Cully. So when I got to Whitney Camp that August, I found Auntie Flora and Uncle Cully settled in at Camp Deerlands along with Children. There was Pam and there was Witty and two others too babyish to mention.

But not too babyish to mention was a Some One Else. And when my eyes met the eyes of this Some One for the first time, there came upon me an all-over melting, and I leaned against Gerta who stood there on the dock beside me at Camp Deerlands—otherwise I would have fallen on my knees, for they were as jelly.

Now there had been a few of those weak-in-the-knees attacks before—such as at Maidenhead, every time I saw David Medina Milford Haven. Then there was that other time in Monte Carlo at the Grand Hotel—the unknown boy taking our luggage down for our departure. It had come over me then too, as weakly I had thrown myself into the car, turning to stare at him through the window as he piled our suitcases in the back. How I held on to the sight of him—holding on and on to the melting into him as we drove away, wondering what this feeling was and if it would ever come to me again.

Well, there was no wondering anymore. I dared not speak for fear the stammer would return, preventing even utterance of the magic I Say. Who was this person who dissolved my eyes into the brown of his? Who was this who stood in front of me, here by the lake at Deerlands, rendering me fluttering and speechless?

This is Johnnie Russell, Witty said. And I looked away, for now I could give a name to the shaking that possessed me. Johnnie Russell Johnnie Russell Johnnie Russell. And whatever small part of myself there had been was now forgotten, all forgotten, for I belonged only to Him.

Blueberries

Over and over again running through my head was a song, and over and over the words of this song went through me until it soared over the lake and along the deer trails that led through pine forests to the place where He breathed. And I would burst with the aching for Him and with the wondering if He even knew I existed. Silently, if people were around, I would sing to myself, but loud when in my room alone—out loud, in celebration that on this earth there walked the likes of Him:

> *For I'm fall-ing in love with some-one*
> *Some one boy*
> *Yesss—I'm fall-ing in love with some-one*
> *Head a-whirl*
> *Yesss—I'm fall-ing in love with—some-one*
> *Plain to—seeee—*
> *I'm sure I could love some-one*
> *Mad-leeee!*
> *If—some-one could on-leee love meeee!*

About to explode, I could not understand why everyone else went around eating and sleeping as they always did. How would I live until I saw Him again?

I had not long to wait, because the very next morning He came over to Camp Togus, with Witty, the two of them in a rowboat. Yes, and for no particular reason that I could make out—other than—could it be so?—to see—me! Gerta was already there, and although I hadn't told her yet what had happened to me, she knew something was up, and I found myself in a game of Ping-Pong, Gerta and I against Witty and Him. It was all I could do to hold the racket, much less hit the ball, and soon the game got so lopsided we stopped playing.

Let's pick blueberries, I said, and I wandered off into the bushes. But no one followed and I lay on the ground and scrounged my face in the desperate piny needles and wondered what was to become of me. . . .

Turning over, I looked up into the sky, but instead of the blue it was His face, for He stood looking down into my face and smiling. I lay there unable to make any move at all, and He just stood there, both of us without a thing to say to each other, until I couldn't stand it another moment and, jumping up, I ran as fast as I could through the blueberries, ran and ran, until I got to my room and threw myself on the bed and cried and cried.

I was *so* mad at myself—so *mad* at myself. And now—now—there would never be a chance to see Him alone again—never never never. . . .

Sand Kissing a Moonlit Sky

Gerta had run after me and put her arms around me and asked me what was the matter. I told her I was crazy for the love of Him and what could I do what could I do? But he's going to be here for the whole month, she said. He's visiting Witty and he'll be here all of August until they go back to school, to Newport, to St. George's. I could not believe it. And I think he likes you, too—*really*, she said.

I got off the bed and went to look at my face in the mirror. Hopeless—the tomato squishiness of it, what from the piny needles and the crying. Filling the basin with cold water, I stuck my face in and blew lots of bubbles. It would just have to get back together before I saw Him again.

Which was the next day and the next day and the next. Now I knew He was in love with me too, and we took a lot of chances meeting in out-of-the-way places so that the others wouldn't find out. These out-of-the-way places were mostly on the deer paths that trailed through the woods between Togus and Deerlands. Hard to decipher at first glance, but by now as etched on my mind as the lines in the palm of His hand, these paths had seemed always to lead nowhere—until now. Now they led to blue heaven and you and I and sand kissing a moonlit sky—words from "The Desert Song," another of my favorites to sing out loud when alone, or to myself when at the dinner table and He wasn't present. When He was present, we held hands at every opportunity and there was no need to talk at all as we followed the paths far into the secret forest—the tufted moss around the roots of trees and the fungus which grew out in jutting hedges from the bark, sometimes a deer as it leaped far ahead of us, startled, and then a surprise, the call of a loon and the lake suddenly upon us. We paused at its edge and the strange answering cry of another loon came to us from across the water, and He leaned over to kiss me—but I pulled away. My hand too. I was frightened, but the most frightening thing of all was that I didn't know why. Had this not filled my dreams?

Let's go back, I said. Why why won't you let me kiss you? He said. I said nothing, because there was not one single reason I could think of. Why, He said, why? And He tried to stop me from walking away. No, I said, no. Then when we had almost reached the camp I glanced over my shoulder at him, just for a second.

I'll tell you tomorrow, I said, praying my knees would hold up. Tomorrow—yes, tomorrow. . . . Certainly by then I would be able to come up with something.

Cashews and Sugar-Loaf Mints

There was not one thing I could understand about any of this. *Why* was I so scared to kiss Him, when it was what I wanted more than anything else in the world? Frightened . . . frightened . . . so frightened I could not even talk to Gerta about it.

And the more I thought about a reason, the more scary everything became. Then I started keeping count of how many hours were left until the Promised Meeting next day in the tool shed at Camp Kiloquah. This countdown made it all even worse, and I still hadn't come up with one single reason to give Him when here I was on my way through the forest, about to arrive at Kiloquah. Soon I would be face to face with Him, and there it was, ahead of me, the tool shed—but no sign of Him anywhere at all. Maybe He would not show up. Pray that this was so, but pray pray pray that it was not so.

Inside . . . there He was. He came right up close to me with the brown of his eyes. . . .

Turning away, I said, I can't kiss you—because—because—because I—because—there is this other boy who thinks I am in love with him and—and—and I—I—(what was I saying? what movie was this from?)—and I guess—well, you know—it's not, I guess, fair—fair to him—to him—(what him? as if there could ever be any other him in the whole world but this Him!)—to kiss you—until—until—well, until—you know—until I can tell him that I'm not in love with him anymore—anymore anymore anymore . . . (Oh, God!)

He took my hand and said, When do you think you'll be able to tell him? I could not believe it. Not believe it. That He believed. He believed what I had said.

Soon, oh, very soon, yes, very very soon, as soon as I get back to school then I'll see him and on the first day I'll tell him tell him tell him.

Let's go for a walk, He said, still holding my hand, and we went on into the woods as though nothing had changed. And it had not, it had not—except that now we talked a lot to each other, making plans about when we would meet, and how we would meet when the summer was over and He was in school and I was in another school far away. We could keep writing to each other every day just as we did now—we had our own secret hollow in a tree on the path through the woods where we left notes for each other—until vacation, and by then we would have figured out a way to be together. And by then I would be sure to have figured out a way to be unstricken by fear of kissing Him.

But of course He knew nothing of any of this. I let Him go on thinking that my reason was a true one. Lucky I had not received my first Holy Communion yet, because if I had, it would have to be confessed in the confessional, this lie I had told. But I didn't feel guilty about it—why, I have no idea. Maybe I could talk to Father Feeley about it. No . . . better to keep things as they were . . . with the cashews and the sugar-loaf mints.

The Other Johnny

Parting from Him made my stomach turn inside out. But we promised and promised and promised to write every day. And soon soon my complicated Romance would be straightened out, and I would no longer be afraid to kiss Him. That is how it was when we parted, and how it was afterwards, for weeks and weeks, in letters to each other.

Then Christmas was near and I became like the Little Countess with her calendar, crossing off the days until He would be visiting Witty at Old Westbury Capital. I still didn't know what to do when the time came about the kiss situation, but last time I had thought of something, hadn't I? So—

Also . . . since then I had met, or rather *seen*, a boy, here and there, who went to a nearby school. This boy was a few years older than me and didn't know I existed. But I certainly knew *he* existed. And how! His name happened to be Johnny too. Johnny Delahanty. I guess you can feel weak in the knees about two people at once, because I really did, every time I saw him, even though I didn't really think about him all that much, because He would be showing up soon and I wanted to concentrate on that. Still, from time to time when writing to Johnnie Russell I found myself putting Delahanty instead of Russell, but that's as far as it went.

Then the longed-for moment was here. The feet of Johnnie Russell were right here, at Old Westbury Capital, actually touching the floor of Auntie Ger's living room. I wondered on what spot on the carpet they stood as I ran through the halls to meet Him. . . .

But when I did—something had happened, for He did not look like Himself. Could it be that I too looked different? And, worse still, something else was different. My knees—*that* is what was different. Nothing happened to them, nothing at all at all. They felt just as they always did—when He was *not* here, that is. And that tie? What was that? I had never seen Him with a tie on (not only a tie but one with squiggles printed on it) or wearing a proper suit. In the Adirondacks it was always shorts and those shirts with the short sleeves and the sneakers. Now in this suit and tie he looked just like the other boys in school. What had happened to blue heaven and you and I and sand kissing a moonlit sky? I must have struck him in some odd way too, because he couldn't think of much to say either. . . . And as for a kiss—it was unthinkable now. All I could think about was how were we going to get through the next couple of days, what with him staying right here at Old Westbury Capital and all.

Well, we did somehow, what with all the cousins around and Hortense with another tree to get up. But when he left I felt sad. Not because he was leaving, but because He had never really arrived . . . the Johnnie I knew in the Adirondacks—that wasn't the Johnnie who had been here these past few days.

It was all most puzzling, and finally I stopped trying to sort it out and just hoped that I'd see him once in a while, and that when we did, we would be friends.

Buona Sera, Old Westbury Capital

Come along, Comet—come along, Comet—come along. It is Aunt Gertrude's voice as she climbs the stairs, coming up slowly, urging along dachshund Comet with his long hair who will be trailing behind her like a snail. Soon they will pass the door of my bedroom, and although I must sleep without a light in my room, when Aunt Gertrude is here I am allowed to keep the door ajar until she passes by to say good-night to me. Before she goes on into her room, she will pause for a moment outside my door, waiting for me to give a sign that I am still awake— not that a sign is necessary, for I am always awake to her step on the stairs and her voice as it comes closer. I know that once she finds I am still awake, she will stand for a moment in the doorway, and the words she will say are, as always, *Buona sera, Gloria—buona sera.* She will be dark against the light of the hall, and I will answer, *Buona sera,* Aunt Gertrude, *buona sera,* before she closes the door and I am in darkness but cannot sleep. . . .

But this night it is different! The door does not close. Instead, Aunt Gertrude comes forward into my room and sits beside me on the edge of the bed. Comet has chosen to remain in the hall waiting for her. My hand rests on the sheet and she reaches out to touch it. I bless the shadows, for I do not know where to look or what to do. This demonstration of love baffles me, for the hope of it has long abandoned me. Neither one of us speaks as we sit here through eternity. . . .

I hope you know how much I love you, Gloria? It is said as a question, not as a statement. But what is there to say?

My eyes close and silently I recite the litany of love her letters have conveyed to me. They are in the drawer by my bed, and I can see her writing on the page as it curls around each word of affection and love. Somewhere there must be a clue. For the person who sits beside me here on my bed is not the same person who writes the letters in the drawer. But now as she holds my hand, saying, Do you know how much I love you, Gloria?—I know the answer to all that has bewildered me. And I say to her—

Oh yes, Aunt Gertrude, I do know, I do, I do, I do!

But what I know may be different from what Aunt Gertrude thinks I know. She may believe I know she loves me, and this is true—I do know, now that she has said it. But words hard come by are always too late, and she will never be able to bring herself to say them again. . . . And so Aunt Gertrude and I will keep trying to find each other, but it will be, as it is now, forever too late.

Sunday

Dearest Gloria

You are close
to me every minute.
I can feel your arms
around me + mine
around you. You must
eat a lot + get
very strong so we can
be "Girl Scouts".
I love you + will see
you soon

Auntie Gertrude

Another Unfortunate July

When another July came my mother rented a house in Old Westbury, about twenty minutes or so from Whitney Capital. It belonged to the Le Boutilliers and had a library filled with books, and on the front page of each book, in thick black ink in the same scrawl writing—This book belongs to Peggy Le Boutillier. I read one book after the other, and, although I never met her, by the end of summer I felt I knew a lot about Peggy Le Boutillier.

I also knew a lot more about myself, because two things were to happen that summer that were quite a surprise in one way or another.

First, when Tootsie Eleanor and I got to the Le Boutillier house, it was a shock to find that Consuelo-Tamar not only was there but was to be there all of July—yes, every day of it.

Then the second shock came a few days later when I got the Curse. It was a shock because, although I had heard the Curse here and the Curse there from older girls in school, no one had ever really talked to me about it and I thought it probably had something to do with a witch or some such thing, and I did not connect it with what was happening in my own body. I thought the bleeding would stop, but it didn't, and finally I got so scared I told Tootsie Eleanor. She was really nice about it and explained it to me—sort of—but anyway she did make me feel there was nothing to be afraid of and that all girls got it around my age and that I should expect it every month from now on. Do boys get it too? No, they don't, she said. But eventually they have to shave every day—that's *their* Curse—ha, ha! But I didn't see what was so funny about that or what it had to do with me.

Then, without telling me, Tootsie Eleanor went and told my mother what had happened, and to my horror I was called into my mother's bedroom. She had not quite started getting herself together for the day and lay against the pillows with her hair spread out all around her in those silky waves. Come sit by me, darling, she said. Oh God! We just sat there while she looked up, examining the ceiling, as if words might be written up there for her to say to me. . . .

It's okay, Mummy, I said.

Okay? What do you mean, okay? What is okay, darling?

Tootsie Eleanor told me—all about it—about—the Curse.

Now she looked right at me and smiled. Oh, darling, I'm so glad, so glad—so glad. Now I must jump into my bath, otherwise I'll never be ready for lunch. Where *is* Wannsie? And she pressed the bell on her bedside table up and down, up and down. Did anyone tell you who's coming this weekend? Bea Lillie! Yes, isn't that divine? She's here from London and arriving in time for dinner tonight—so divine, too, because she and Tamar haven't seen each other in ages and ages—not since Deauville, I think—and won't it be fun for you to meet her after having seen her in the play? She's very amusing, just as amusing offstage as on—hand me my robe, darling. Where *is* Wannsie? She pressed her finger again, up and down, on the bell, over and over—and in came Wannsie with pajamas all pressed on a hanger. Here they are, Modom, she said in her Scotch way. Now you run along, darling, my mother said, I'll be down soon. Why don't you go—go—yes, why don't you go for a quick swim before lunch?

Maybe it was all right to swim after all. Tootsie Eleanor had said I shouldn't for a few days, but maybe she had made a mistake. I had better go and ask her.

Instead of Tootsie Eleanor I met Consuelo-Tamar on the way downstairs. She never talked to me, but this passed without comment as when we saw each other it was usually with other people around. Face to face, as it were, it was another matter. I hoped to slip by unnoticed and I thought I had until I heard her say, drawing it out in that sly-puss way of hers, Lit-tle Glo-ria. . . . (How I hated my name when visiting my mother. At least at Auntie Ger's I was Gloria without the Little Little before it.)

Lit-tle Gloria . . . ? And now, as she went on, my body chilled. Could I get away with going on down the stairs, as if I hadn't heard her?

How much do you weigh? Consuelo-Tamar was now at her most purringest. . . .

It was true. Fatness had descended upon me in recent months, and I hated my fatness with every day that dawned, and I dreamed hated dreams of my fatness with every night that darkened. Was fatness forever and ever to be my lot? My mother's highest accolade was thinness—Why, look at Connie Bennett, she's so thin, she could swallow an olive and it would show! *That* is what my mother held in highest esteem. And now, never never never would I be able to attract her favorable attention with the Fatness I had become.

You better watch out, Lit-tle Gloria—she made that sound, in her seductive manner, that was meant to be a laugh—or—or—you might end up as wide as you are tall! Wouldn't that be something . . .

It would indeed.

My mother went to the city now and then, I guess to go dancing with Mr. Mendoza. Blumie's name did not come up at all anymore, and along with him the Rolls-Royce had also disappeared. Oh well, too late to meet him now, so I stopped thinking about Mr. A. C. Blumenthal and my mother. But still on the lookout for a father, I concentrated on Mr. Mendoza—Roberto—and my mother. For it did not take much to see they liked each other a lot. But did they like each other enough to *love* each other a lot—enough, that is, to get married? When he was with us I thought yes yes yes, but when he was away I thought no no no.

If only I could lose some fatness, to fit more—more into the overall picture, if you know what I mean. But they had such a good time together, I don't think my fatness came into it that

much, if at all. Still, you never could tell about things. If I had thinness so that my mother could see the olive and its tiny bulge sticking out through my stomach, who knows what might happen? Why, Mr. Roberto Mendoza might love me enough to want to be my father. And if *that* happened, my mother might love me enough to want to be my mother. . . . *N'est-ce pas?* as Mademoiselle Ruel would say.

That is the way I had it all figured out, sometimes. Other times . . . well, I just didn't know what to think about any of it at all, and I'd go back to the library and read *Gone with the Wind*.

Melba Melsing was on a Mexican trip with someone that summer—a beau from the Eastern Shore of Maryland. I wondered if he knew Godmother Stewart and if he had Arabian horses on his farm the way she did at her castle. There was a lot of sly talk going on between the grown-ups about Melba's new romance, and Aunt Toto couldn't wait to tell Bea Lillie about it. Lowering her voice, she winked and said, Ward is *very* bed-worthy! What did *that* mean?

Melba and Ward, Ward and Melba . . . I don't know, Ward sounded much too cold a name to go with the loving beauty of Melba Melsing. But you couldn't tell all that much about a person without seeing him, and I would have given anything to know what he looked like. I thought of Melba and Ward on the sands of Mexico with the blue heaven above. And picturing them thus, it came to me that Melba Melsing was—fat. Yes she was. Odd that I had never thought of her fatness until now. When she was there in front of me she didn't seem fat at all. She was just right. It was only when she wasn't here and I envisioned her in my mind, on the sands with Ward, that this came to me, this awareness of her fatness. Then—I don't know why, but it gave me hope about my own fat situation. Not that I intended to remain within this fatness—not by any means. Soon all would be taken care of, and then my mother would see who could swallow an olive!

As for Diane and Melsing, they had been put away in a camp somewhere in the Poconos while Melba was with Ward on the sands of Mexico. I wondered if Melba and Ward did a lot of tangoing when night came and they were no longer on the sands. Wouldn't Melba be something with a mantilla and a red rose! Or maybe they spent most of their time in bed—being worthy. Whatever, I bet Melba would come back with some great new songs added to her repertoire.

My mother was in a good mood almost all the time. And I guess it was because of a very handsome—*very* tall—Mr. Roberto Mendoza. So much so that one day she went into the city, and when she came back next day—

ALL HER HAIR HAD BEEN CUT OFF!

I was stunned. Well, not *all* of it, but most of it. And recoiffed into what was called a pageboy bob. It was still parted in the middle, but it now ended just below the chin, in a soft undercurl continuing on all around her neck in a straight line. Roberto's wild about it! she said, and her charm bracelets jingled while she fiddled at it to fluff it under.

Well, he may be wild about it, but I was not. Not at first. Then a few days later I guess I got used to it, because I was wild about it too, only . . . I wished she had let me have the cut-off part. What had they done with it? What had become of it at the hairdresser's? Had it been swept up into a cruel pile on the floor, mixed up with all the other cut-off hair that day?

As for Mr. Roberto Mendoza, he came out on weekends, but only for lunch, and there was no fooling about staying in guest rooms over the garage, because there wasn't any guest room to stay in. I wished he had stayed, though. Because when he was there, my mother always got herself dressed up in print silks and everyone laughed and told funny stories even though there was no Melba around to sing.

California Here I Come, Summer 1937

It was all too much for me—even before we got on the Super Chief train. Every morning I would wake up and the first thing in my mind would be my mother! trip! Hollywood! It was all I could think about, and every day I expected something to happen—like one of the Tweedles coming to tell me it was all off because Justice Carew did not approve of the idea. But no—here I was sitting in a drawing room on the Super Chief with my mother and Tootsie Eleanor, and I kept thinking it must all be a dream and soon I would wake up and be back at Old Westbury Capital in Mr. Harry Payne Whitney's bed in the room down the hall from Aunt Gertrude's.

We had mountains of luggage, but Wannsie was along to keep it all in order and make sure none of it got lost. My mother looked very beautiful in a new silver fox cape—a present from Mr. Roberto Mendoza perhaps? Then again perhaps not, because he had not been around much of late. Whatever, it made her look more like a movie star than ever, and I couldn't take my eyes off her, what with the cape and the hat with its veil just covering her eyes, making her even more mysterious. But she talked on and on in that singsong way and I sat riveted as she told Tootsie Eleanor and me one thing and another about Hollywood, and all the movie stars who were friends of hers, and how soon we would be meeting them. I was speechless, unable to believe all this was really happening to me.

But it was—and the Super Chief was chug-chug-chugging along, faster and faster, and I was going along right with it, clippity clippity clippity, closer and closer and closer to Hollywood. And now my mother was saying, Shall we dine here in our drawing rooms or go to the club car?

We had three connecting compartments, all neat and complete with everything anyone could wish for. And I was to have the top bunk bed for my very own during the whole trip.

What would you like to do, darling? my mother said.

Let's eat in the club car, I said.

She was so beautiful I just wanted to be seen sitting beside her.

All right, darling, she said, we'll order a drink here first and make a reservation in the club car.

She pressed a little bell and soon in came a waiter. Tootsie Eleanor and I ordered ginger ale and my mother said, Brandy and soda, please.

When our drinks arrived, there was a plate of sandwiches on the tray, little sandwiches cut out in shapes like those you see on a deck of cards—there was a club and an ace and a heart, each filled with something tasty. Then the train slowed down and made a stop, and soon after that there was a knock on the door. Come in, my mother called out.

And the door opened and there was a boy holding an enormous bouquet of red roses—dozens and dozens of them, with the longest stems I had ever seen. They were all blurred and crystally, seen through the cellophane, and there was a big red bow placed in just the right spot, and pinned to one of the ribbons was an envelope with Mrs. Vanderbilt written on it.

Oh, my! my mother said. Who can these be from? And she reached over and took the bouquet. Darling, go get Wannsie, will you, she said to me, and ask her to get a big vase somewhere to put the roses in.

I'll find her, Tootsie Eleanor said, and out she went, leaving me with my mother in the garden of red roses. Without disturbing the bow, my mother unfastened the envelope from the ribbon and opened it.

Oh! she said, sounding surprised. From Maurice! Isn't that sweet of him!

Maurice? *Who* was Maurice? That's the first time a Maurice had come up. My mother was charmed, utterly charmed by what

Maurice had written on the card, and she tucked it into her purse which was on the seat beside her. I would have given *anything* to know what this Maurice person had written on it. . . .

The next day we arrived in Chicago and my mother took me and Tootsie Eleanor to the Pump Room at the Ambassador East Hotel for lunch while Wannsie stayed behind to attend to things. It was the thing to do, my mother said, to while away the time between the change of trains. It was one of those long lingering lunches with petits canards and cognac, and by the time we got back on the Super Chief it was almost dinner time. When the door of our compartment opened, it was like walking into another rose garden—for there, along with the other red roses which Wannsie had carried from one train to the other, was another cloud of cellophane, and inside there were even more red roses than the first bouquet of red roses.

Oh, my! my mother said. Oh, my! Who could have sent these?

I could have given a good guess.

Wannsie took my mother's silver fox cape from her shoulders and my mother sat down in front of the bouquet and turned up the cobwebby veil covering her eyes, arranging it delicately over the curling black feathers of her hat before taking it off. Wannsie disappeared with that too, and my mother leaned back against the carpety plush of the seat, resting her head on the square of lace that was pinned to it. She turned and looked out the window in a pensive movie-star way . . . and for a second I thought she was going to cry. But instead she looked back to me and smiled. Then she reached over and delicately took the envelope off the bouquet.

Oh! she said, and she studied the card carefully. Then she said in that surprised way, My! from Maurice! So pretty! Isn't that sweet of him! Wannsie, find another vase, will you, and a brandy and soda, and ginger ale for Miss Walsh and Miss Gloria. And she put her head back against the seat and seemed to drift off to sleep. . . .

Every day on the train my mother slept until lunch time, and some days we had all our meals in the drawing room. But there were lots of things to do on the Super Chief train. I was reading and reading, and we played Parcheesi, and, every day at one time or another, my mother and Tootsie Eleanor and I would be sure to catch each other's eye and we would all start to sing— Wannsie too, if she was around—

> *Cal-i-for-nia, here I come!*
> *Right back where I start-ed from. . . .*

Al Jolson had sung this song in a movie; only we sang it

> *Cal-i-for-nia, here we come!*
> *Right back where we start-ed from. . . .*

But then it happened. We were singing and laughing away, all of us, when—suddenly—what was happening? What? My mother looked as if she were starting to cry, and then she was laughing again, but it was like half laughing and half crying. Which was it? I became so frightened, for I knew that if she was sobbing, her tears would become a river rushing—out the window, farther and farther away—and I would be pulled along with her, and so would Tootsie Eleanor and Wannsie too, and there we would all be, floating out the window on a river of tears. . . .

When we got off the Super Chief there was so much luggage it couldn't all fit in the trunk, so some had to be piled around us in the front and back seats of the car, and even at that Wannsie had to follow behind with the rest of it in a taxi. I was dying to see what Hollywood looked like, but all I could see from between the suitcases was palm trees sticking up and lots of flowers around the flat houses we passed. Of course, there were no movie stars around on the streets anywhere at all, and I hadn't expected there to be. But, somehow, I think I did expect all the people we saw walking around to *look* like movie stars even if they weren't.

We drove and drove and drove until finally there we were at the Ambassador Hotel, being shown up to our rooms. In the living room of our suite there was a big silver bucket filled with crushed ice and two bottles of champagne—and everywhere on the tables bouquets of roses, all wrapped in cellophane.

My mother stood in the doorway looking around the room. Oh, my! Who could have sent these?

Well, here we were in Hollywood—and I wondered what was going to happen next.

What happened next was that we went to Maureen O'Sullivan and John Farrow's house to swim. They were great friends of my mother's, and I got all dressed up to meet them. Then, when we got there, everybody was in bathing suits. So my mother and I changed into bathing suits and we all sat around the pool, but nobody went in swimming. Maybe later.

The house and pool house and everything were all perched, up and down, on a hill that was covered with millions of flowers all in bloom. There was even a tiny chapel with an altar and a tiny confessional—for tiny confessions?—with an emerald-green velvet cushion to kneel on.

Maureen O'Sullivan was the first movie star I had ever come face to face with. I kept imagining her as I had seen her from the dark of the movie theatre as Tarzan held her in his arms and flew her from one tree branch to another. But now she was expecting a baby and it was a whole different scenario. She was so beautiful—but the surprise was not that she was beautiful but that she was real.

There was a long drawn-out lunch by the pool and everyone kept putting suntan lotion on, because the sun was really hot hot hot. Some swam, some never did. When it was time to go, Maureen O'Sullivan said, We'll see you soon, and then she looked right at me and said, Come for a swim anytime—and she actually gave me a hug. On our way back to the hotel, my mother told me that Mr. Farrow had said to her that I had "It." What is

"It"? I asked her. Oh, "It" is what Clara Bow had—you wouldn't remember her, you're too little, but "It" is what she had. I thought if Clara Bow was in the movies and had "It," "It" must be okay, and I couldn't wait to get older and find out what it all meant and what "It" felt like.

Soon after, Maureen O'Sullivan's baby girl was born and my mother and I visited her in the hospital. We saw the baby through a glass window. It was the first time I had ever seen a baby that small. So *that* is how it was when we started out in the world, when nothing at all had happened to us yet. . . .

Then we went back to see Maureen O'Sullivan and sat next to her, beside the high bed where she lay propped up on a lot of pillows, with vases of flowers all around her. She had a grosgrain ribbon of pink around her dark lovely hair and she looked really happy.

They talked about how beautiful the baby girl was. Then, after a while, my mother said in a low voice, Did you have a difficult time, Maureen?

And Maureen looked over at me, and then back at my mother, and said, just as though I couldn't hear her, Is it all right to talk in front of—? and she looked over at me again.

Of course that put my mother in a spot, so what could she say except Oh, yes, of course.

I was all ears, expecting to hear what it was *really* like to have a baby, but Maureen O'Sullivan changed the subject and I didn't find out *anything*. Still, it was so astonishing just to be there, it didn't matter.

One day my mother took me to Metro-Goldwyn-Mayer to visit the sets where movies were being shot. There we sat with Joan Crawford in her trailer dressing room. My mother kept saying Joan this and Joan that, and Joan kept saying Gloria this and Gloria that—they sounded as if they'd been friends forever. I could not get over how big Joan's eyes were. They really popped out at you. Did she put belladonna in them the way my mother had in Paris? Or were they just that way naturally? Of course I

didn't ask any personal questions or say anything at all, because
I couldn't think of anything not personal to say. All I could do
was try not to seem too bowled over by being in her poppy-eyed
presence, and I tried to act as if I fitted right into the Gloria this
and the Joan that.

Not too long after I met another friend of my mother. Her
name was Ketti Keven and she was also an actress who had been
on the stage once and then from time to time in the movies. But
now she didn't work unless parts came along, because a big movie
producer had loved her so much he was taking care of her for
always and she wouldn't have to worry about a thing ever again.
Who was he? I wondered. It was mysterious, but that was the
only thing about Ketti that *was*, because everything else about
her was all unmysterious, for she had noisy ways and made jokes
about almost everything. Not mean jokes, but jokes that made
my mother giggle, until their giggles turned into gales of mer-
riment and laughter, not merry to me at all because I was left
out of it, not only left out of what was so funny but out of what
was going on between them. What was it that was going on
between them? I couldn't figure it out. Then there was that
hairdo, which at first I'd liked but now didn't like at all. At first
it had seemed yellow and soft as cotton, but now it appeared
mustardy and hard as steel wool. And what about Maurice and
the roses? Why had they stopped coming after that avalanche the
first day we arrived?

Olives

One day, while dawdling over lunch at the Brown Derby,
my mother had a spur-of-the-moment notion to go visiting, just
the two of us, and as we got into the glossy limousine waiting
for us outside the restaurant, she gave the driver an address in
Beverly Hills and off we went. I still had no idea where we were

going or whom we were going to pay this unexpected visit to.

We pulled up at a house that looked like a pretend Aunt Gertrude's house at Old Westbury Capital, and out we got and walked along a brick path with hibiscus on either side, up to the front door, where my mother pressed the bell. Soon a butler answered and my mother said, I'm Mrs. Vanderbilt and this is my daughter—is Miss Bennett at home?

Come in, madam, won't you please, said the butler. And we followed him in to a huge beige-on-beige-on-beige living room, where even the piano was beige, and the flowers on tables, placed here and there, were in beige vases. Could the flowers be real? I had never seen beige flowers before.

The butler disappeared, and soon a door opened on the landing at the top of the curving staircase, and out came the thinnest person you ever saw. This thinnest person was also beige, wearing a long beige dressing gown with gorgeous beige hair parted on the side and cut like a bell, which swung around her face every time she moved. And following behind this beige person was a handsome man with naturally black curly hair all over his head, and you could even see some of it on his chest, and he had the whitest teeth I had ever seen. (Were they natural too?) Soon he was putting his arm around all that beigeness and they were both hugging each other and looking down at us from over the banister and laughing.

Gloria! how wonderful to see you!

What a couple! They both started on down the stairs towards us side by side, as if they were dancing a two-step.

You know Gilbert Roland, don't you, darling?

And Gilbert Roland flashed his white white teeth at us and said, Oh, and you've brought Little Gloria along too!

I could have hit him for that Little if I hadn't been so goggle-eyed.

Now the butler was back, asking what everybody would like to drink—and I tried not to stare at Connie Bennett's stomach to see if she had, or had not, swallowed her olive that day.

Gilbert looked as if maybe he'd just gotten out of bed, for his shirt was buttoned up in a hasty way; and Connie, now that I was up close to her, had no makeup on at all—not that she needed it, for she was luminous throughout in that beige-on-beige way that hovered about her.

All through this visit I could not think of one single thing to say. All I could do was to sit there hoping I looked old, really old, for it was terrible to be here in Hollywood at last and to be stuck in my babyish thirteen.

And as for the olive—no, she had not had her olive that day—yet. For everything my mother had said about Connie Bennett was true. She was indeed thin—so thin that had she swallowed her olive that day, we all certainly would have remarked upon it.

My mother was in such a good mood after the success of our unexpected call on Connie and Gilbert that when we got back into the limousine, instead of telling the driver to take us back to the hotel, she gave him another address in Beverly Hills.

Where are we going now? I asked her.

I thought it might be fun to pop in on Marlene, don't you think so, darling?

Marlene? Marlene—Dietrich!

And I tried to say in a most casual way, Oh, yes, yes, yes, Mummy, what fun fun fun to pop in on Marlene Dietrich—Oh, yes.

It was only a few blocks away, but this house was much smaller than Connie Bennett's and was cute looking in an unreal way. It was surrounded by a picket fence, but it was not this that was surprising, because every house in Beverly Hills had its own unusual style about it, often like a version of some other style. These different styles of houses existed together side by side, screened as they were from each other by the strategic planting around them. So there was nothing especially surprising about this house set cunningly among the other

Aunt Gertrudy–style houses around it. What was surprising was
that I had always pictured Marlene Dietrich living in the Taj
Mahal, and here we were in front of her house that looked more
like another version of the house in the Andy Hardy movies.

You'd better wait in the car, darling, my mother said, I'll
go on ahead to see if Marlene's at home.

I watched her as the chauffeur unlatched the gate for her and
as she walked on, along the pathway, through the dainty garden
right up to the front door. And I watched her as she stood waiting
for the door to open. And when it did, I watched her disappear
into Andy Hardy's house as the door closed behind her.

And I kept on watching the door . . . and waiting and waiting
and waiting . . . waiting for it to open, and for her to come back
out and wave to me, wave to me, to come on in. . . .

But it did not, it did not open; and it went on and on, the
waiting and waiting, on and on. Why didn't the door open—
why?

How about some music? the driver said, and he switched on
the radio . . . and we waited and waited and waited. . . .

Maybe something had happened. But . . . what?

Maybe I should get out of the car, walk through the gate of
that picket fence and down the garden path, the way my mother
had, right up to the door—and when I got there, ring the bell—
to see if everything was all right.

But somehow I did not think my mother would like that
idea. She had said to wait to wait to wait, and wait I would.
And wait—is what I did.

Would would—would you—turn the radio off—please please
please please, I said to the chauffeur.

And just as it clicked off, the front door opened and there
she was coming towards me, my little mother coming towards
me in her white dress made of silk. And she was beckoning to
me—but instead of a Come On motion, it was a Stay Back
motion.

And I sat there not moving at all at all at all, until there she was sitting beside me in the back of the limousine saying, Back to the hotel, please, driver.

Then she patted my hand with the white crochet of her glove and said, Marlene is resting—she didn't feel up to having visitors, so I only stayed a minute, darling. Oh, there will be lots of other times to meet her—I promise you—oh, and guess what? She's going to send you an autographed picture—isn't she a pooks! I told her you were one of her biggest fans.

I did not want Marlene to do that—really I didn't—and I wanted to say this to my mother. I wanted to say, Please, Mummy— I wish Marlene Dietrich would not do that.

But I didn't say anything at all. My mother was silent too. . . .

I wondered what she was thinking about. I wondered what the inside of that Andy Hardy house was like. Not that I cared— no, not one bit!

Place Cards at the Banquet

Here we were, alone together for hours and hours, my mother and I, driving along the coast of the Pacific Ocean, on our way to the castle of Miss Marion Davies and Mr. William Randolph Hearst for the weekend.

Tootsie Eleanor needed some time off, which is why she wasn't in the car with us. It seemed funny to be sitting there without her, and I wondered what my mother and I were going to talk about.

I never could quite decide if it was considered necessary to make conversation while inside a car, driving along, if you had nothing to say. After all, it was not like being in a living room or at a party. Would it be considered polite to just sit back and look at things passing by and not say anything unless you really had something to say?

Not that I didn't have tons and tons of things I would like

to have said to my mother. . . . But the more things crowded into my mind, the more silent I became, for which one should I bring up first? And even more of a dilemma—how to begin?

Of course, I never did, because long before we reached Santa Barbara my mother ran out of conversation, and when she ran out of conversation, I ran out of conversation too.

Maybe if I started singing "California, Here We Come"— but somehow it didn't strike me as a good idea, because here we were, weren't we, and so there didn't seem to be much point in singing about it. Unless, maybe—if I changed the words to Cal-i-for-nia here we are! But are didn't rhyme with from, and there was no way around that. Not that things had to rhyme, but—oh, well . . .

So we sat silently for miles and miles, until my mother rolled down the window between us and the chauffeur and said, Can you tell me, driver, how can I turn on the radio back here? So that took care of that.

Now I had been to castles before—like Aunt Gertrude's castle at 871 Fifth Avenue and so on—but never ever to a castle like this castley-castle of Mr. William Randolph Hearst's at San Simeon. It was something!

And so were the guests. For here they did *all* look like movie stars, even though some of them were not. One of them, a Baron Hubert von Prussen, looked eerily like an actor rigged up to play the part of Prince Hohenlohe in a movie. I kept looking at my mother, hoping she wasn't going to fall for him. He deigned to talk to me for a bit as we sat around the Grecian-style lake-sized pool.

How old are you? he said.

Sixteen, I said, and looked straight at him.

But he didn't flinch, and later I stewed about in a torment, afraid that he would repeat what I had said to my mother and that I would be discovered in the lie I had told. Finally, in desperation, I told my mother what I had said and pleaded with her to back me up. Of course, darling, she said, and didn't seem to think a thing of it!

Mr. William Randolph Hearst was behind the scenes most of the time and appeared only in the evening just before we went into the Great King Arthur's Hall for dinner. Everybody snapped to and shaped up the moment Mr. Hearst stepped into the Great Hall, always appearing through the same door. He was tall, so tall, and everybody hushed quiet waiting for him to speak, which he sometimes did, sometimes not—mostly not. But when he did his voice came out tiny, so squeaky-tiny it was amazing to hear. Miss Marion Davies always seemed to wear the same shapeless slacks and dusty-colored matching blouse. She certainly liked to talk more than Mr. Hearst did, but she kept glancing over at him a lot, as if she weren't all that sure that what she was saying was the right thing to say.

We all sat at a long long banquet table, the longest I had ever seen except in the movies. Mr. Hearst sat in the middle of this table and my mother sat at his right, which I knew, of course, to be the place of honor. Then on down down down, to the very end of the table on either side, sat all the other guests. Miss Marion Davies sat opposite Mr. Hearst, and when it came to either end of the table, no one sat there at all. My place was on one side down near the very end. And it turned out the best place to be, because—seated next to me was Philip Kellogg.

When I had first met him I thought he was Gene Raymond—he was that good looking. He was in his early twenties, and I was certain, for it was too good to be true, that it was all a mistake that he had been placed at the banquet table next to thirteen-year-old me, and that by the next dinner he would be placed elsewhere.

But it wasn't a mistake. Every meal, there we were, once more, side by side. At first I thought, He'll never ever speak to me! But he did he did! I found out that he was a film cutter at Metro-Goldwyn-Mayer Studios and he not only had worked on many of my favorite movies—he actually was a friend of Bette Davis. Of course, he was a grown-up and I was not, but he talked to me the way one person talks to another person. And I kept hoping he wasn't just being polite in that grown-up way grown-ups had now and then, sometimes. And I prayed that when the weekend at San Simeon was over, it would not also be over—all over—between him and me. For I wanted more than anything else to be his friend.

And then it was good-bye good-bye, and I held my breath and wished and wished and wished—so hard—until I heard my mother saying, Good-bye, Phil, good-bye, good-bye, and how we must all get together in Los Angeles—next week.

And he was saying, Yes, we must—and I could tell he really meant it. And I floated up up up into the sky like a balloon with Phil Kellogg written all over it.

Then a few days later he came by the Ambassador Hotel to take us to Olvera Street for dinner—my mother, Ketti Keven, and me. Tootsie Eleanor stayed at the hotel resting and having room service.

We had never been to Olvera Street before, and it was like traveling across the border into Mexico, only of course it was right here in Los Angeles. Everything about it was Mexican— the streets, the shops, the restaurants, the food. Everything! And the music! Here and there, groups of three or four musicians would stroll around, thumping on guitars and singing. In the streets and everywhere you could hear them. And then when we went into a restaurant for dinner, there they were again, only this time with more guitars and more singing, and they came right up to our table to sing to us—

Ay ay ay ay
canta no llores
porque cantando se alegran
Cielito lindo los corazones.

And I knew that I could never again hear that song without thinking of Phil Kellogg, and my mother, and Ketti Keven, and the candles shining all around us as they were that night on Olvera Street. . . .

By now I had become much more used to Ketti Keven, and now that I got the drift of her, so to speak, I thought I understood what it was about her that my mother liked so much. Mainly it was because she was easy to be with and laughed a lot and made everything seem like it was fun—almost everything. I even, more or less, got to be quite taken again by her hairdo, even if it was a bit too tangly. Of course, she was still noisy as ever, yet maybe that was one of the things my mother liked best about her. She was so quiet, my mother, and Ketti Keven was so noisy—somewhat in that Nada-like way, only of course nowhere near as elegant and bewitching. Anyway, Ketti Keven seemed here to stay, and I never did get much chance to see my mother alone.

We saw a lot more of Phil Kellogg too, and for the first time I knew what it was to really have a conversation with a grown-up person, a person who was a grown-up and who listened to me and didn't treat me like a baby. And although I still hadn't given up my search for a father, I did not think of Phil Kellogg in that way at all, although I didn't know quite why. Was it because he talked to me as an equal? Could that be it? But fathers should do that too—or didn't they? As I had never had a father, I didn't really have much of an idea *what* it would be like. It was all most perplexing. But whatever it was, it was somewhere right in the middle between being weak in the knees and talking to a father. And it meant much to me.

So for want of a better word to describe my feelings for him, I thought of him as . . . friend. Yes, the more I thought about it, that was just right, for that is what he was. Phil Kellogg was my friend.

The Snow Queen

There were only two more days left and we would be back on the Super Chief, only now it would be

Whit-ney Cap-i-tal—here I come!
Right back where I start-ed from. . . .

And how did I feel about that? Really, I didn't know how I felt about any of it, because I was confused about so many things.

The night before we were to leave, my mother said she had a surprise for me and that I must have a long nap in the afternoon because we would be up very late, on and on, into the night. Of course I couldn't nap or close my eyes or think of anything else, imagining what the surprise could be.

Finally nine o'clock came around and my mother started dressing and so did I. She gave me some of her Ardena Fluffy Milk Bath and I lolled in it in my most movie-star way until the water got cold. Then I kept adding more and more hot water, until finally there were no more bubbles left and I had to get out.

I took ages dressing, building up to the moment when for the first time *lipstick* was to be permitted to touch my lips. The effect of the faint blush of Tangee was thrilling, and I couldn't wait to get my mother's reaction.

The dress I was to wear was a white dotted swiss, hopelessly infantile, but I was determined not to let that ruin the evening. My mother was to wear white crêpe de chine, bias cut, with pearl beads speckled about all over it, and over all this, a cape of white fox fur that went right down to the floor.

When I saw her all ready to go, she looked like the Snow Queen from my book of fairy tales, and all I could say was, Oh, Mummy, you look beautiful, over and over again. So beautiful— so beautiful . . .

How I longed to touch her, but I didn't dare. We got into the limousine, and I sat as far away from her as I could on the seat so as not to disarrange her dress and the cloak that protected her. . . .

We drove and drove and drove through the night, and above us there was a moon and lots of stars twinkling—and then the coach stopped, and a knight in splendid uniform opened the door and assisted the Snow Queen from her carriage, and then turned to me and held his arm out for me to descend.

And we walked along a crimson carpet in stately fashion until we came to the castle door, and over this door were stars, as if they had fallen down from the night sky and clustered themselves, one around the other, until they razzle-dazzled on and off above the door—

T-R-O-C-A-D-E-R-O

blinking on and off, on and off

T-R-O-C-A-D-E-R-O

off and on

T-R-O-C-A-D-E-R-O—

Then other knights came forward to escort us in, into the spangly light, in and down the steps on into the castle ballroom, on past the round tables holding bowls of lavender roses on cloths of pale yellow damask, past tall candelabras of gold holding ivory candles, each flame sheltered by a shade of fringed silk . . . on through gardens of delight, until at last we reached our table . . .

Loretta Young and Dolores del Rio welcoming us . . .

Penguin-suited men, handsome—and if not handsome, fascinating—and if not fascinating, mysterious! . . .

But above all else, and fairest of all the fair to see, was my mother. . . .

Because I could see—it was plain for all to see—that all the others—yes, even the beauty of Dolores del Rio and Loretta Young—all were as dolls made of wax, and my mother was . . . ? She was . . . ?

What? Who was she? And what was it that I wanted?

I had to know, for without knowing I would be in a never-never land floating throughout the world, forever an Impostor. Yes, even years from now, even when I entered the grown-up world—if I did not know the secret of her, it would all be for nought. . . .

And I looked around me into the beauty everywhere, for if not my mother's, surely one of those other faces would tell me what it was I searched for.

And I looked back at my mother, sitting there, unaware of me, as she leaned over, talking to a stranger. And then I saw that it was *me* she leaned towards, it was *me* she spoke to, and that *I* was the stranger. And it came to me, and I knew what I had to have before my soul would rest. I wanted to belong—to belong to my mother. And in return—I wanted my mother to belong to me.

One and One Equals Two, August 1937

There was something about Old Westbury Capital very much like a kingdom, for no matter where you were or where you went, and no matter what might happen elsewhere, there it would be, waiting. No, not waiting—for Old Westbury Capital did not *wait*. It simply was there, and so it would be for always and always, forever and ever. Amen.

And sure enough, just as it always remained in my mind during the times I was with my mother, now I was back and everything was set in exactly the same place I knew it would be.

Only it was not! For soon after I got back, Tweedle Crocker showed up bearing tidings. At first I thought it was some kind of joke, only it was not in Tweedle Crocker's nature to spend time kidding around. For whenever he came with a message, he said what he had to say, and once the message had been relayed to me it was in and out, quick as quick could be. And this time was no exception.

So things started out as they always did, with Your Aunt Gertrude has asked me to tell you. . . .

Then as usual he got straight to the point: Next Saturday your half-sister, Cathleen, will be driving out here to Old Westbury to have lunch. Mrs. Whitney will of course be here also, having driven out the night before.

Sister!

Yes, sister—that is, your half-sister.

Half-sister?

Yes—he looked over at the door as if she might be arriving any moment.

I didn't know I had a sister!

Half-sister, he corrected.

Are you sure this is true? (I knew it must be, but it was all so . . .)

Didn't Mrs. Whitney advise you of this fact before? A look of bewilderment was hidden somewhere in the dough of the Tweedle's face.

No, she didn't—no one did—I never knew I had a sister— I mean a half-sister.

Well, you do now, he promptly stated, looking over at the door again, well satisfied, and he started twiddling his fat thumbs.

It was most annoying, this habit of his—thumb twiddling. It was usually a sign that he was becoming bored and soon would be getting up to leave. Only this time I didn't want him to, I wanted him to stay and talk to me, stay for hours telling me about my sister—my sister—my sister.

Why didn't Auntie Ger tell me? Why didn't anyone tell me, not even my mother?

Well, there was no reason for Mrs. Vanderbilt to mention this to you. After all, Mrs. Vanderbilt has nothing to do with this half-sister of yours, now, does she? Nothing at all.

Why doesn't she? (I wanted to pounce on his twiddling thumbs and crush his fat hands into a mass of jelly.)

Well, well now, he said, and he meandered on slowly, explaining it all to the poor backward child, teaching her that one plus one equals two—from your father's first marriage to Miss Neilson, this was their only issue. Miss Cathleen Neilson. They were married at one time, your father and Miss Neilson, and their child, the only child from this marriage, was—is—Cathleen—now Mrs. Lawrence Lowman.

Married?

Before. Yes, your father was married once before he married your mother, so surely you can understand that Mrs. Vanderbilt—that is, your mother—well, she has nothing whatsoever to do with this matter, nothing at all.

And my sister is *married*? (I had envisioned something more along the lines of Gerta.) How old is she then?

Cathleen is now Mrs. Lawrence Lowman—yes, and married, of course—and would be—well, let me see—well, she would be about your mother's age—yes, precisely. What a coincidence!

But why—I still don't understand why no one had told me about her. Why?

It's not for me to say at this time. You'll just have to take my word for it.

What word? Word for what?

Well, Gloria, there must have been good and sufficient reasons, mustn't there? Now, that's all I'm permitted to say.

And he stopped twiddling and got up, and out he twaddled, out through the door and into a car, and he drove away just like that, without saying another word. And there was I, waiting and waiting for Saturday, trying to picture what she would be like, this sudden sister who I never knew existed.

Then the most incredible thought came to me. Perhaps *she* would be the one to bring the letter, the letter I knew my father had written to me before he died—the letter I had waited so long to receive. Yes, perhaps that was what Tweedle Crocker had meant by good and sufficient reasons, because it was all part of a plan, and soon—it was now only a matter of time—I would be meeting my sister whose name was Cathleen. And she would hand me the letter, Special Delivery, the letter from my father, and everything, yes, *everything*, would be put right and fall into place.

Dear Diary

It is over. The lunch. The meeting. They have left, and here I am back in my room trying to put the pieces all together. With me in the room is a sausage dog sniffing around and making me nervous. I am not partial to dachshunds, but maybe, in time— who knows?—they say you can get used to anything. I just wish he hadn't already been named Fritz. I know my sister—(SISTER— just think of it. It seems so funny to write it, and the word keeps pushing around on my tongue—*sissss-ter*—as I say it over and over again to myself. *Sissss-ter* . . .) Anyway, what I started to say was that I know my sister meant it as a getting-to-know- you, break-the-ice kind of present, for how could anyone be shy with this cunning thing running around, leaping up on chairs and sofas and sniffing at people's feet in that doggy way? Even those few iffy moments between Fritz and Aunt Gertrude's long- haired dachshund, Comet, turned out okay after a few growls. Cathleen says she has eight dogs, all just like Fritz and almost as cute, and that they all get to sleep in her bedroom at night and I should see them fighting for a place on the bed. Gee, I really look forward to seeing that. Ha, ha! They must have an awfully big bed. Anyway—Fritz! Fritz, stop that! Gosh, now he's peeing on the rug—and they said he was house-trained. Come on, Fritz. I'll take you out for a run.

Later—he's really quite a nice dog after all. Somehow when I got him out and running around, he lost some of that shimmy-

ing motion he had in the house that was making me jittery.

Now to get back to my sister, Cathleen . . . she is *very* quiet. Tall, and—yes, definitely sophisticated. And wears lovely things— especially that turban she had on. I have never seen anyone wear a turban except in a Sabu movie. Now that I think of it, there is something indefinably Oriental about her, and she has the same eyes I do and which everyone calls the Vanderbilt eyes. Maybe we have Javanese blood? Many of the Dutch married with the Javanese, didn't they? I'll ask her about it next time I see her. Wouldn't this be thrilling if it were true? Maybe she was so quiet because she's as scared that I won't like her as I'm scared she won't like me. But I think she did like me, even though she didn't say much. She did look at me in a friendly Javanese way, and smiled at me too. Often. So did Larry. He was really nice, and nowhere near as quiet as Cathleen. I loved that black dress she had on, and it went so well with the turban. The dress had flecks of white here and there all over it, and the turban was the same print, only it was white and the flecks were black. I wonder what color her hair is, and how she wears it when she's not wearing a turban. She had loads of bracelets, but only on her left wrist—all shapes and sizes, gold links with charms dangling, and on her fingers ruby rings. The one I liked best was a gold snake, twisting around her little finger in the most friendly way with flinty ruby chips for eyes. Her hands are gorgeous! Almost as beautiful as my mother's, with the same long long tapering nails, ovals all shiny with the prettiest shade of coral lacquer brushed right down to the tip.

Yes, she is very beautiful, and I can't wait to see her again. When? I wonder. As they were leaving, Larry said, See you soon, and then my sister said, We'll all have dinner together in New York, we'll go to a restaurant. But when?

This has been quite a day! And why did I ever start thinking about that silly letter? It was always a stupid idea anyway, and I should be thanking my lucky stars I have a sister instead of mooning over some dumb letter that doesn't even exist and never did. And that's what I'm going to do right now, right from this moment on—forget all about it—the letter, I mean. Cross my heart and hope to die, I am going to forget all about it.

I wish Cathleen could see Fritz right now. He looks like he's in a coma, but he's only fallen asleep, passed out at the foot of my bed.

Nick and Nora Charles

Last night they took me to a restaurant for dinner. And I saw her hair because she wasn't wearing the turban. It's a kind of—well, it's hard to put a color on it, but on the blond side. Definitely on the blond side—but not in that white goldilocks way of Jean Harlow's—more toasty-like and natural. Now that I think about it, there's something about my sister that's a lot like Myrna Loy—but Myrna Loy *only* when she's with William Powell, when they're together in a Thin Man movie, playing Nick and Nora Charles. Not that Larry looks like William Powell, because you couldn't say he does, but when you see him with Cathleen, when you see them together, there's something about the air of it that's so like Nick and Nora Charles. Now all they need to make it perfect is that fox terrier dog (what's his name? the one that's always yapping around in the important scenes) instead of all those dachshunds running around. And boy, do they have a lot of dachshunds running around. All over the apartment, all so cute you can't tell one from the other.

They live on Park Avenue in a not-too-big apartment. It's all done modern with not many things around to make it cozy, except for fruit-shaped English tea caddies placed around on tables. On one table will be an apple of burl wood, and on another a pear of some other kind of wood, all polished to a burnished glow. My sister says she collects them. She smokes all the time in a most sophisticated way, using a gold cigarette holder. She also drinks a lot of Coca-Cola, sometimes one right after the other, with only one cube of ice in it. They have a Gauguin painting on one wall, a real one just like in a museum. And on another wall a Daumier, which I didn't like—it's all dark and has judges spooking around in the background conferring in that murky way they have. I got to see their bed where all the dachshunds sleep, and it *is* enormous, about as big as Auntie Ger's.

We went to Jimmy's Oyster Bar for dinner. It had sawdust on the floor and hundreds of different choices of fish on the menu. Larry did most, if not all, of the talking, and my sister sat there looking inscrutable, smiling from time to time, murmuring a word here and there, while I just listened. I didn't speak up because I wanted so much to make a good impression and was afraid of saying something that would make them think less of me. Of course I kept hoping the conversation would finally get around to my father, but it never did. Maybe next time—maybe Cathleen is waiting for the right moment, when we're at home instead of in a noisy restaurant. I mean, she's my mother's age, which means she was also nineteen when my father died, so she must remember things about him, because she knew him all those years before he died.

She had on different bracelets this time, but the same snake ring twirling around her little finger. Maybe she wears it all the time. After dinner they had demitasses and Cathleen took from her purse a round gold compact, the biggest compact I've ever seen, with angels on the lid. She handed it to me across the table so I could examine it. The angels were enameled and each one was doing something different, like sitting or standing or flying, and each one had an appropriate expression on its teeny face. Paul Flato made it for me, Cathleen said. It sounded too unsophisticated of me to ask who Paul Flato was, so I said, Oh, did he really?—how lovely! Larry's sister gave me the angels, she said, on a charm bracelet. I collect angels, you know (of course I didn't know, but it was one of the most grown-up things I'd ever heard of). And so I took the bracelet to Paul and he had the idea of putting the angels on a compact—and she looked at herself in the mirror inside of the lid, in a most critical, preoccupied way, dabbing tenderly at her face with the fluffy puff. It was the kind of soft thing my mother would call goofoo feathers. Yes, it was definitely a goofoo-feather puff.

What would my mother think about Cathleen? I don't think she ever sees her. Maybe they don't like each other. Maybe that's why I hadn't known about my sister until now. But my mother doesn't seem to have much to say about anything these days, so it must be something else. Cathleen's hair is pulled back kind of like my mother's used to be. I wonder how it looks hanging loose and if it waves the way my mother's did, and if it's as long.

There was no dawdling over demitasses at this dinner and no petits canards and no brandy, only more Coca-Colas. Then it was time to leave, and they dropped me off at the castle on Fifth Avenue, where I spent the night because it was Friday and the next day I had to go to my mother's for the usual weekend visit. (Could I tell my mother about meeting my sister? Better not— too complicated.)

Next time they're going to invite me to their house in Stamford, Connecticut. Maybe that's why Cathleen is waiting to talk to me about my father. I mean, maybe there is so much to tell me about him that she needs a whole day and then some.

Cathleen and Larry kept going on and on about Fritz and how was he doing at Old Westbury Capital and what new frolics was he up to? Fritz was doing just fine, thank you, to the manor born was Fritz; so we talked on and on about that until I couldn't think of one other thing to add to the Fritz question.

I wonder how tall he was. My father, I mean. Maybe I'll find out the next time I see her.

Night Hunters

My mother is going to a costume ball and she and Aunt Toto go on and on about it all the livelong day. They're in a real dither trying to decide what to wear. It's ages away, this fancy-dress ball, but to hear them go on about it makes it seem as if it's happening tomorrow night and they've been caught without a stitch to wear. Now the pace has eased up a little as they come to a unanimous decision. A Miss Yvonne has come into our lives and she feverishly sews and snips away at bolts of creamy white velvet which have been spread out on a table in that room on the top floor.

It was in this top-floor room—in fact on the very spot where Miss Yvonne's sacred table now stands—that a weekend ago a settee had been placed, and on this settee my mother had sat, with me placed close beside her. We had been so placed by Aunt Toto for photographs she was to take. It was all part of a game that I wasn't supposed to know about—but, good sport that I am, I went along with it. Actually, I went along with it because I was thrilled to be with my mother in this just-we-two situation, not to mention the niftiness of being the center not only of her attention but of Aunt Toto's as well. Aunt Toto, in her artful way, had draped a silk scarf over a Brownie camera. This scarf had tiny toy wooden soldiers printed on it, rows and rows of them, and they bobbed around the room over the Brownie in a casual way, as Aunt Toto tried to pretend the camera wasn't pointed in our direction and hopped around, chatting up a storm. The scarf was one I had seen my mother wear, but I knew that Aunt Toto had one exactly like it, so who's to say which scarf was which. There was a moment at the start when I could have pulled away and said, The jig is up! But I didn't—and then it was too late. So there we all were, caught up in and accepting the rules of this particular little game. Only sometimes Aunt Toto was naughty and would cheat and lapse into Spanish, and in between the Spanish the name Hearst popped in rather a lot—and from that I guessed that these pictures were being taken especially for Mr. Hearst and that they would end up in his newspapers. Oh, well . . . But would I ever get to see them?

But by the next weekend the settee my mother and I had sat on had disappeared, and this room was now dedicated to Miss Yvonne and her comings and goings. She would arrive early, this Miss Yvonne, long before my mother and Aunt Toto were awake, entering the house with a singular energy, intent upon the task at hand. She spoke not at all, nor did she look to the right or to the left as she entered, and if the lift didn't happen to be on the ground floor in readiness, she would disdain the wait and race through the air in her garb of puce, up the stairs to her aerie on the top floor.

Not only was there the rippling cream of white velvet in this sanctuary on the top floor, there were laces, soft as my mother's skin, to be made into jabots, and tendrils, curling into the feathered white of plumes, to be placed on the velvet black richness of hats to be worn with this fancy dress, for my mother and Aunt Toto would make their appearance at the ball dressed as ladies of the court of Marie Antoinette. Elsewhere across the city, at M. Antoine's, there were also serious doings—for to complete the costumes, wigs were to be fashioned. Yes, and not only that— it was deemed necessary that they be of real hair curled into white ringlets. But whose curling white hair would be cut to cover the beauty of my mother's tresses? It would never be known, because M. Antoine never divulged important secrets.

Every weekend I would arrive expecting the costumes to be finished, but they were not. And each time I would glimpse Miss Yvonne coming in or going out. And that's all I saw, for no one except my mother and Aunt Toto (and of course Wannsie) was allowed to enter the room on the top floor, for to do so would be to disturb the concentration of Miss Yvonne.

But all things come to an end, and here I am at my mother's and there is no sign of Miss Yvonne or her snippets anywhere in sight. Not only that, but my mother and Aunt Toto say they have a surprise for me—which must mean that the costumes are finished and that I will see them.

And now I have not only seen the costumes but seen my mother and Aunt Toto *in* the costumes. *Sans gêne*, as the Twins so often say. And it is a sight to behold, for my mother pirouettes back and forth in the long mirror of her boudoir, entranced by the double image of her luscious magnolia self . . . only it is not her double image at all—it is the image of Aunt Toto as well, swinging to and fro so pleasingly beside her. Together they waltz around the room, with white flower bell skirts swinging, for there are petticoats of hooped steel beneath the skirts, making the velvety waves fall just right. And next to my mother's skin are the jabots of lace, frothy as the white of egg in a bowl of floating island, and on the hat a feather rests over the crown reaching forward over the brim, as if hoping to touch the beauty of my mother's face.

But this is *not* the surprise. The surprise is that at my mother's request, stitch by stitch, Miss Yvonne has also made a costume for me, identical in every way to my mother's—and it's just awful. Rooted to the spot, I stand in this ridiculous getup as the Twins in their Dresden way cavort in the background, and I want to run run from the room so that my fatness is no longer reflected in my mother's boudoir in this hideous way.

But this is not the end of it. No—I have been told that a special occasion has been arranged for me to wear this fancy dress. Not a party, because it's obvious that my fatness is too much of a muchness to accompany my mother and Aunt Toto to the ball— not to mention my babyishness, which is much too babyish to boot. No, it's something else that has been cooked up—a real treat. There's to be another photograph session, only this time it's no nonsense. Mr. Hal Phyfe himself is coming right here to this house, and traipsing behind him will be assistants bearing lights and cameras, and I am to squeeze my fatness into the fatfulness of this steel hoop of a skirt, don this feathered hat, and sit next to my mother, right here in the living room. And I know, I just know, that this time I will not be able to pretend it isn't happening, because it is, it is! And I wish I could die!

But no such luck, for here I am all rigged up and standing around waiting for the assistants to get the lights bright bright bright so that no detail of my mother's beauty will be missed and no detail of my hooped-up fatness will slip by either. Mr. Hal Phyfe is thin thin and tall tallest and winsome as can be— why not, because he is a most famous photographer who photographs my mother every year, to make certain her beauty is properly recorded.

Slowly down the stairs my mother now is making her descent. The cherubim and seraphim herald her arrival—all turn towards her as, drawn out of our lowly selves, we stand in awe and wonder at this apparition. On her head even the hated wig of white sits in beauty, and I dare not imagine the preposterous apparition of mine which has been pulled down to cover my fat hair, for, yes, M. Antoine has created a wig of white, from who-knows-whose hair, for me to wear. It is identical to my mother's, right down to each strand. I am indeed, piece by piece, a dressed replica of my mother—and more's the pity.

But now Mr. Phyfe has unfrozen himself and is no longer a statue, and there is much hugging and kissing as he and my mother exchange foolish banter, while around her all the minions ooh and aah. Soon surely the floor will open and I will make a merciful descent into realms unknown. But no, it is another descent I make, for unknown hands are pushing me into the sun which circles my mother, as she sits in perfection, while the lowly ones adjust the oceans of velvet around the hoops. Yes, I am to sit on the arm of her chair and lean in close to her just as though we belonged together. Oh, the cruelty of it! From this pool of white light I peer out through the blaze into caves of darkness as voices echo through caverns, for our every gesture is directed into attitudes of tenderness, while other voices flicker in and out mumbling about fuses blowing and more light on Mrs. Vanderbilt's right cheek—and all I want to do is to shrink into a tiny ball and hurl myself off the face of this earth forever.

Smile, Little Gloria, smile. It is the voice of the dragon from somewhere far at the distant end of the cave. And I try I try I try, but instead my face turns into a pumpkin with no candle inside and a mouth going down instead of up. Beside me my mother remains valiant, but I can sense that her endurance is waning. What will happen if she too collapses into a miserable pumpkin?

Little Gloria, lean closer lean closer to Big Gloria.

Now my eyes have grown used to sunbursts, and if I squint, I can make out the shadow of the dragon bending over a pillar of stone as it stands immovable and silent, and I can see it is not a dragon at all, nor is it a pillar of stone. It is Mr. Hal Phyfe calling from the cave's hollow darkness, while others, in mysterious ways, drift silently around the cave, still fiddling around, adjusting things.

That's better that's better, Little Gloria—only smile, please, smile smile smile smile!

In rage I lean over to take my mother's hand, but it is spread out just so, and her fingers, all five, placed just so—the long nails of mahogany red presented just so. How heartless to disturb such symmetry. So I pull back.

Little Gloria, put your arm around Big Gloria—arm around her arm around her.

And I do, without hesitation. And now I reach over and, without disturbing her hand, my hand circles her wrist, lightly and gently, so gently, I will her towards me—but it is for nought. She gazes out through the blaze of sun into the abyss, hooked to the image she projects, and I know that she is not aware of my intent at all. And the dragon's teeth click away, and I see how it will look, this picture Mr. Hal Phyfe is conjuring up, when framed in silver and standing on a table somewhere in my mother's house, or on the piano maybe. Others will look at it and my mother will look at it, but no one will look at it as I do, for to me it will always be a picture of a greedy little night-hunting rabbit, in pursuit of something . . . but what? A mother perhaps? Yes, that's as good a name for it as any . . .

Good-bye Gerta, Autumn 1938

Gerta lives in a white house—big—high up on a hill, across the woods from Aunt Gertrude's house at Old Westbury Capital. We keep trying to devise a way of stringing wire from her room to mine for sending notes secretly in a basket back and forth to each other across the distance, but so far we haven't worked out the details. Bozo Bean is Gerta's father. Her mother is Aunt Gertrude's youngest daughter. She never has much to say because Bozo Bean says it all.

Gerta and I went up to her mother as she sat cross-legged on the grass near their house to ask her if we could go riding that afternoon. But she sat there pulling at the grass without saying anything until after a while she said, We'll see, we'll see, we'll see. She didn't look up at us and it came out serious, as if this were a very important question, when it wasn't, not at all. There she sat, tugging the blades of grass in front of her as if that would help her come to a decision. But it didn't. All she said was We'll see we'll see, over and over again.

So we went back into the house and knocked on the door of the library, where we knew Bozo Bean would be. He sits there most of the day, straight up, in an enormous dark leather chair with wings on either side, smoking his pipe and looking over papers. What these papers are we do not know, but whatever they are he spends most of each day attending to them.

Who is it? he barked. It's me Daddy, Gerta said. Come in come in come in—he sounded interrupted—but I didn't want to go in and I turned away and said to Gerta, I'll meet you outside.

Instead, I went into the front hall, near the door leading out to the gravelly circle of driveway. There was a China person there I wanted to see, a fat mandarin seated cross-legged on the hall table right in the center. He had a scary smile that never left his face and if you touched his head it nodded up and down up and down. So did his hands stretching out from the tubby folds of his china robe, palms down in an unfriendly way—the painted nails of Fu Manchu, up and down, nodding. I was afraid to touch him, but I always ended up doing it—and of course nothing happened, it never did. After all he was only made of china, and I could end it all in a second by smashing him to bits. Or could I? I kept looking at his face nodding up and down, up and down, with that knowing smile, until I got so scared I started out the door. But then Gerta appeared. And I knew that behind the closed door of Bozo Bean's library something terrible had happened. She put her arms around me and started to cry so hard no words could come out.

What is it what is it what is it? I said.

She took my hand and pulled me, running, out across the driveway, running gravelly gravelly, the crunch under our feet like chalk scratched wrong against the blackboard—running running to her mother sitting on the lawn. But there was no one there—only the patch where she had torn at the grass, a patch as if maybe a squirrel had crouched there nibbling at one particular spot. . . . Gerta sobbed and sobbed and her fist pounded at that spot until all you could see was a round circle of earth, black and rich, mashed into a hole, with the green spreading out clipped and even around it. . . .

He never wants us to see each other again—ever ever ever!

And she pulled me down beside her and I started to cry too. Why? Why? Why?

He says I'm to be sent away to school, to boarding school, and that you are too, to another school another school a different school, and I'll never see you again again ever ever because— because you—you'll—grow up—grow up to be—like—your mother—your mother—mother mother—and and and—he says— he says—bad bad bad—in-flu-ence—influence influence—on me— You me—

She started choking; it was terrible to see.

Dad-dy—Dad-dy—that's what Dad-dy said—said never again—ever—to see you or write again never ever ever—to you— as long as I live—live—live—and we can't be best friends anymore ever again again—again—

Never?

Never never never. . . .

And I ran from her, across the grass, across crackling chalk, through woods and back to Aunt Gertrude's . . . and as I ran the crying dried up, yes it did, because although I knew I'd never see my best friend again, what I knew better still was that I didn't have to say good-bye to her or to anyone else ever again— because I'd already said good-bye to Big Elephant, and that good-bye was the Big Good-bye, the one to last me for the rest of my life . . . so I'd never have to say it again ever, would I? Would I?

New Friends

And here I was fourteen years old and still had the fatness upon me and it was time for me to be sent to boarding school. It was to be Miss Porter's School in Farmington, Connecticut. Yet with all these good-byes around—it's too bad there were no good-byes to fatness. For not one pound had I shed before that first day when all the new girls gathered in the main building at Farmington to get to know each other.

In our tweed skirts and buttoned-down-the-back Brooks Brothers cardigans, we stood around and sniffed at each other in an offhand way, as yet no alliances formed, no sides taken, no scapegoat selected. All had equal chance—or so it seemed as warily we waited, each in her own way, fat or thin, for the other to make a first move.

But I did not have long to wait. Quite soon one girl favored me from among all others. I was to be her Star, so to speak, to torment. And although she had fatness upon her too, her fatness had authority and a wit of sorts—that is, if you called ridiculing someone wit. Now of course you can make a joke of anyone, if that's what you want to do. You could take the most serious person you know, or do not know, and make a joke of this person. Take Mrs. Eleanor Roosevelt and even the President himself, and you could turn both of them into a joke. Not that I compared myself to them, but although I may not have put it into words, I did think of myself as someone with serious intent. Still, it was clear that Olga Benedict did not think of me like that, and I knew that unless I thought fast, all would be lost.

Not only was Olga a presence by her very fatness; she was an obstreperous presence in all her ways. She delighted in shouting from where she sat at the end of one of the long tables where we took our meals down to me sitting at the other—better still if I sat across the room at another table. These sallies were usually about my mother, but sometimes Auntie Ger would come into it—only she pronounced Auntie Ger "Antiga" and spoke it as if it were some new obscenity.

Hanging over all this was the hazing ritual which traditionally took place a month after school had started. At a breakfast—an occasion with all faculty barred—certain chosen ones were thrown into the arena. Over the cornflakes and the Post Toasties no humiliation was out of bounds, for never would it be known to the faculty what had transpired behind those closed doors.

Well, well, I would have to get moving. Something would have to be done about that. But what?

Bonavishski Buttercup

Well, I made her my best friend, that's what. Not only that, but I gave her a new name—Bonavishski Buttercup—which *she* thought hilarious. I put up with her drivel and even sometimes made myself laugh with her. And eventually I even got to like her—then later to love her. Her authority was, of course, masquerade more than anything else, but I went along with it, and one day the cruel prattle stopped and she started picking on someone else, a blond buffy person with hair (could it be a wig?) and hefty ways more suited to driving a truck than to mincing around the campus of Miss Porter's School in brown and white saddle shoes. God knows what went on between them, for many weird things went on at Farmington, but whatever it was, it soon ended, and there I was with none other than Bonavishski Buttercup back at my side, claiming me as her best friend.

There was another girl who joined forces with us—Caroline Jennings from Little Rock, Arkansas, with the look of a Botticelli angel, soft accented ways, and tales of hayrides and exotic Southern doings far away. Together we called ourselves the Stout-Hearted Men, inspired by the spirited song sung by Nelson Eddy. And so it went, with this unlikely triumvirate presenting a united front as we paddled along through the days of the fall semester.

Whenever talk came up about the longed-for vacations, Bonavishski became oddly silent. And after a while, after much probing on my part, I found out that it was because Olga Benedict had no place to go. Her mother was off somewhere in Mexico and her father off somewhere with someone else. So I ended up asking Tweedle Crocker to ask Auntie Ger if I could invite The Buttercup to stay with me at Old Westbury Capital during vacation. He wrote back that it was acceptable. So we had that to look forward to as the semester progressed.

During the week there were various diversions once classes were over. Counting each other's stacks of Brooks Brothers sweaters was one, for the competition about this was fierce, and there was much totting up as to who had accumulated the most. Then there were the weekly bets as to which basement window a certain worker would choose next time, for every week he picked a different spot in which to expose himself to us. Along with this went the bets as to which worker it actually was, for there were more than one of them around the school, and each of us had her own particular opinion as to which one ours really was.

But better than anything were the every other Saturdays when the headmistress of Miss Porter's School, the tea-shoppy Mrs. Keep, permitted us to have boyfriends call on us at her house. Even better than the tea party was the piano in her living room which she allowed to be played. One of my boyfriends was Kirk Browning, and he played the most honeyed music on Mrs. Keep's piano every time he came on one of those Saturdays. He went to Northchurch Academy nearby, and I was always so proud that it was me he had come to have tea with at Mrs. Keep's, in spite of the fatness still upon me.

As for the testy Mrs. Keep, after the first hellos she only spooked around in the background in a cold-muffiny way, and by then nothing mattered but Kirk Browning and Gershwin on the piano.

Hold Me Close, Bea Wain, and Rock Me

Receiving letters at Farmington was also looked forward to . . . especially letters from—yes! it had happened. Not only had I come face to face with Johnny Delahanty at last, I had actually danced with him, and now we were writing back and forth to each other at least once a week.

This had all come about because he had been in Miss Bonnie Mae Murray's dancing class and so had I. During my last year at Green Vale, dancing class met from time to time at one or another of the members' houses, and I had almost fainted when I walked in to Mimi Harriman's living room and there he had been, standing with his back to me, talking to George Howard and Charlie White, who were two boys in my class at school. Miss Bonnie Mae Murray was a stickler for doing things in a formal manner, but she also had a dimpling doll-like air about her, and no one in dancing class was afraid of her. It was just the opposite, because we always knew that she would see to it that everyone circulated around—no easy thing to do, for the boys always acted as if they would much rather be someplace else than where they were, and had things been left up to them, well, it's for sure that they would have stayed in a group on one side of the room while we shifted about on the other side of the room fidgeting at the flowers in our hair and pretending not to mind. So when I had seen him across the room with his back turned away, I couldn't take my eyes off him until suddenly he turned around, and I quickly turned my back to him so he would think I hadn't seen him.

Records were stacked up by the gramophone and the music was starting. Just as it did, Miss Bonnie Mae took her elegant cane from against the wall and started beating time with it in a tap-tapping way on the floor, which was the signal for the boys to choose partners. They lingered in a group in their self-conscious manner and got a move on only when Miss Bonnie Mae Murray tap-tapped again, swirling around on her spiky high-heeled pumps, saying in her singsong voice, William, wouldn't it be nice to dance with Nuala? And Trubee, you dance with Babette. And Johnny, you with—Gloria! And there he was coming towards me, and all I could do to keep on my feet was to hold on to the sound of Bea Wain singing—

> *It's been so long*
> *Since we had that date every night at eight*
> *It's been soooo long*
> *Since I held you tight when we said good-night*
> *It's been sooo long . . .*

And here I was with Johnny Delahanty's arms around me, moving across the floor, with Babette and Trubee and Nuala and George gliding around us, as if it were all meant to be.

> *Honey, can't you see what you've done to me*
> *Let me get back in your arms where I belong—*

Bea's voice was pulling my heart up, up into my eyes—

> *'Cause it's been oh so-oh long . . .*

Yes! where I belong . . . belong—belong. For wasn't it true that since the Caravan had disbanded, there was no place in the world for me because I was an Impostor—an Impostor not only at Whitney Capital but also at my mother's? And although it had not yet been discovered that I was an Impostor, it was only a matter of time. And what would happen then? The North Winds will blow and we shall have snow and what will robin do then, poor thing, what will robin do then? Whatever it was, would robin not be an Impostor there as well?

Play it again—again, again, again. . . . Hold me close and rock me, rock me . . . back where I . . . belong . . .

But Bea Wain had stopped singing, and Johnny had broken away, and Miss Bonnie Mae Murray piloted him over to Wissy

West, because now the music had started up again, and his arms were around her as she did a fancy dip and snapped her fingers to the tune of "Bob White" in that peppy thin way of hers. It was over, all over—over. Never again would his arms be around me. . . .

Well, they were not around me again during that first dancing class of Miss Bonnie Mae Murray's. But the next week something extraordinary had happened. Johnny Delahanty drove to Old Westbury Capital just to see me and to show off his car. This car was called Brünnhilde, and its top was made of canvas and could be snapped on or off just like that. He asked me to go for a ride in Brünnhilde, but the Mademoiselle said no. It didn't matter anyway, because even though we didn't go anywhere, just to sit beside him in the front seat was thrill enough for me.

Now there had been no mention of kissing or anything like that at all, but he did write me a lot at Miss Porter's, and it was weak-in-the-knees every time I saw my name in his writing.

I had heaps of plans swirling around in my head, none of which he knew about. I was certain that someday, in the not too distant future (for hadn't my mother married at eighteen?), I would be Mrs. John Bradley Delahanty, Jr., and as such would live in one of those little houses that we drove by on the way into New York from Old Westbury Capital. Each house was identical to the house next to it, and they went on, row on row, each like the other, each with a little row-on-row garden that went with it. One of those houses would belong to Mr. and Mrs. John Bradley Delahanty. And inside, in our very own kitchen, I would cook him savory dinners every night when he came home from the office. And softly from somewhere the gramophone would be playing "You'd Be So Easy to Love." . . . Ever since Big Elephant had left, my heart had been like a great bowl on a table, and into it the sadness came. But now it would be there no longer, for inside the great globe, swimming around in an easy way, we would have two blushing goldfish, very contented. To begin with, these would be our only pets, but later, when her own conclusions she'd get on the telephone to give directions to her broker. These conversations were usually long and one-sided, with Naney Morgan doing most of the talking. I never got a clear picture of what the stockbroker was about, except that he was a good listener, and the Little Countess really loved to get him open-eared at the other end, especially when she went into details about stock in Campbell-Taggert, a bakery said to be a dark horse winner. Then she'd go into a whole thing about Jacqueline Stewart having tipped her on to this, and on and on about the muffins and millions of prune popovers made in the Campbell-Taggert style, until it all got really boring and I wondered how the stockbroker was ever going to get off the phone.

Then it occurred to me that each day there must be loneliness for Naney because she didn't really have any friends in New York, what with the Infanta Eulalia across the ocean and all. Of course she chattered with everybody who worked at the Hotel Fourteen, but that was only on her way out, or in, after her dinner. Also to ramble on with were the waitresses who worked at Schrafft's and Caruso's, along with the blind man from whom she got the *Journal-American* every evening. But that was not the same as having a friend the way she did when my Godmother Jacqueline Stewart was in town.

So this is why I was really happy when I got her letter saying she had met someone who had just arrived at the Hotel Fourteen but who liked it so much she was going to remain as a permanent resident. Her name was Mrs. Fox and she was a blond divorcée— Naney did not quite put it in those words, but that's the impression that came through in her letter. With Mrs. Fox was her son, a very good-looking young man named Albert Fox who was two years older than me and was to start boarding midterm at Northchurch Academy right near Miss Porter's. Naney said I would meet him in due course when I came to see her at vacation time, and wasn't that nice, Little One?

And sure enough, the next time I went to our gypsy Caravan at the Hotel Fourteen, there sitting in the living room part was the children came, we would have dogs and a cat, and a few hamsters, maybe—maybe not.

It was all I could do to keep these plans to myself, because I was dying to tell him about them. But I kept quiet, waiting for the right moment to present itself.

And while I waited for this right moment, I tried not to think too much about . . . Impostor! But it was true, wasn't it? Not only at Whitney Capital and at my mother's but at Green Vale . . . and now it had followed me to Farmington, and I was beginning to wonder if it would be so forever. I knew the difference. In our Caravan, with Big Elephant and the Little Countess, I was not an Impostor. But since then, in every other place I walked, I belonged nowhere, for I was an—Impostor! And with that knowledge came the dread of discovery.

And with the unmasking there would follow the descent from grace. But to where? The memory of the Caravan was becoming more and more elusive to me, but, most frightening of all, the *idea* of the Caravan was also receding farther and farther away. And without it, what would I do? And who would I be?

But maybe by that time I would be Mrs. John Bradley Delahanty. I thought of what it would be like to have our own Caravan and, once in it, never to feel like an Impostor again for as long as I lived. Wouldn't that be something! Light filled me, and I wrote over and over again Gloria Delahanty Gloria Delahanty Gloria Delahanty, over and over again, Gloria Delahanty Gloria Delahanty . . . until my finger got so sore I had a bump on it and had to stop.

Chaperones

During the day, the Little Countess took a lot of time going over what was what in the stock market, making elaborate charts from the listings in the *New York Times* and predicting why one stock would be more attractive than another. After coming to a blond divorced lady, thin and pretty in a Helen Vincent sort of way—just like her, in fact, because Helen Vincent usually played the divorcée-friend parts in movies I'd seen. Sitting in another chair was Albert—only everyone calls him Bertie, Mrs. Fox said, so you must call him Bertie too. As yet, Albert-Bertie had not spoken up about anything. But the Little Countess was right. Bertie was very good-looking indeed, and tall but not too tall. We all sat down again after shaking hands, and Bertie and I both made a distinct effort not to stare too much at each other.

On a table there were petits fours with pistachio icing all over them, and on the top of each were little blobs fashioned to look like flowers. They nestled on the plate in pleated paper cups, and I got up and passed them to Mrs. Fox. Oh, no, thank you, she laughed in a coy way and patted her stomach. I'm trying to lose five pounds! Naney Morgan took one, and when I passed them to Bertie he took one and ate it in one bite. There was also a choice of tea or hot chocolate with marshmallows to float on top. We all sat there, eating or not eating. Naney Morgan and Mrs. Fox talked a blue streak to each other, while Bertie and I sat silent and I racked my brain trying to think of something to say. But try as I would, my mind whited out.

Do you know a restaurant called the Queen Mary? Bertie finally spoke up, taking another petit four.

Oh, the Queen Mary . . . the Queen Mary . . . no I don't, I don't think I do—where is it?

It's on Fifty-eighth Street right near the Plaza movie theatre.

Oh, I said, I—then I picked up a marshmallow and bit into it, not wanting to let on that the only restaurants I had ever been to in New York City were the Sherry-Netherland Hotel, on those Sunday lunches with my mother, and Jimmy's Oyster Bar, but they could not really be called restaurants, not in the way this Queen Mary restaurant sounded. Oh, I found myself saying gooily through the marshmallow, oh, yes, I've heard a lot about it, a lot a lot.

Then Bertie said, in a smoldering Heathcliff kind of way, Would you like to go there with me for lunch one day?

I looked over at the Little Countess, but she was in the middle of some long harangue with Mrs. Fox, going into the between-us details of her divorce from Mr. Fox, and I knew I would have to wait until later to know if I could accept Bertie's invitation to the lunch at the Queen Mary restaurant.

I knew there would be a better chance asking the Little Countess than asking Tweedle Crocker to ask Auntie Ger. For at Auntie Ger's there were chaperones here and chaperones there, and you could hardly even go into the bathroom without a chaperone following you right in. But it was not only the chaperones, it was the detectives who stood vigil day and night and whom I wasn't supposed to know about but found out about anyway from overhearing some boys talking at Green Vale, speculating on who at school had detectives and who did not. Deenie Hutton's name was mentioned as definitely having one, and then Mary Lou Osborn's name came up, and then there was my name right along with Deenie's and Mary Lou's! The way they talked about it made it sound like a much-to-be-desired attribute, a symbol of stature. But try as I could, it was impossible for me to view it that way. There was something freaky about it, definitely, and the next time I saw Deenie and Mary Lou, I wondered if they knew they had detectives too or if they were as unaware as I had been until I overheard that conversation. Well, I wasn't about to open my mouth about this to anyone and I kept quiet. It was up to them to find out, each in her own way, as I had.

In any event, I was longing to find a way to accept this sophisticated invitation to lunch at the Queen Mary restaurant. I could see us now, Bertie and me, at that secluded rendezvous. . . .

I finally did go, but not with Bertie—not alone, that is. The Little Countess and Mrs. Fox followed us, edging slowly down the steep stairs that led from the street into the cavern of the restaurant. It was startling to go from the sun-blazed day, cut off suddenly as the door closed behind us, and descend on down the steps into the basement restaurant with its underwater lighting and sheltering alcoves. Centered among the tables like an island was a buffet table and on it hundreds of platters and little plates offering the myriad choices of a smorgasbord.

Instantly it became for me a place of heady glamour, and I longed for the time when Johnny Delahanty and I could have a rendezvous to lunch here alone. For surely, although I had never been in one, this Queen Mary restaurant with its dark discreet corners must be like—*exactly* like—the nightclubs and cabarets my mother frequented when she went out with Roberto Mendoza. I could see them holding hands as they sat in one of the alcoves, heads in profile, almost touching as they confided to each other their most secret hopes and dreams. And did these secret hopes and dreams include me? Somehow, sitting there in the shadows of the Queen Mary restaurant, it seemed to me that I did belong— did belong in whatever hopes and dreams my mother and Mr. Mendoza had as they leaned close to each other over the princely smorgasbord. . . .

But then, as I looked around me, the darkness of the Queen Mary restaurant reminded me of another darkness—the movie theatre darkness. And the more I thought about this, the more it came to me that it was all much too much like being at the movies, much too much so to be—real. But maybe imagining my mother and Roberto Mendoza in this setting was what *made* them real to me. For the people in the movies were real to me, and my mother and Mr. Mendoza were not, so perhaps imagining my mother and Mr. Mendoza in this setting made me feel closer to her, and less fearful of her. But then Consuelo-Tamar came to mind. . . .

What of her? How did she fit into one of the cozy alcoves at the Queen Mary restaurant? Not at all at all at all. Having her there would ruin everything.

More chèvre Laura? Mrs. Fox said to the Little Countess. I'll get it for you, Naney, I said. No—no, thank you, darling mine, nothing more for me.

And we all crept up the steep stairs again—and suddenly there we were, all on the street, in the sunlight blazing around us. . . .

Invitation to the Dance, Winter 1938

There was to be a dance at Northchurch Academy, and Albert Fox had invited me to go. At first I was all excited, but then I started getting frantic about what to wear to cover my fatness.

I envisioned something purple-colored and trailing, with mauvy flowers—lilacs perhaps?—strewn about over the skirt, on up around the strapless décolletage defining me in a most seductive way. All of which was fine—except it did not in any way fit the reality of myself when looked upon in the mirror. For try as I would, the fatness remained upon me, and every time I looked in the mirror I longed for a miracle to have taken place. I longed that it would be Katharine Hepburn who smiled back at me instead of the same Fat Impossible Me.

And now there were only two weeks left between my fatness and the dance at Northchurch Academy, and even if I starved myself it would only be a drop out of the bucket of my thick fat self. I stewed about all this a great deal and ended up, as I knew I would, wearing the same dress I had worn to Miss Bonnie Mae Murray's New Year's Eve dance. This dress had many memories, because in it I had been held in the arms of John Bradley Delahanty as we swirled around the floor. Only now, for the dance at Northchurch Academy, to my mortification, it had to be let out, otherwise I couldn't have hooked it up over my fatness.

Only one other girl from Farmington had been invited to this dance—a thin thin Sara Debevoise, from Boston, hair cut

TO GLORIA VANDERBILT AT THE RITZ

On New Year's Night, 14-year-old Gloria Vanderbilt stepped vividly into the corridors of 1938 at New York's Ritz-Carlton Hotel. No longer the gangling little girl for whose custody her mother Mrs. Reginald Vanderbilt and her aunt Mrs. Harry Payne Whitney fought a famous court battle three years ago, Gloria is now rapidly maturing into the sub-deb class. Here she is shown dancing in a white chiffon evening frock at a party for "juniors" at the Ritz. The same day her guardian officially reported that her estate was $4,025,004.

in a pageboy bob, like my mother's, only of a tawny blondness. Everyone called her Lombard, because she looked like guess who. She had an erminette jacket and a brother called Regis Malcolm Debevoise who was Bertie's best friend at Northchurch Academy. I hadn't met Regis yet, but I had heard a good deal about him from Bertie. Lombard was, of course, all set as to what she was going to wear to enhance her thinness, and this choice waited in her closet, pristine and twinkly.

And so the days went along until here we were, the Thin One and the Fat One arriving at Northchurch Academy for the dance. It was kind of a shock to walk into the hall where the dance was to take place. I had imagined it would be at least somewhat like dances were in the movies, with couples swirling and dipping about, and I had not been one bit disappointed by Miss Bonnie Mae Murray's New Year's Eve dance, which had taken place at the Plaza Hotel. But at Northchurch Academy it was like going into a gymnasium—which, of course, is exactly what it was.

No one there seemed to know anyone else, and little clusters formed to stand looking suspiciously at other little clusters, while the band played in an in-and-out-of-tune way, as if they were still rehearsing and hadn't gotten the hang of it all yet. Kirk Browning was nowhere to be seen—he was in the infirmary with laryngitis. We spotted several other boys in the distance, but they lurked around as if they didn't know us. As for Bertie and Regis, they were glued together in a sulky manner in a corner.

It was all so uncomfortable, and I kept glancing at Lombard and her thinness, expecting *her* to do something. But she seemed just as out of it as I was, and so we stood around like that and I wished we were back at Farmington, or that Miss Bonnie Mae Murray would suddenly appear and get us all dancing together in that way she had of turning everything into a party.

But no one came forward. And it all got more and more peculiar. Then, just when I thought I couldn't stand it another minute, Bertie and Regis lurched out of their corner and came across the room straight at me. Bertie took my hand in a panic and said, Follow us—come on, come on! And he took my elbow and I was running with him on one side with Regis on the other— running in my Fat Dress, across the empty dance floor of the gymnasium, running away from Lombard, running past everyone as they gaped at the spectacle of us running—running—Bertie pulling me up the stairs with Regis behind—faster and faster— and as we ran I could hear shouting between the music—

Come on, catch them, catch them, catch them—they went that way—up the stairs—

Now it had become a chase, with Bertie and Regis and me running running away, running up the stairs, running from the hunters who pursued us. Faster and faster we went, for now Regis had my hand as well, pulling me along faster and faster, until—

There they were, Bertie and Regis, scrambling up a ladder which Bertie had pulled down from the ceiling. And there I was, my dress tearing as I scrambled up behind them.

We threw ourselves down on the attic floor, Regis pulling the ladder after us, and as the darkness surrounded us, we were Foxes escaped into their lair—and free of danger.

But of *what* danger? And why was I here in the attic of Northchurch Academy, in this unlikely dress, crouching on a mattress in the dark, between Regis Debevoise and Albert Fox? All around us from the courtyard below, from all sides around us, came the shouting shouting shouting. . . .

Regis lit a candle, and as I crept over to the half-curve of window my dress ripped on something jagged. Below us a crowd was gathering, people running running to join them as, there below us, they waved fists and shouted up at us. But what were they saying? And why? I couldn't make any of it out, and I wanted none of this to have happened or to be happening, and I was filled with the desperation of why it had. And what did it have to do with me?

For something was going on at Northchurch Academy, and the something had nothing to do with me, nothing at all. Whatever it was, it had to do with Bertie and Regis, and it got scarier and scarier as the shouts grew louder, and I felt part of some nameless thing that Bertie and Regis knew about but I did not. Regis and Bertie knew, and so did the crowds shouting up at us, and I looked at Bertie and said, What *is* it? What *is* it? What is going on, what is happening, what are they shouting about? But he did not answer me, and Regis stayed silent, and I did not know where to turn.

Then a powerful hammering came, as though the floor were going to crash under us, and the voices shouted from below—

Open up, Albert, Regis! Come on, open up! Put the ladder down—now!

Albert hesitated . . . and Regis took his hand and said, Come on, Bertie—it's all over.

No one had taken my hand, and on my knees I scurried over to where the ladder was and tried to lift the trap door up. Hands below pushed at it, and then Regis and Bertie came over to help me, and what with all the hands trying to get it open, finally it did open, and we climbed down the ladder, down into the crowd of faces, boy faces and girl faces and faculty faces, all come from the courtyard below and now piled, one on top of the other, on the stairs, staring at us, my hands all sooty and Bertie's tie askew and the three of us something to see. . . .

Of course, I was blamed along with Albert Fox and Regis Debevoise, and no matter what I said or how I tried to explain how it had all come about, there was nothing to say, really, for I did not know myself how it had happened, or why it had happened, or what any of it was about. . . .

Until a few days later . . . seeping down and through Miss Porter's School like typhoid. Sara Debevoise's brother had been expelled—expelled—expelled—expelled from Northchurch Academy. And at the same time—expelled—Albert Fox. But why? For what? What?

Because they're both *pansies*, that's why—didn't you *know*?

Marian Sweetser was the first to say it, and everyone looked at Sara Debevoise as if waiting for her to say something.

What did that mean? What did Marian Sweetser mean when she said they were pansies? Pansies were flowers. What did she mean by saying Bertie and Regis were flowers? Boys were not flowers . . . girls were, sometimes.

Sara Debevoise started to cry and ran to her room. What do you mean, Marian? I said. What do you mean, pansies? What is that?

You should know, she snickered—you of all people should know. Why, haven't you read about your mother in the newspapers? Everybody else has.

And over me there came a chill and it crept everywhere within me, for I knew now that what she said had to do with the one something that had been discovered during the Trial—the thing that was so terrible about her that would make me terrible too—the thing that I had torn myself apart about with the wanting to know—but also the not wanting to know. For if I did know, it might be so terrible I would no longer be able to live and I would be struck dead—dead—dead.

Well, now I knew. But what did I know? Because the most terrible thing of all was that although I knew, I still did not understand. . . . Help me, someone, help me help me help me. . . .

Help me, Naney, help me, Naney Naney . . . But everything at the Hotel Fourteen was all wacky, what with Naney trying to calm Mrs. Fox down, and Mrs. Fox trying to calm Naney down, and in between all the frantic phone calls trying to get another school to accept Albert quickly quickly quickly after, as Mrs. Fox put it, all this unpleasantness at Northchurch Academy. The Little Countess rolled her eyes around and walked up and down the halls muttering that it would soon all blow over, and not to say too much in front of the Little One Little One Little One. . . .

I wanted so much to talk to Bertie about everything that had happened at Northchurch, but he was so upset every time I saw him, I thought I'd better wait until he brought it up. But he never did, and the more silent about it everyone was, the more frightened I became. I could tell he missed Regis a lot, because Mrs. Fox and Mrs. Debevoise had been back and forth from New York to Boston on the phones and had firmly decided that Regis and Bertie must never ever see each other again and must not write to each other or have anything to do with one another at all. Ever ever ever!

Help me, Big Elephant, help me help me . . . But how could she? Even if I had been able to write to her, how could she answer me in a letter while sitting at the desk of Mr. and Mrs. Ambrose Schiller in far-off Freeport?

And to say Help me to Aunt Gertrude through any of the Tweedles would be unthinkable.

Also unthinkable to talk about it to Miss Mary Nearney Mount. Tootsie Eleanor had long since said her good-bye, and the French one also said *au revoir*; and in their place, brought in by Tweedle Dunnington, was this Miss Mount from Virginia, whom he highly recommended. Tweedle Dunnington knew her family well, and Miss Mount was doing us all a real favor by taking this job temporarily, until she made up her mind which of the many clamoring suitors she would deign to accept in marriage. This occupied most of her time—one could almost say *all* of her time—and it would have been out of place to bring up Albert Fox and Regis Debevoise and the terrible thing that had happened at Northchurch Academy.

And so it lay within me. And as the days went by, it settled into me like a woeful darkness, and the fear of it became a part of me. And then, more terrible than anything else, I grew accustomed to it, until one night when I went to bed it came to me that a whole day had gone by and I hadn't thought of it at all. Not even once.

.   .   .

There was a big surprise waiting for me at spring vacation when I got back to Old Westbury Capital—no more Miss Mount! Hooray and hallelujah! And what a relief that she had already left by the time I got there—no need to go through exhausting charades, trying to find polite ways of saying good-bye and all that.

For instead of good-bye it was hello—and to the most marvelous person I had ever met in my entire life!

Her name was Kate Drury, and she had such loveliness of character—she was so just right in every way. And she kept on reminding me of someone—but who? Mummy Anne, of course! She was the big sister I often dreamed of having. And although I felt this way about Kate, I didn't feel in any way disloyal to my half-sister, Cathleen, because Cathleen—well, I don't know, with Cathleen it was just different. For one thing, she was the same age as my mother. But that wasn't it really, for age had nothing to do with it. It had to do with something about Cathleen—something that could only be called inscrutable. Not that this made me love her less—on the contrary, it fascinated me. But, well—I could never tell her things the way I could to Kate.

I could tell Kate all about Johnny Delahanty and the blushing goldfish and the house we would live in when we were married. And I could tell her all this because I knew that she wouldn't laugh at me. And she didn't. She realized that it was serious to me, and I could talk it over with her from every point of view. And she understood. And because she understood, hope came to me that it was *not* a silly thing to wish for dreams to come true. So many others around me believed that it was childish to dream.

Especially the Little Countess, who had big plans already mapped out regarding my future. For I was to make a rich rich rich rich coup of a Marriage, and it had to be to someone I was not in love with. For when it came to marriage, love had no place in the scheme of things—so thought the Little Countess. No place at all. And soon I had to barricade myself from the knowing sneers here and the knowing sneers there that accompanied Naney Morgan's most casual remarks whenever she could work them into the conversation.

I especially avoided going to the movies with her, for she always took the opportunity to disperse loud comments during love scenes between poor-but-in-love couples.

Aie! Aie! she would say, making certain the unseen audience in the dark theatre wouldn't miss a word, Aie! Aie! Aie! *Little* do they know! Hmmm! And out of the corner of my eye I could see her straighten up in her seat as she leaned towards the screen, pushing the force of her will towards it. Listen to *that*, will you! Aie, aie, aie! *Wait*, just wait—they'll find out soon enough!

The shush-shush-shushing around us would grow louder and louder, but even the Quiet, lady, quiet—*will* you be quiet! coming at us from throughout the theatre had little effect upon her, and often it made things worse. For she would only lower her voice slightly and temporarily, saving her energy for the next foray. And when they came, these further declarations of love between the poor-but-in-love couples on the screen, her voice would rise again, spurred on to louder shifts and groans and Aie-aie-aies, until, sitting beside her, I sank deeper into the seat, hating myself for hoping no one would think we had come to the movie together.

I don't know which was worse, being at the movies with her, or after, when the movie was over. For inevitably I would find myself in an argument with her. It was like being pushed onto a roller coaster—once on, no getting off—the hopelessness of it. For I knew that I would never be able to change the Little-do-they-knows and the They'll-find-out-soon-enoughs and the Aie-aie-aie!s—all her views on what was what.

Now it may sound as if Kate and I did nothing but have serious conversations all the time, but that would be misleading, because much of the time we just had fun together. She was the first person *ever* who laughed at things I sometimes said, things that I thought were funny but nobody else did. It was such an incredible feeling to observe something and then say it out loud and make her laugh. Because that is the best—to laugh with someone because you both think the same things are funny.

So at spring vacation this is what I came back to when I left Farmington and all the terrible things that had happened there. Nothing had been the same after that night at the dance at Northchurch Academy—not that things had been so hot before, but at least I had put a muzzle on Bonavishski Buttercup and had heard Kirk Browning play Gershwin on Mrs. Keep's piano. *And* Johnny Delahanty's letters, all nicely tied together with a ribbon of white and read over and over again as I searched for signs and portents. (There was also a much smaller pile from Phil Kellogg, gathered carefully together with a ribbon of royal blue, and read over and over again too—only, of course, not so often as those from Johnny Delahanty.) So, all things considered, swell things had happened along with the terrible things.

And now with Kate Drury by my side—well, things were really looking up.

Sophisticated Lady

I had a picture in my mind of how good it would be if Kate and I could go somewhere for a vacation, just for a few days, somewhere away from Old Westbury Capital, away from the Hotel Fourteen, somewhere I had never been before, somewhere where there would be no one I would know and where no one would know me. And, to my surprise, Kate was able to convey this feeling to the Tweedles, who in turn passed it on to Aunt Gertrude—presenting it in a favorable way, I guess, because soon after, Kate and I took off to one of those inns, highly recommended by Duncan Hines, in Connecticut, where we would stay until it was time for me to go back to Farmington when the spring vacation was over.

This Duncan Hines–style inn was on the edge of some woods, and we settled into one of the cottages near the main building, which had once been an old farmhouse. We had our meals there or not, depending on our mood, because each cottage had a neat little kitchen in which to cook up peanut-butter-and-jelly sandwiches and so on.

We settled ourselves in in a most cozy way. I brought all my Bea Wain records with me, and a portable phonograph, along with my current passion, which was a record of Duke Ellington's "Sophisticated Lady." Kate was really a good sport about this, because I played it over and over and over again and never tired of hearing it. It had a mysterious attraction for me, this Sophisticated Lady music, and the Sophisticated Lady words persistently haunted me—I knew not why. And over and over again I would play it, each time thinking, This time I will find out why—why the music and the words possessed me so in this eerie way. It had something to do with my mother, but not really, for it had more to do with two girls who had been briefly at Green Vale the last year I was there. Images of them drifted in and out of my thoughts continuously—images I tried to hold on to but which always eluded me. . . .

Lying on my bed I would look up at the ceiling, absorbed into the music, possessed by the mystery of

> They say—into your early life romance came,
> And in this heart of yours burned a flame—
> A flame that flickered one day and died away.
> Then, with disillusion deep in your eyes,
> You learned that fools in love soon grow wise.
> The years have changed you, somehow;
> I see you now . . .
> Smoking, drinking, never thinking
> Of tomorrow—
> Nonchalant
> Diamonds shining, dancing, dining
> With some man in a restaurant.
> Is that all you really want?

No—sophisticated lady, I know—
You miss the love you lost long ago—
And when nobody is nigh
You cry. . . .

Anne Martin—Nancy Martin—at Green Vale—the two sisters who never mingled with the rest of us, for they were much too sophisticated, much too nonchalant, and we were all much too unsophisticated, much too babyish, for the likes of them. Every day they would appear at school with their straight honey hair, in their leopard coats, wearing silk stockings. How skillfully they maneuvered themselves on their high-heeled pumps as they went from class to class. But that was only the half of it, for they wore—makeup! To *school*. And it wasn't just Tangee. It was movie-star makeup and with it nail polish and lipstick to match. And every day there on their eyelids would be a different color shadow that reflected the color of their dresses. There was even gossip that they had been seen in the theatre in Locust Valley, in the balcony, holding hands with two boys who didn't go to Green Vale and who looked more like Men. Not only that, but in her other hand each of them waved a long cigarette holder which glowed in the dark as nonchalantly they puffed away all through the double feature. Through the halls of Green Vale they trod as nuns do, always walking together in twos. And even though many of the girls pretended not to notice them, most of them were pea green over their showy ways.

As for me—I viewed them with open-mouthed adoration. Everything about them enthralled me, and I would have given anything to be admitted, even for a minute, into their sisterhood. But none among us had been so favored except for Lowrie Flagg, a girl in a classroom down the hall from me. She became a creature of wonder and I longed to know the secret of why, among us all, *she* had been chosen, for could I discover this, I too might have a chance to be admitted into the magic circle. But it was not to be, and except for Lowrie, they stayed mostly to themselves and never made friends with anyone else at Green Vale. Then, after being there for only one semester, the Sisters Martin vanished, and no one knew where they had gone. Except, of course, the envied Lowrie, and we were too proud to ask her. Wherever it was, I would never forget them. Never! But why? It had something to do with . . . I don't know. What was it? Something to do with having had in our midst, as part of us, two who could be observed closely—two girls who were already *there*— there in that other country. For not only had they reached the grown-up world, they *belonged* there, or so it seemed. And perhaps once *I* was there, I would find that I belonged there too, and no longer would I be a stranger in the world—no longer an Impostor.

Overnight

Of course, at other times, when I wasn't playing "Sophisticated Lady" on the phonograph, I thought a lot about Johnny Delahanty. And there were moments during the day when I would look at the time and say to Kate, Right this minute it's ten past five in California—what do you suppose *he's* doing right this *second*?

Because that's where he had gone—to California to visit his uncle for the spring vacation. And then Phil Kellogg would come to mind—he was on the West Coast too—and I would wonder about him and what *he* was doing that very second.

Still, I couldn't bring myself to talk even to Kate about Albert Fox and Regis Debevoise and the terrible things that had happened. But then whole days would go by when I almost didn't think about it at all. Every morning we walked around in the woods, and on afternoons when it rained we went to the movies in Stamford. I read too, and Kate and I speculated about who the other guests were. Most were ancient couples who spent most of their time sitting around and eating. After a while it all got a bit monotonous and even "Sophisticated Lady" lost some of its allure. As for Farmington, I tried not to think about how soon I would have to go back.

Then, two days before I was to go back to Miss Porter's, I woke up in the night with the worst pain in my stomach. It really hurt. I thought I was dying. Kate called the desk at the inn and they said they would try to get a doctor as quickly as possible. Finally a doctor showed up, but he didn't know what it was, maybe my appendix, and where did I live, and if it wasn't too far away, I'd better get on home fast so my own doctor could see what was up.

All the way back on the drive to New York I was in and out of the pain. Once we got stalled in traffic, and it became a knife and stayed twisting around in my stomach until finally we made it to Fifth Avenue and Aunt Gertrude's castle.

There, waiting for us, was trusty old Doctor Santa, and with him was another doctor I hadn't seen before. His name was Doctor Weeks and he called an ambulance, and soon I was being taken into an operating room where I was given ether. This ether drew me into the waters of a warm stream, and I was pulled along by unseen hands until I woke up in a room at the Doctors Hospital.

And there, right on the bureau, floating around in a jar, was my appendix. It was disgusting, but I couldn't stop wanting to look at it. Doctor Weeks was a whole other kettle of fish from Santa Claus. The nurses were wild about him and so was I. Much sprightly flirtatious banter went on whenever he appeared. And of course my appendix, drifting around in the jar like some weird fish, also brought forth lively comments.

But the most interesting comment of all to me was when the doctors said that because of this appendix thing I would miss the opening of the spring semester at Farmington! Which was no sorrow to me. But it did put me on tenterhooks, stewing about the moment when I would have to go back there. The spectacle of this filled me with dread, for it would mean drawing undue attention to myself, turning up in midterm as it were.

But now the day had arrived—not to go back to Farmington, though, for everyone agreed that I had to convalesce for a while before being able to return to school.

I looked at the disgusting thing floating in the jar on the bureau and decided to leave it there as a souvenir.

Then I got off the high bed for the last time and started getting my things together to leave. I took my dress off the hanger and slipped it over my head—and as I did, the strangest feeling came over me, because my dress slithered down around my body like a bubble and hung there as if it were still on the hanger. . . .

I stood there quietly, without breathing, and tightened my fist around the fabric that fell around me. In my hand were bunches of cloth, and if I hadn't been certain that this dress was mine, I would have said, Oh! This is a mistake—this isn't my dress. Why, look—see, it doesn't even fit!

And can you imagine? Without even looking in the mirror I could tell that the fatness was no longer upon me . . . that without my doing anything at all, overnight it had simply sloughed off, all of it, sloughed off and disappeared.

I—could—not—believe—it!

I tiptoed over to the mirror and stood there for a long time. I looked at my body, and I looked at my face, and I looked again at my body—

And I thought about a new dress . . .
> and Johnny Delahanty . . .
> > and red lipstick . . .
> > > and Duke Ellington . . .

And I couldn't wait—
> Couldn't wait—
> > To get out of that hospital room—
> > > Out into the world—
> > > > And get moving—
> > > > > Moving—
> > > > > > Moving!

But was I nonchalant? Alas, no! I was much too excited about this thin new person who turned out to be—me! And every day I would wake up feeling thinner, and yet I would jump from bed and run to the mirror, for maybe it had all been only a dream and the fat might still be attached to my body like an awful jellyfish. But no, it didn't come back. So how could I take it nonchalantly? I would just have to wait, that's all. For as surely as the fatness had vanished, there would be a day when I would wake up and, overnight, the nonchalance would have come to me and with it the sophistication. And for now all I had to do was wait and try not to be too impatient.

Every day Kate and I had discussions about clothes. In fact, that's all I wanted to talk about. And don't think they weren't serious, because they were—very serious indeed. And not only about clothes but about what to wear *under* the clothes—that too got a lot of attention. For up until now I had never given it any thought at all, because, as I said to Kate, what does it matter if a slip has a tear here or a touch of lace on it or not? After all, no one knows it except me. But that's exactly what *is* important, Kate said. *You* know it, even if no one else does. And I thought about that a lot—a lot—and I put down Pretty Underwear— adding it to the long list of things I hoped to get. After all, I had to cover my thinness with something, didn't I? And why not have it pretty as could be?

On the top of my list of Things To Wear I had written BLACK DRESS, for to me a black dress was the ultimate—the Ultimate Sophistication. Others might dream of the Sisters Martin and their spotty coats, but for me a black dress headed my list any day of the week. My mother often wore black dresses, and when you came right down to it, there was no denying that it was the most grown-up thing to do. Definitely. And Kate hadn't laughed at me when I told her of my longings for this black dress. Maybe she could get through to Auntie Ger about it, through the Tweedles or some such channel. Time would tell.

So this is how we talked on and on through the days. At first

I had to rest a lot, and some days Kate had the chaise taken from the porch and put out onto the flagstone terrace in back of Old Westbury Capital. It was lovely to sit there looking out over the vast lawn, on down the hill and into the meadow below. Lovely to see the daffodils starting to flower all around us as we talked about clothes and made lots of plans for the future. Both of us had a hankering for red shoes. And I couldn't wait! No one had said a word about going back to Farmington, and as the days went by and I was up and around more and more, I tried not to think about the day when I knew one of the Tweedles was bound to show up and say it was time to go back.

When the day came, it was not one of the Tweedles. Guess what? It was Herself—Aunt Gertrude! She said she had to talk to me and it was serious. Very. I was so startled that *she* was sitting there, actually about to tell me something serious in *her* own words and not have it told to me through an interpreter, that I didn't have time to panic before she told me what it was.

Gloria, she said, it's very difficult for me to have to tell you this—

Now I did start to get a little jittery. What *was* it?

Very hard, she went on.

What? What? What is, Auntie Ger?

I have even told Mrs. Keep that *I* will *personally* make the long trip up to Farmington to talk it over with her.

It? I wanted to scream What? What was *it*?

But—I am quite astonished—Mrs. Keep is adamant about the matter and said that even this would—well, even this would be of no avail, because a decision has already been reached, a unanimous decision by all concerned.

What? *What* decision? What?

Well, Gloria, it seems Mrs. Keep does not want you to go back to Farmington.

Why? Why, Auntie Ger? I said.

It's most unfortunate—she feels you do not fit in. But more than anything else, she feels the publicity surrounding you is

too—too—*disrupting*—that was the way she put it. Not only to
the other students but—more than anything else, Mrs. Keep
believes that it reflects badly on the school. . . . She took from
the table a package of Benson and Hedges cigarettes and fussed
with the wrapper.

Here—let me open it for you. And I cracked the paper around
it.

Thank you, she said, and I lit the cigarette for her.

Yes, she went on, it reflects badly on the school, and therefore—
she took a long puff—therefore Mrs. Keep thinks it is not in the
best interests of the school, and that is why she has requested
that you do not go back to Farmington. . . .

Ever? I said.

Well—yes. That is, if you want to put it that way.

What other way could it be put? But I sat there unable to
say anything at all at all at all, for I didn't know, really, how I
did feel about it. Because after the suddenness of this pro-
nouncement, I could feel a great whoosh of relief streaming through
me. Yet another part of me felt awful, and it was that part of
me which finally said, Auntie Ger, isn't there *anything* you can
do?

No, my dear, I am afraid there isn't. I have, as I said, offered
to make the drive up there to meet with her about this, but my
offer has been turned down. Unfortunately. And under the cir-
cumstances . . . well, surely you see my point.

I certainly could. Now—why did I say I wanted to go back
when the truth of the matter was I did not want to go back. The
truth of the matter was that as we sat there with our sad faces,
I felt not only relief but hope, and with the hope, high spirits—
so high that I thought in another minute I would have to sing
or burst with it! Yippee. Hi-ho, Silver!

Instead, I found myself saying to Aunt Gertrude, in a whis-
pery voice, Oh, Auntie Ger, what is going to happen now?

I'll have to give it a lot of thought, Gloria, she said, and she
put out her cigarette and seriously lighted another. Right now

you must put it out of your mind completely, and just think about recovering your strength and being up and around again.

Up and around again—yes! Up and around again, up and around again in a new black dress, seen dining in the Queen Mary restaurant, so nonchalant, so sophisticated—not even Bonavishski Buttercup would recognize me. And as for Mrs. Keep—if only I had had the opportunity myself to tell her how much I hated the idea of having to go back to Farmington. Maybe I should write her a letter. But no—for of course she would never believe me and would only think I was doing it to save face.

In the days that followed I sometimes found myself brooding over it and then not brooding about it at all—just the opposite, for the hope would come over me again and possess me. And so I went in and out of it, wondering what was going to happen now. For surely I had to go to boarding school somewhere. But where would it be? Where?

I looked to Kate for the answer.

Aunt Gertrude's Decision

There was a lot of consulting back and forth between Aunt Gertrude and the Tweedles, and the result was that I was to enter the Mary C. Wheeler School in Providence, Rhode Island, for the fall semester. I knew Kate Drury had recommended this school to Auntie Ger, and so Wheeler must be a really good school and I was looking forward to it.

As each day passed, I came to realize more and more how happy I was that I didn't have to return to Farmington. In my mind I kept going over the conversation Auntie Ger and I had that day she told me about Mrs. Keep's decision. And the more I went over it, the more I thought about the part Auntie Ger had taken in all this.

For I knew that Aunt Gertrude always got what she wanted, and I was sure that had Aunt Gertrude wanted Mrs. Keep to change her mind she would have persevered and not given up so easily. And this got me to thinking that perhaps Auntie Ger really had given it serious thought, and that she could see things ahead in a way that I could not possibly see them because I had not yet entered into grown-up territory. One of the things she may have seen was the unfairness of the reason Mrs. Keep had given for not wanting me to go back to Farmington. It was not my doing that so much publicity had settled around me, not my doing that it followed me everywhere, not my doing that there was no escaping it. Perhaps Aunt Gertrude had understood this from every point of view and even from points of view I couldn't know about yet, and in doing so Aunt Gertrude had come to her own decision—that there must be a school somewhere free of prejudice, a school that would accept me and where I would have a chance of belonging. And this is why she had not pressed the matter with Mrs. Keep. When the truth of this came to me, I felt closer to Auntie Ger than I ever had in all the years I had lived at Old Westbury Capital. If only I could talk to her about this. But every time we were together the opportunity was never just right, and then the moment would pass and she would say, What did you do today, Gloria? and I couldn't bring myself to tell her that what I did was to think about her and Mrs. Keep and Farmington, and all the things that had happened there. It did help to know, though, that all this may have gone into the conferring with Kate, resulting finally in Aunt Gertrude's decision that the Mary C. Wheeler School would be the one for me.

Soon after Aunt Gertrude's decision she asked me if I would like to have the living room of the Cottage to decorate in any way I wanted. Oh, boy—would I! By decorating, Aunt Gertrude meant an indication here and a touch of something there, to give it a look other than the Englishy look it had now. No walls repainted or new furniture or anything like that, but otherwise it would be my room to do whatever I wanted with, and I could see friends there when they visited, because it would be my very own place.

It was really swell of her to think of this, and I knew right away how I would decorate it. For the minute she told me about it, I knew I would do it—Egyptian. And I couldn't wait to get a move on with these changes. But before anything else, the most important move was to get my portable Victrola and my records settled into the Cottage. Once this was done, I was ready to go on with the rest.

Across from the Plaza Hotel, Kate and I had discovered an Egyptian store, and we hotfooted there right away. I had a modest budget for the decorating, but I found everything I could wish for at this Egyptian store. I draped a cotton spread over the Cottage sofa, and even if I had traveled to Egypt I couldn't have found a more Egyptian-looking print, with a background of pink sand color and personages bearing fruits with enigmatic symbols bordering the proud figures. To place in front of this sofa, I found a tray, round with brass and copper inlays, and it rested on a tripod of wood. Significant designs—hieroglyphics? —were hammered into the tray's surface, and on it I placed the lidded brass pitcher to serve the Turkish coffee, fine as confectioner's sugar, that I would make for friends, and four tiny cups of brass from which to sip the rich brew, which I had renamed Egyptian coffee. Then there were two large pillows, variations on the pink sand theme. And with the money left over after these purchases, I bought a package of incense, musk-scented, which added just the right touch. Exotic but American cozy.

Now that it was all together, it looked even better than I thought it would. Even Auntie Ger approved. Then when I showed her the Egyptian coffee pot and the little cups that went with it, she suggested that it might be nice to have an electric two-burner stove put inside the closet, where it would just fit. Nice! It would indeed. And she waved her magic wand and there it was, installed overnight. And not only that—there was a surprise, for a little icebox had been fitted right under it, neat as a pin, and next to the two burners, an oven, small as could be, but just right for broiling a meat patty or two.

So there it was, not only did I have a room all my very own, I had an Egyptian room all my very own—and an Egyptian kitchen all my very own as well. Not to mention my very own Egyptian coffee.

It was a big step up towards reaching grown-up territory. And I kept looking around me . . . and wondering what it would feel like if I ever got a black dress and really high-heeled red shoes.

The Force

Juliana Force—the most positive of names. The romance of the Juliana, tempered by the talisman—force. Like Aunt Gertrude she wore a hat even indoors, and it sat on her tangerine hair as though it were a jaunty crown. There were always friends around her and an air of lovely things about to happen.

Her house was the Whitney Museum of American Art. Her domain, the top floor, was transformed into a secret garden. The museum was close to a house Auntie Ger owned at 60 Washington Mews, and she and Aunt Gertrude were friendly as could be. Not simply in the way of friends, but in business ways as well. Mrs. Force had worked with Aunt Gertrude in founding the Whitney Museum, and I knew that Auntie Ger listened to what Juliana Force had to say. Not only that, she could always get to Auntie Ger *immediately*. I don't know why it hadn't occurred to me before—the fastest way to get a message to Aunt Gertrude was through this most positive of messengers. After all, the Tweedles, when you came right down to it, were only minions. Yes, the minions of Aunt Gertrude.

There had been something on my mind for the longest time, about my mother and Justice Carew's decree—those weekend

visits to her and the fateful thirty-one days in July. They stretched
before me in an endless future and took away all spontaneity. If
only I could sometimes just pick up the phone and say Mummy,
let's have lunch today. I often wanted to. Instead, the time clock
of Justice Carew hovered over us, growing bigger and bigger as
the days went by, until soon it would *become* the place I inhabited
and I would be living inside a huge clock instead of inside a
room of my own.

Without telling anyone I called Mrs. Force. Right away she
said Oh, Gloria, I'd love to see you, come for tea.

And soon I was on my way through the labyrinths of the
museum, past the guards, up, up to the top floor. On her front
door there was a brass mermaid knocker. When I tapped it the
door opened immediately and there she was.

Come down my primrose path, she said, giving me a hug,
and I followed her along a hallway strewn with primroses and
meadow grasses. I kept looking down at the floor—the flowers
surely were real?

It's fabric, she said smiling. You see, I always wanted to
walk down a primrose path, and when I saw this print I knew
I'd found it. So I had the material cut out and glued to the floor,
it's shellacked over, of course, so it doesn't get scuffed.

It was astonishing. But so was everything else about this
place as I noted each and every detail to think about later. On
a table as you entered the living room there were anemones in a
Bristol-blue vase, and the walls of the room had been lacquered
its same exact blue, and against one wall a cabinet, inlaid with
mother-of-pearl, held a collection of Bristol-blue glass. The man-
telpiece was covered with a mosaic of seashells forming designs
of fruits and flowers. On it there was a clock tiered like a wedding
cake and decorated with white paper lace, crystal candelabra of
emerald green on either side. Some of the chairs had been covered
in watermelon velvet, others in citron satin, and above them
hung a Tamayo painting. On the red lacquer tables were ebony
boxes with scenes of unicorns and Russian princesses, others of

porcelain with mottos. "Remember, my friend, all things have an end" and "Love and Live Happy"—things like that. And next to the fireplace was a child's chair of white lacquered carved wood, and sitting on it was a doll in Red Riding Hood's cape staring at something in the distance, calm as you please.

When Mrs. Force had invited me for tea I had expected a cup and a lump of sugar. Now we entered another room, where a white wicker tea wagon had been placed, and on it the prettiest array of food you could imagine. But this room could not be called a *room*—it was a gazebo, with trellises and twining Morning Glory vines painted on the walls around us. And on the floor there were cool blue and white tiles, and around, here and there, baskets holding orange trees with plump baby oranges dangling from the branches. We settled ourselves on a curlicue sofa, the wicker starchy as Battenburg lace.

Now let's see, Mrs. Force said, scanning the tea cart. Today it's tea I brought from Claridge's on my last trip to London. Their special mixture, you know, and one of my favorites.

From the teapot she removed a tea cozy encrusted with multicolored caviar-size beads and poured the tea into mauve and gold cups.

Sugar? she asked. Dipping a silver leaf spoon into a bowl, she held out a confetti of crystals. Lemon? Or cream?

Oh yes, please, I said, lemon.

Spread out on the tea cart were delicacies I had never seen before. There were little soufflés of gruyère with whipped cream on top and a sprinkle of cayenne, round tissue paper-thin sandwiches of cucumber and chopped sweet onion. Centered on another plate were coconut drops surrounded by black walnut lace cookies. But that wasn't all—another dish, heart-shaped, held a coeur à la crème with Bar-le-duc jelly close at hand.

I didn't know where to begin.

A Victorian tea, you might say, Mrs. Force said absentmindedly. Now, what shall we start with? Later I'd like you to try a sorbet de pêches. I discovered it in Portugal, made from fresh peaches, you know, but the secret of it is cracking the peach stones and pounding the kernels into the fruit—that's what gives it the flavor. The glass of kirsch doesn't hurt either. Now let's see. And she gave considered thought to each dish before popping a coconut drop into her mouth.

All through the Victorian tea we chatted away—that is, when our mouths weren't full. And soon it was quite an easy matter to bring up the reason for my visit—to ask her if there was any way it could be arranged that my mother and I could just see each other when we wanted to, on the spur of the moment as it were. Would Aunt Gertrude agree to it? For if not, all would be lost. Only through Aunt Gertrude could the Judges be approached.

Mrs. Force nodded, without comment, to everything I said, but I knew she was listening. And later, as we walked along the primrose path back to the front door, she put her arm around me. You'll be hearing something soon, very soon, I'm sure, so try not to worry about it, Gloria, and do come and have tea with me again. I always love to see you. I will, I will, thank you, thank you, I said. For what a lovely time we had had together. And as for tea—why, it had been a banquet!

Soon after this I *did* hear. For Fish-Face came a-calling to give me a message from my legal guardian the Surrogate Foley— who, Fish-Face relayed, had taken all things into consideration and concurred that my mother and I could see each other whenever we wanted to with no more set jurisdiction regarding those times. Of course, Aunt Gertrude had had to approve my request before it had gone to the Surrogate, and oh, thank you, Juliana, and blessings on your force. How would my mother regard the matter? Fish-Face went on to ask. Did I feel up to talking to her myself or did I want him to?

No, me me, I'll do it I'll do it, I said. Next time I see her.

And I did. I asked her if we could see each other alone, just the two of us. We met in the Palm Court of the Plaza Hotel and I couldn't even make myself wait until we ordered lunch. I plunged right into the middle of everything and I wasn't frightened of her at all, not one bit, because right away she said, Darling, this will be so much easier for *both* of us. It's a terrible, well, strain, isn't it, the other way?

Yes yes yes. I was so happy I started to cry, and so did she.

She looked so exhausted sometimes. My little mother. And then I wasn't afraid of her anymore, and all I wanted was to put my arms around her.

But another day I'd see the Little Countess and she would roll her eyes around and say something like, My telephone—she's trying to get it tapped. *That* woman! Just like that lawyer of hers Burkan did when he hid a tap in the curtains of my bedroom at the Hotel Fourteen before the Custody Trial! Yes, she is, she is, that's what she's doing!

And soon it was muddy again, and once again the snail crept under the leaf and the fear came back into my heart.

For Ever and Ever

After the triumph resulting from the Victorian tea party with Juliana, there was no stopping me.

I went straight to the Little Countess and asked her if she thought that now that this change had taken place, there might be hope for another change. For I had never stopped hoping that someday I would once again be permitted to see Big Elephant.

I went straight to Naney Morgan about this because I knew she would understand better than anyone else how much this meant to me. And if it was not to be—well, it would be less painful to hear the news from her than through the usual channels.

The Little Countess listened, really listened, to my every word, not saying much one way or the other. And this was always a good sign. It meant she had heard what I said and that she was brooding over strategies, plotting the best course of how to manipulate the situation.

Let me see, Little One, she said, let me see what I can do—
and she withdrew into a place of deep thought.

It took over a month, but when she came to me and told me
her methods had been successful, I was so overjoyed I didn't think
to ask her how it had come to be. Nothing mattered but that
from now on I could see Big Elephant any time I wanted to!

Soon I was in Aunt Gertrude's car and Freddy was driving
me to the house of Mr. and Mrs. Ambrose Schiller, where Big
Elephant had lived since the trial. Now, on all the letters written
to Big Elephant I had always put Care of Mr. and Mrs. Ambrose
Schiller, 2727 North Ocean Boulevard, though it wasn't a Boulevard—what it really was was an Avenue. But Big Elephant
fancied Boulevard because, she said, It just sounds better, Peach
Pie, so that's what I always put on the envelope. And now I
knew there really *was* a Boulevard, and I was on it, spinning
along fast as in a dream.

I trembled in the car, and I trembled when we got onto the
Boulevard, and I trembled even more when the car stopped in
front of number 2727—and I didn't stop trembling until I was
in the front door and her trunk was around me. Then it stopped—
the shaking, I mean.

We didn't say hello or anything at all. . . . After a while we
went into the kitchen and Big Elephant started making cambric
tea. I hadn't looked around much, but Mr. and Mrs. Ambrose
Schiller were nowhere to be seen. Maybe they were in an upstairs
room somewhere. The kitchen was tidy as tidy could be, and I
wondered if the other kitchens in the long row of houses were
as tidy as the kitchen of Mr. and Mrs. Ambrose Schiller. Certainly
from the outside everything looked alike—row on row, one house
right next to the other; so they might be all alike on the inside
too. It made me think of those Russian dolls made of wood: one
doll opens to another doll exactly like it, only smaller.

As if reading my mind, Big Elephant said, Mr. and Mrs.
Schiller aren't here today, and she lumbered about, puttering
around with potholders and things. They went out for the day

so that we could have a chance to see each other alone together.

Oh! paradise. I hugged her again. It was funny to have grown so much taller while she hadn't grown at all, and now—why, I was almost as tall as she was.

Soon we were sitting side by side, cozy as could be, in Mr. and Mrs. Ambrose Schiller's dining room. The table we sat at wasn't all that cozy, for it had kind of a mustardy-wood clumsy style about it, and the matching chairs didn't help much either. But I didn't notice any of this until later, as I lay in my bed before going to sleep, going over in my mind's eye every detail, recapturing it all, just as it had taken place, each blissful moment of it, one right after the other.

Big Elephant was the only person I knew whom I felt completely happy with. And I had forgotten what it was like to be this content, what heaven on earth it was just to be with her in a room like that and not have to do anything at all except be myself. . . .

Once upon a time it had been like that with Naney Morgan too, but lately something had crept into us, and I couldn't please her about anything, and I couldn't please myself if I took on her opinions about the important things. And more and more as the days passed I found myself slipping away from her while she, in another direction, was slipping away from me.

So now with Big Elephant it was no longer just the memory of the Caravan, for once again I knew the contentment of pure love as we sat here in the dining room of Mr. and Mrs. Ambrose Schiller. A blessing settled over us and even Smokey Bear, Big Elephant's grouchy old cocker spaniel, felt it too and stopped growling around in that annoying way, as he had been doing ever since I got there. And the other dog, Lolly, a caramel cocker spaniel, stopped her cringing ways and settled down onto a pillow in the corner and started snoring. I was home, safe in the Caravan, and I tried not to think that soon I would have to leave. Maybe a miracle would take place and I could stay here with Big Elephant for ever and ever, and we would never have to be apart again.

A Lesson in Good Taste

No, Gloria, you cannot have a black dress, Aunt Gertrude said. It would be most inappropriate.

Besides, summer's coming, she went on. And to be well dressed you must wear the appropriate thing for the occasion. Perhaps next winter or the next one after—perhaps—we'll have to see. But I don't think so. Really, you are much too young to be wearing black. It would be most inappropriate.

I was in Auntie Ger's room standing in front of the full-length mirror, going over what I would wear to a Choate weekend, looking at my tweed skirt, the matching jacket, and the hated babyish blouse with its Peter Pan collar, fervently wishing it would all turn into a black dress. Maybe if I pulled my hair back and held it in a knotted chignon at the nape of my neck. . . . Yes. Decidedly. This did make me look older. Much. Sophisticated too. Only to get the full effect I would have to let my hair grow a bit longer so it would stay up properly.

And what about the red shoes, Auntie Ger?

The red shoes . . . the red shoes . . . She was looking at my hair pulled back into the chignon, about to make some comment on it.

Yes, Auntie Ger, I pressed on, remember the red shoes? Kate and I saw some in Best and Company in Garden City.

Oh, yes—the red shoes. Yes, Gloria, do get the red shoes— that is, if the heels aren't too high. That would be inappropriate.

Oh, no, Auntie Ger, not too high at all, not at all high— in fact just the opposite.

I looked down at my moccasined feet and could have done a pirouette right there in front of Auntie Ger's mirror. Instead, I let my hair fall back around my face again and leaned close to the mirror. Drawing my cheeks slightly in, I was dying to ask Aunt Gertrude if she thought I looked like Katharine Hepburn.

Maybe a little bit? But she would laugh at me, I was certain of that, and I kept silent, thinking about Katharine Hepburn. Now *she* was appropriate in every way, and so I understood what Aunt Gertrude meant about being well dressed. But I still craved a black dress. How to get around that? Katharine Hepburn would understand, I was sure—not only understand but even find a way to make Aunt Gertrude see it from her point of view—make Auntie Ger see that a black dress was in fact the most appropriate thing for me to be wearing. Well, I could find a way, given time, too—and until then, there I would be, all through the summer, dancing around in my new red shoes!

Egyptian Coffee, Summer 1939

At the subdeb dances a few months before, I had met The Sparkling Betty Lewis! She would be arriving soon at Old Westbury Capital, and so would my old chum Bonavishski Buttercup. The Egyptian room and I were all ready and waiting to receive guests, and I was all ready and waiting to brew Egyptian coffee in my Egyptian kitchen.

The Sparkler Lewis had the real reddest hair ever seen anywhere, and it crackled around her face in wavy flames, and you could not stop looking at it and wondering where it was going to catch fire next. She even made Bonavishski Buttercup come across kind of subdued-like. The boys were crazy about her, but she was so swell other girls didn't seem to mind. As for me— now, all of a sudden, since the fatness was no longer upon me . . . well, I had a lot of boys crazy about me too. And all we did was talk about Them—this boy and that boy, and which ones had crushes on us and which ones didn't.

Now The Buttercup was more or less left out of all this, because she still had a fat-ness situation. You might even call it serious, for it was not baby-fatness, which I now knew is what I had on me before my appendix was removed. About ten pounds

of fatness-of-baby had disappeared after my operation. But the
fatness of Bona was of a much more lingering nature, and it did
not have the baby-fatness style about it at all. It clung to her
like lard and wouldn't go away, and it had about it an air of
permanence which boys did not take kindly to. So that was why
there was not much buzzing around Bonavishski Buttercup. Of
course, she made up for a good deal by being funny in that stand-
up comic's way of hers, but it was often at the expense of someone
else and made people edgy instead of carefree. Not that she
directed her barbs at me anymore, because she didn't, or at The
Sparkler Lewis either. She didn't dare do that, because when it
came to making people laugh, The Sparkler Lewis could match
The Buttercup any day, only The Sparkler way was bubbly and
made everyone like to be around her. So soon after this visit was
under way, we knew something was in the air; and because there
was no boyfriend buzzing around The Buttercup, The Buttercup
started buzzing around me.

Wishing

Every Saturday there was a dance at the Seawanhaka Yacht
Club, and one Saturday as we were getting ourselves ready to go
to it I said, It's really a gyp that we aren't allowed to drive to
the dance in Brünnhilde. I was still trying to get Auntie Ger to
let me have a ride in Johnny Delahanty's car, but she wouldn't
even let me sit in it while he drove around the circle in front of
Old Westbury Capital, which was no distance at all, so at this
point it was a closed issue.

Oh, well, said The Betty Sparkler philosophically, fussing at
her hair with a brush, think of all that wind with the top down.

I wouldn't mind that at all, said The Buttercup, who was in
her usual quandary about what to wear.

She stood in front of The Betty, hogging the mirror and

bravely pulling at the zipper on the back of her chartreuse tulle
dress. This chartreuse tulle was the one she always ended up
wearing, no matter what else had been taken into consideration.
Come on—help me zip it up, will you? I can't seem to get
it—and she patted at the folds in a petulant way.

The fact was, there had been no date for The Buttercup until
a last-minute inspiration when Albert Fox had been called into
action and hurriedly invited out for the weekend so that The
Buttercup wouldn't be without a date for the dance at the Seawanhaka Yacht Club. Luckily he had no other plans, and now
here he was at Old Westbury Capital in the Cottage, getting
ready to go to the dance just like we were.

My date of course was Johnny Delahanty, and The Betty
Sparkler's date was Benson Rose. And now The Buttercup was
all set with Albert Fox. But she still didn't seem too happy about
it. Maybe it was the chartreuse of the tulle. She kept turning
sideways and looking at herself in the full-length mirror and then
at The Sparkler standing there behind her in pink—in bright
bright pink. It was something to see, because the pink was so
bright no one would ever have thought of putting it near the
firecracker of her hair. But wow! Surprise, surprise—the chem-
istry of the combination turned out to be dazzling.

I hope Johnny's going to like my dress. Betty, what do you
think?

At first when I put it on I was sure about it. Now I wasn't
so sure. The all-white of it looked—well, all-white, next to all
that pink and red and crackle. Still, the camellia in my hair
didn't look bad at all. It was just the right size, and it made me
feel pretty, especially from the side.

The Buttercup and The Betty stopped looking at themselves
in the mirror and turned around to look at me. Now we were
all looking each other over, and Bona was saying how divine I
looked, and I was saying how divine Bona looked, and Betty was
saying how divine Bona looked too, and it went on and on like

this until we ran out of adjectives. And so armed, out we went, all excited and ready for the evening ahead.

Most of the parents also went to the Seawanhaka Saturday-night dances, so there were plenty of chaperones. The grown-ups all mingled together, and when they weren't dancing they sat at round tables and told jokes and laughed a lot. The boys and girls mingled at other round tables or strolled out onto the big deck that stretched around the Yacht Club. The club itself was more like someone's big house instead of a stuffy old club. And if you walked past the boats moored at the dock, on down along the deck, you finally came to the end of it and to the steps leading down to the sand and the bay.

My knees still got weak every time I saw Johnny Delahanty. I longed to kiss him, and we had, once. But although he was eighteen and I was fifteen, he was much more afraid of what we felt for each other than I was. The opportunities we had of being together alone were not that many, but the few times they occurred I gave no thought to anything else and would have gone on and on with him, into the melting of it, had he not each time become afraid and pulled away. Now, soon—at summer's end—he would be leaving, going to college at Cornell, and I would be going to Wheeler, and I wondered if he would forget all about me, because I knew I could never forget about him and all the plans we had made for the future. . . .

Benson Rose was twirling The Pink Betty on the dance floor and her hair was sparkling around as she laughed, while boys kept cutting in, wanting to dance with her. They kept cutting in on me too, but all I wanted to do was dance with Johnny Delahanty and have his arms around me.

Bertie was maneuvering The Buttercup in and out through the other couples, only it was more the other way around, because although Bertie was tall and Bona was not so tall, she made up for it in other ways, and she seemed to have a much firmer grip on Bertie than he had on her.

The Betty was always saying catchy phrases—things like Sure— glad to! Only she slurred the Suuuurrre until it sounded like a new word and it was somehow funny and made everyone laugh. Of course, Bona tried to pick up these speech patterns right away, and so did I. But we only sounded like the copycats we were as we tried to say other phrases the way The Betty did, such as I'm mad for you! and Egad, what a cad!

Now I was dancing with Jack Fraser, and out of the corner of my eye I could see Johnny Delahanty coming towards me . . . and then I was in his arms and the band was playing "Wishing" and I closed my eyes and leaned against him.

Wishing will make it so—
Just keep on wishing
And cares will go—
Dreamers tell us dreams come true—
There's no mistake—
And wishes are the dreams we dream
When we're awake. . . .

He leaned closer to me as we danced, and then the music stopped and he said, Let's go outside, and we went out onto the deck.

All around us was dark and still, and he took my hand and we walked along past the boats as they flap-flapped against the moorings. Then there was no sound at all except the water lapping and sometimes the summer breeze in the sea grasses; and when we came to the steps, we took off our shoes and walked out over the sand. Now there was no light anywhere at all except from the moon, and we sat down on the sand and looked out over the water and at the moon reflected on it. The sand was still warm from the heat of the day, and I wanted to take my dress off and lie there beside him in the hot summer night. And now through the hot summer night the sounds of the band came to us, for the music had started up again, but it was all far away and came to us, now and then, only as the memory of some other life long ago and now forgotten. . . .

We couldn't stop kissing each other and touching each other, and I knew that this time Johnny wasn't scared, and I said to him, I love you, Johnny, and through the darkness he looked into my face and I could see the soft shining blur of his eyes, and then he kissed me, and his hand touched my breasts, and I lost all mind and said again over and over I love you Johnny I love you Johnny I love—

But then he pulled away and stood up and walked over the sand, down to the edge of the water. In the moonlight I could see the dim shadow of him, standing there with his back to me, and I ran to him and put my arms around him. What's the matter? What's the matter? What's the matter, Johnny?

We can't, he said. We can't.

Why? Why can't we? I said.

We mustn't, that's all—I don't know what to do.

And now he was angry and we were walking back over the sand fast. I didn't know what he meant and I didn't care, all I cared about was being close to him.

On up the steps we walked, on down the long dock, and then we were back on the dance floor and the band was playing "Roll Out the Barrel." The camellia had gotten mixed up in the sand somewhere, and there was sand in my shoes; but nobody seemed to notice us, and I ran into the powder room and looked at my face.

I stared and stared at it . . . I couldn't believe it . . . for I was sure it would be unrecognizable. But it wasn't, no, it wasn't. I kept looking and looking at my face, but it hadn't changed at all. . . .

Escapade

Who knows who first came up with the idea, because it seemed as if The Betty and The Buttercup and The Me all came up with it at the same time. It was the best idea any of us had ever had!

And now the moment was here and all our plotting and planning was being put into action. No red shoes or sneakers on this occasion, for to be appropriately shod it would have to be bare feet, that's all. So here I was creeping down the stairs to the appointed meeting, shoes in hand to put on later.

I was creeping because it was ten-thirty at night and all was still and quiet and dark at Old Westbury Capital and I was on my way to a rendezvous—a secret rendezvous. But first I must get past Sharkey, who would now be in the pantry sitting reading his newspaper, whiling away the time until he made his next rounds at eleven o'clock. Sharkey was the night watchman at Old Westbury Capital, and by now we knew his nightly duties right down to the last detail. This was crucial to our plan, for if he caught us, all would be lost.

Of the twenty steps on the curving staircase, I knew that the fifth and third ones creaked, but once past them I was home free and speeding down the hall to the Cottage, where The Bona and The Betty would be waiting.

And there they were in the dark of the Egyptian room, shoes in hand, shuffling around in their bare feet and whispering.

You should see my bed! said The Buttercup. No one would believe it wasn't me in there. I put tons of pillows under the sheets and then I got the mop from the broom closet and spread it out on the pillow at the head of the bed—and it looks just like my hair.

Come on, come on, let's get going, The Betty said, and she opened the french door of the Egyptian room and we followed her out out into the night.

It was quiet, too quiet, and there was no moon. We ran along, keeping close together on the little pathway that led to the circle driveway at the front of the house. Having done test runs of our route, we knew the hazards of the driveway with its gravel and the scrunching sound it made, but now in bare feet it was no joke. Still, it was the only way to get to the hill facing the house. Once on the hill, we would circumvent the rest of this pitfall altogether and sail on up the hill, through the woods, and on down to the main driveway—where Johnny Delahanty and Benson Rose would be waiting for us in Brünnhilde.

At least that's what we had thought. But it was even denser in the woods on the hill, and there was a lot of dissension within the troops and a lot of mumbling about which direction to go in. More stumbling . . . until a blinking on and off—fast—of lights, a signal from Brünnhilde guiding us on—and there we were, all piled in, reckless as you please, driving in Brünnhilde along the roads of Old Westbury Capital through the night with the top down and the wind blowing our hair every which way, without a care in the world, just as though it was the most natural thing to be doing.

Our destination: Rothman's! In bounds by day *only* if chaperoned and off bounds by night chaperoned or not. What went on inside making it forbidden when dusk descended? We made our entrances, each in his own style, assuming attitudes appealingly blasé. Or, we hoped, if not blasé at least old enough to get us seated at one of the oak tables we coveted. Once ensconced with our Coca-Colas in front of us we relaxed enough to glance around. In a way it was kind of a disappointment. The only difference being that at night it was more crowded and noisy than when we had been there chaperoned by day. Oh well, it gave me courage to concentrate on the task at hand. For it had been in my mind for a long time to penknife initials into the top of a Rothman's table along with all the other initials carved there by passing strangers over the years.

Has anybody got a penknife? I said, for in the hasty getaway I had lost mine. But no one had, so I said, Oh, well, next time. Because I really wanted to get that J.D. and G.V. carved right in there, right into the top of that table, linking us together for ever and ever.

After a while I said to Johnny, What time is it?

Time to get back, The Betty said. We'd better get going.

Getting back in the house was even scarier than getting out of it, because we got back late and our timing was off and we almost ran smack into Sharkey. It was one o'clock in the morning when I looked at the clock beside my bed. The pillows stuffed down under my sheets were just as I had left them. Nothing had been touched. I felt as though I had been away somewhere on a long trip—Bokhara, perhaps. I took the pillows and threw them on the floor and got into bed without even brushing my teeth and instantly fell asleep.

Gee Whiz, Bona!

At first I didn't know what it was all about. We were strolling among the shrubbery in Aunt Gertrude's rose garden, and everything started getting all mixed around. Bona's feelings for me were getting mixed around, and my feelings for Bona were getting mixed around. After all we had gone through to be friends, now it was toppling over here in the shrubbery, for suddenly we were not walking but rolling around playfully on the grass at the edge of the garden, and something had to be done to put an end to it before it all fell under us and around us and over us and by then it would all be too late.

Gee whiz, Bona. Golly, Bona, quit it, will you! and I pushed her away.

She started giggling, but there was nothing giggly about it and I tried to get up off the ground.

And then we were both standing, and it got all peculiar and neither one of us could look at the other and I just wanted to die right then and there.

Because how could we ever get back from where we were to where we had been before this . . . *this?* Never, never, never. How could we? Never! And it spoiled everything. Everything!

Bona looked down at the bushes and with her fingers started pulling the petals of one of Auntie Ger's roses. She looked all funny, and it was a miserable thing to see, and I felt sorry for her instead of angry and scared.

Gee, Bona, I said . . . Come on, let's go back inside, okay?

The petals were all torn away, yet she kept on pulling, and now she was reaching over and doing the same thing to another rose, only this time it was a red one.

Quit it, Bona, I said. Look, look . . .

She stopped pulling at the flower and tried to throw it across the lawn, as though she were skimming a stone far, far out across a lake. I looked across the lawn too, and then I got really frightened . . . . We were almost touching—

But I pulled away and started walking through the shaking sunlight of the rose garden, calling back to her, Come on, come on, come on back with me into the house!

Do you really want me to? she said, not moving.

Of course I do, I said, and I turned to her and looked at her and again said, Of course I do.

But did she believe it?

Did I believe it?

She followed me back through the rose garden as easily as we had entered it, as though nothing had happened. And after all, nothing had.

Soon Bona's visit would be over. Soon she would be gone. And when she was gone, I never wanted to see her again.

Mrs. Vreeland and Camels and Rubies

Our escapade to Rothman's had been brought off without a hitch—no one had discovered anything about it. And soon afterwards, The Betty and The Bona went their separate ways, for they had other fish to fry this summer now that their visit was over.

Most days I went to the Piping Rock Club to swim and lunch, and there he would be—Johnny Delahanty—and a lot of other chums to pal around with. Johnny was still the one I got weak in the knees over, and I kept longing for another chance to be alone with him. But days and days went by and though we would keep seeing a lot of each other, there were always other people hanging around.

Johnny had a sister whose name was Patricia, and she was very beautiful. She was grown-up—at least nineteen and a half— and so of course she never noticed me much, but I certainly noticed her and studied everything about her. I loved to say her

name over and over again—Patricia Delahanty, Patricia Delahanty—for it had the most rolling warm sound to it yet was
princessy at the same time. In conversation with Johnny I always
brought her name up whenever I could. Everyone called her Pat,
but I never did—only Patricia. She was a debutante with photographs of loveliness appearing often in the rotogravure section
of the newspaper, so she had things on her mind, what with
boyfriends and so on. I desperately wanted her to like me. And
as for Johnny's mother—well, I would have died for *her* approval.

One afternoon when I got back from Piping Rock I looked
at the phone messages which were always placed on the table in
the front hall. I couldn't help reading one that was really for
Auntie Ger—once I caught sight of my name on it I read the
whole message. It said: Mrs. Vreeland called Mrs. Whitney and
hopes that Louise Dahl-Wolfe can photograph Miss Gloria for
Harper's Bazaar magazine—will Mrs. Whitney please return Mrs.
Vreeland's call at her earliest convenience.

Harper's Bazaar magazine!

I couldn't believe it.

It was just simply the best magazine ever, and as for Louise
Dahl-Wolfe—I knew all about her photographs and already had
lots of them pasted in my scrapbook along with pictures of Patricia
Delahanty and other similar fascinating subjects.

But Aunt Gertrude would never let me do this. Be photographed for a magazine? Never. Never!

It must have come about after that drive a few weeks ago
from New York to Old Westbury Capital. Cathleen and Larry
and Mrs. Vreeland were all coming to have lunch with Aunt
Gertrude, and I sat in the front seat with the chauffeur while
Mrs. Vreeland sat in back with Cathleen and Larry. And talk
about sophisticated. When it came to that, I felt as though I had
never known what it meant really, not until now. And I couldn't
wait for Aunt Gertrude to see Mrs. Vreeland's black dress. For
on this hot hot day Mrs. Vreeland was wearing the most cool
cool dress of black you ever saw—yes, a cool black sheath of some

cobwebby kind of material, sleeveless, and skimming over her body like a second skin. And the black of her hair was pulled into a black snood, fishnetty and smart as could be. Now what would Aunt Gertrude have to say about that? It would have to make her change her mind about the inappropriateness of black for summer. Because no one in the world could be more appropriate than Mrs. Vreeland, and I wanted to memorize her every word and gesture so that I would remember them forever.

Now she was talking about a trip, riding on the back of a camel—there was a lot about roo-bies—joo-els—and feathered ploomes—and what a marrrr-vel-lous unn-du-lat-ing as the camel moved across the sands while she directed the party in and out among the pyramids—and how smooooth it had been, not only getting on the camel but getting off the camel. . . .

Then Larry called out to me from the backseat, where the three magic ones sat, saying, Gloria, tell Mrs. Vreeland how you've decorated your room in the Cottage.

Oh, yes, Gloria. Only when Mrs. Vreeland said it she pronounced it GLA-riA! and it came forth like a sound from the trumpet of an angel, heralding tidings of great joy.

Yes, GLA-riA! How have you done it? Doo tell me.

Egyptian, I said proudly.

Egyptian. But how marrr-vel-lous.

Really, she was impressed. I could tell

So this phone message waiting on the hall table for Auntie Ger came, no doubt about it, as a result of my meeting Mrs. Vreeland that day. Well, I wasn't going to get my hopes up, because there was no way at all that Auntie Ger would allow me to do it. No, she would say, no, Gloria—and that would be that.

But she didn't. She said—yes.

And it was no time at all before I was standing in my closet with Mrs. Dahl-Wolfe and two most sophisticated and glamorous editors called Muffin and D.D., and we were all going through my clothes trying to decide what I should wear for the photograph. It took ages, but finally they persuaded me to wear a white blouse with a round collar, and over it a nubbly knit white sweater that was more jacket than sweater. The picture was going to be in their October issue, so it shouldn't look too summery. Then we looked through my jewelry case and came up with a leather heart-shaped pin, red of course, with white leather piping around it and a white leather bow in the center from which dangled two little red leather hearts. The D.D. one pinned it on the left side of the sweater, and they all stood back in a row to get the full effect of it.

I like it, D.D. said, while Muffin looked over at Mrs. Dahl-Wolfe, not saying anything yet.

Yes—yes—so do I, Mrs. Dahl-Wolfe nodded in a preoccupied way.

And then I thought I was hearing things, for Mrs. Dahl-Wolfe was saying, Gloria, I think we should try a little pancake, don't you?

Boy, did I. And Muffin opened up a bag all jumbled up with pencils, tubes, pots of rouge, and lipsticks. She fished around in it and came up with a flat compact, big as the one Paul Flato had made for Cathleen, only this one was white plastic. She took it into the bathroom and came back dabbing a damp sponge over the milky-cocoa color.

Close your eyes, please, just for a minute, will you, Gloria? And she cautiously dusted the sponge over my face, patting softly around my nose and over my eyelids and even down around my neck—then a few dabs of something else here and something else there—and after a while she said, Okay, you can look now.

I opened my eyes. My skin looked much darker, almost as if I had a tan, but it was dramatic, for everything on my face looked—defined. It was like meeting a new person, and I couldn't think of how to introduce myself to her.

How do you like it, Gloria? Mrs. Dahl-Wolfe was standing back looking at me attentively.

Oh, I like it, I said. I really like it a lot.

Maybe a speck more color—just here, Muffin, Mrs. Dahl-

Wolfe said, touching my cheekbone, and Muffin moved in and deftly brushed sable across my face in an upsweep movement.

There—that's *perfect* now, Mrs. Dahl-Wolfe said. Let's get started.

I spoke with Mrs. Whitney just before we left, D.D. said. We were all trooping down the stairs with the equipment to go out to the lawn in back of the house.

Yes, Mrs. Whitney called herself, because she wanted to make sure we had received her message about photographing Gloria anywhere we like *except* in front of any of Mrs. Whitney's sculptures. So we must make sure they don't show at all, even in a long shot.

They all stood still and scanned the lawn, looking around for Aunt Gertrude's sculptures.

Oh, I said, there's only one of them here—the one of Diana the Huntress—and that's out in the front, in the center of the driveway.

Oh—we didn't see it, Muffin said, and they relaxed and started roaming around looking for a spot that pleased them.

I went over to the big oak tree in front of the house and sat down underneath it on the grass. It felt good, and I called out to them, How about here? And they all came over and thought about it.

Let's try some right now, Mrs. Dahl-Wolfe said, and she started click-click-clicking away, all around me.

I took a deep breath and leaned my head back against the trunk of the oak tree and took to it all the way a duck takes to water.

We're Off to See the Wizard

There is to be a gala party for the entire cast of the movie *The Wizard of Oz*. It is to be at the Waldorf-Astoria Hotel, and my mother has been invited—and I am to attend it with her.

That means we'll meet not only Judy Garland but also Mickey Rooney, for he is escorting Judy to the gala! Billie Burke will be there, and Ray Bolger, and Bert Lahr, and other famous movie stars who will gather to give homage to *The Wizard of Oz*. It must be taking place in a banquet room if it's to hold all these people. How many Munchkins will be there? Probably only a few representative ones, because they couldn't possibly get them all in, could they?

My mother is being escorted by Prince Paul Chachavadze, and I am to invite someone to escort me. But who? Not Johnny Delahanty, because he is in California again. I know—Jack Fraser would be perfect. And my mother likes him a lot too. He goes to Choate and I met him the weekend I went to the school festivities as Shearen Daniel Elebash's date. Betty Lewis and I were both there that weekend, along with our favorite chaperone (ha, ha), Big Elephant, and we all stayed at The Wallingford Inn. Big Elephant sat around most of the time when she wasn't pussyfooting around the inn, while Betty and I did our own puttering around elsewhere.

Jack Fraser is so handsome, but more than that he is so nice and I think he really likes me. You can always tell, when people treat you like a person, it means they really like you. Saturday night at the dance he kept cutting in on me again and again, and the next day at the brunch before the soccer game we really had a chance to talk. And after that we started corresponding back and forth, and then on vacation we went out dancing together, and one weekend he visited at Old Westbury Capital and Aunt Gertrude thinks very highly of him too. He's the best conga dancer, ditto for fox-trot and rumba. Jack has a mother and a father who must love him a lot because he is the most secure boy I know. He is most manly and I feel safe and protected when I stand beside him. He *always* makes me feel beautiful, and he notices things I wear. I'm never really sure how I look, and when he says You look stunning! it gives me such high hopes and I really feel I look my best. So I just pray now that he hasn't got another date for this party—it's next Saturday, and if he can come with us it will really make it perfect. '

He can! Now what am I going to wear? Mummy will be in basic black of one kind or another, I'm sure—I hope she wears the one with the silk fichu cascading down the front and lacy patterns woven in and out of the puff sleeves. What pumps will she wear? The black silk with the diamanté buckles, I bet. I'll have to come up with something really grand so when Jack sees me he'll think I look stunning.

After careful consideration I've decided to wear my almost-black dress—almost-black because, I must admit it, it's only bottle green, but in night light the effect is black—sort of. With it goes a bolero jacket with pom-poms the size of Hershey Kisses on each shoulder, and they bounce about when I do the rumba, somewhat in the style of a toreador (sans bull, naturally). There is nothing babyish about this outfit at all, especially when I wear my Egyptian bead necklace with it—but the best thing about it is that Jack hasn't seen me wear it! It will be a surprise for him. With it I'll put on the new lipstick I found at Elizabeth Arden, called Cyclamen, and it's the best color to wear with sort-of-black, because it's a kind of purply pink that glows on the lips in a soft dazzle, and at the same time there's a wicked look about it that is subtly sophisticated—how about that. So far I dare wear it only when I'm with my mother—too risky in front of Aunt Gertrude—Justice Carew might not like it. No, the more I think about it, not only would Justice Carew not like it, the whole Supreme Court would not like it—so why test their endurance when they have weightier things on their minds, n'est-ce pas?

The night of the gala is here. And what a splendid group we are as we sit in the enormous limousine Mummy has rented for the occasion. Reclining against the grey plush seat, my mother has never looked more glamorous. She *is* wearing the cascading silk, and on her head are soft silky bows that hold in place a patterned veil that sifts over her face in a most seductive way.

Through the veil she smiles fleetingly the half-tilted smile that so enchants—no one smiles like that in all the world. Oh! if only I were a man, how in love with her I would be! I would shower her with presents and surround her with flowers every day, and she would be so happy. But I am not a man. I am her daughter, her *only* daughter, and all I can do is try to be thin and please her.

Anyway, I know I please John Morrison Fraser, Jr., because when he saw me in my bottle-green-almost-black, he said, You look stunning! And for the moment I feel at peace with myself.

Over the black cascades of the fichu my mother is wearing pearls—
not only the ones my Grandmother Vanderbilt gave her but also
pearls someone else gave her. But who? Prince Paul Chachavadze,
perhaps? It seems pushy to ask. But they are lovely, whoever
gave them to her, and each pinky pearl is separated by a pinky
silken knot that hangs just below Grandma's pearls in a most
tender way—pearls are the most tender jewels, are they not?

Mummy and I sit on the backseat while the Prince Chachavadze and Jack Fraser sit on the jumpseats. The Prince and my
mother are keeping the ball rolling in a most pitter-patter way,
and Jack is right in there with it, while I sit back and listen in
the most sophisticated way I can muster. Now we are in a traffic
jam and Prince Chachavadze is singing—some of it is in Russian,
but most of it isn't, and I can tell my mother is getting nervous
at some of the words, which I guess are sort of risqué, because
she keeps looking at the driver who sits in front of us. He is
staring straight ahead as if deaf, but he can't be, of course, what
with the window—well, he is, after all, right in the car with us.

Jack darling—Pooks—(My mother always calls people she
likes Pooks—He's a Pooks, she'll say. And from her that's the
highest accolade.) She tilts her smile at Jack and pantomimes
with her hand as though she's rolling up the window between
us and the driver. Prince Paul swings his head back and forth
like a pendulum keeping time to his song, and now he's clapping
his hands as well. He is getting a bit boisterous! And I'm sure
Mummy has made the right decision, but it does seem sort of
rude, and I hope the driver's feelings aren't hurt. Now traffic is
moving again and Prince Chachavadze has calmed down a bit,
but not much. He really is quite a cutup, which I wouldn't have
guessed unless I'd seen him in action.

The party is not in a banquet room but on the thirty-fourth
floor in a suite of rooms. One of the rooms is huge, and at one
end is a long table, and on this table a city has been built—but
not just any city. It is the Emerald City, sculpted entirely out
of ice, and tinted green. All around it, placed at strategic points,

are platters of things to eat, and all of them stress the Emerald theme. There are green grapes piled high on a silver salver and they've been frosted all over with crystals of green sugar. There is a dish of green figs wrapped in strips of prosciutto ham, and next to it on a green platter are shrimps with sauce verte, and, for a change of pace, bacon strips sprinkled with brown sugar. It is a staggering display, with hardly a place for the eye to rest. Everyone is crowded around the table, looking, but no one is eating any of it. Waiters with sequined emerald-green bowties pass silver trays bearing fluted green goblets of champagne, and many of the guests also wear a bit of green somewhere on their person.

So far not many people have arrived, and Judy and Mickey are nowhere in sight. Neither is Glinda the Good Witch or the Tin Man or the Cowardly Lion or the Wizard of Oz himself, and not even one Munchkin as yet graces the gala. But perhaps they are to descend en masse later. There was a tiny flurry when Mummy and Prince Chachavadze made their entrance with Jack and me following behind them. We were tardy making our appearance as there was some confusion at the entrance about where to check the hats Jack and Prince Paul were wearing, but finally they were whisked away, and now we are part of the group standing around the buffet table admiring the Emerald City and the emerald food. No one seems to know anyone else, and after a while even my mother has run out of Oh!s and Ah!s and we drift over to another side of the room, where our little foursome stands in a row looking across the room at another group standing in another row, looking across at us. But they don't seem to know each other too well, and no one is talking much at all. It's like we are all waiting for something to happen, which I guess is true; and when Judy and Mickey and the assorted Munchkins arrive, then the party will really start. Even Prince Chachavadze is mute as we stand looking across this carpeted ravine at the other guests.

But suddenly there is activity at the entrance, and it's clear

to all that the very important guests are arriving. The Prince
perks up again and we all look eagerly towards the door. A coterie
surrounds Judy and Mickey as in a huddle they are shepherded
in—only it's not Judy and Mickey, for the coterie has pulled
apart and—as though unveiled—standing there in the doorway—
I don't believe it—it's Errol Flynn! He stands there and looks
around the room at the Emerald City of ice, at the groups across
the ravine, and finally at us. Everyone stares at him, but no one
moves forward; he keeps standing there talking to a man who
arrived with him. I guess everyone is too shy and impressed to
go up and introduce themselves, and there doesn't seem to be
anyone around who is the host or hostess. But now someone does
come over to us and introduces himself as a representative of
MGM and chats away to my mother and the Prince Chachavadze.
Isn't it nice Errol's dad is here—he's the one standing beside
Errol—and that's Errol's sister, the one in the green polka dots
standing right behind Errol's dad. They're both here from Ireland
visiting Errol.

But still no one moves around much except the waiters in
their sequined bowties with trays of green champagne, and soon
the man from MGM drifts off and disappears altogether. Time
passes and passes and it now seems as though we've been here
for hours and hours, but still there's no sign of Judy and the
Munchkins. The room is getting bigger, for already people have
started to leave.

Well, Pooks, Mummy says in the plural, to include us all,
maybe it's time to go on to the Stork Club. Prince Paul jumps
at the idea, and soon my mother is looking around for someone
appropriate to say good-bye to and Thank you for the lovely time.
But there's none. Prince Paul decides to take the matter in hand
and disappears into the crowd. Ages go by and he doesn't return,
having gotten lost somewhere while meandering around the halls.

Oh, there he is, standing by the elevator. And now we can
go confidently on our way—to the Stork Club. Imagine! I've
never been there before! So even if Judy and Mickey and the

Munchkins didn't show up, we did get to see the Emerald City and all that green food—not to mention Errol Flynn. And even if, as someone said later, the girl in the green polka dots wasn't really his sister, we did get to see the father.

And now there are lots of other things to look forward to. Soon the band will be playing "It Was Just One of Those Things," and I'll be in Jack Fraser's arms, twirling around the Stork Club, and my mother will be there seeing how pretty I look, and she'll be sitting at a table with Prince Paul Chachavadze, waiting for us to return when the music stops, and . . . Well, I'm on my way to being grown-up at last!

A Picture in a Magazine

The Conga and Xavier Cugat were all the rage, so at the last minute I threw my maracas into the suitcase—who knows, why not, and just in case. Now there was nothing more to do except jump in the car and take off for Providence, Rhode Island. Freddy was going to drive me there, right up to 216 Hope Street, right up to the front door of the Mary C. Wheeler School. I was in high spirits, but not only over excitement to be starting at Wheeler. For in my suitcase, along with the maracas and other necessities, there at the bottom—flat, so it wouldn't get wrinkled—was an advance copy of the October issue of *Harper's Bazaar*. And it had a picture in it. A full-page picture of a girl, a girl who had something lovely and, yes, mysterious about her, in a most interesting way—but who was she? And under the picture the caption read—

Miss Gloria Vanderbilt—She emerges at fifteen, inevitably the next glamour girl. She is not out, but she is already a personality. Her Javanese beauty distinguishes her from her curly-headed contemporaries. Her tastes are definite. At the moment she is interested in things Egyptian. She wears a curious Egyptian bug ring on her hand and has designed her own Egyptian room

in her aunt's house. She was photographed for *Harper's Bazaar* by Louise Dahl Wolfe.

It was mesmerizing. I knew every word by heart and could have drawn an exact replica of the picture of the girl whose head tilted slightly sideways and whose eyes looked dreamily off into some distant country. . . .

I kept hoping Johnny Delahanty would see it, but I would never dare to send him a copy of the magazine—it was much too forward a thing to do. Maybe the Princess Patricia would see it and send it up to him at Cornell—maybe, but then again, maybe not. Anyway, I couldn't leave it behind, and I'd just have to find a place to hide it when I got up to Wheeler so the other girls wouldn't see it.

I looked around and said good-bye once again to Mr. Harry Payne Whitney's bedroom, but I knew it would be here when I got back, with everything in place just the way it always was, and that nothing would have changed. The only thing that would have changed was me. For this minute I was different from the minute before when I had thrown the maracas into my suitcase and closed down the lid. I do not know who I am really, or if I exist at all. . . . Sometimes I even think I am my mother. And although the girl in the photograph on the page of the magazine is said to be me, it really has nothing to do with me at all. Or does it? Maybe I only exist in the magazine. I hope that's not true. I want more for myself than that—oh, yes! much more. I want to know who I really am. And I will—even if it takes forever.

Coo-ee Coo-ee CONGA!

A few hours after arriving at Wheeler I found myself, maracas in hands, weaving along hallways, on down stairs and back up again. Behind me, a girl called Diane Wenger held my waist, and behind Diane, a girl called Charlotte Vroom held sway. And behind Charlotte, for as far as you could see, girls were holding on to each other's waists as I led them to the beat of my maracas and we all chanted—

> Coo-ee-coo-ee CON-GA!
> Coo-ee la bo-ni-ta!

Not only were we doing the Conga, but anyone seeing us would have thought we had known each other for years. Later, I even showed them the picture of the girl in *Harper's Bazaar*, and none of them seemed put out about it at all, and Estelle MacCauley said Gosh! How does it feel to know that there are stacks and stacks of magazines all with *your* picture in it? I hadn't thought of that, but I shrugged my shoulders and thought of Johnny Delahanty and how with all those stacks of *Harper's Bazaar* around there certainly was a good chance he might see it.

My room has twin beds with maple headboards and a night table between. Also a pair of bureaus, one for me and one for my roommate, Julia Chittendin. Two closets of perfect size, and behind another door there's a basin with shelves over it for our toothbrushes and things, and down the hall are showers and tubs and a proper bathroom. Our room has two windows looking out over the backyard of the school; one of them is open, and there's a nip of shine on, shine on harvest moon in the air. Nothing about anything here at Wheeler makes me feel freaky or out of place, and it's with great good feeling that I unpack and start my life here.

During the day our uniform consists of a blue wool skirt, a white cotton short-sleeve blouse with neat collar, and a long-sleeve not-cardigan sweater the same blue as the skirt. Then there are the lisle stockings held up by garter belts, and sensible shoes. But after study hall at five a transformation takes place, and we can change into our own clothes and even wear a smidgen of makeup if we want to. I change into my red sabot-style shoes, which are really comfortable even though they have wooden soles, and now everybody wants a pair. We are also allowed, at certain hours, to walk along Hope Street and go in and out of some of the shops. No movies, of course, and no restaurants, but just to be allowed to go in and out of grown-up territory makes all the difference. Each term we will have one whole weekend off and, later in the semester, a half-weekend free—but that's not all, because if we keep our room in apple-pie order there's a bonus of another weekend. *Quel change* from Farmington, with no weekends off ever and all those nauseating collections of Brooks Brothers sweaters in sappy Easter Bunny colors, worn in that dippy way, buttoned back to front. Everyone says that this school is more like a junior college, and as soon as I stepped in the door

I could sense that everything Kate Drury had said about Wheeler was true. Then there is Miss Van Norman who is the principal and lives on the top floor. She has a most serene way about her and drifts in and out of our everyday comings and goings with gracious white hair piled high in the Gibson Girl manner, wearing dresses with choker collars, and if she has ups and downs, she keeps them to herself. We all look for her high regard, but we do not curry favor, for she gives us the example of her own self-respect. And it is considerable.

For the first time in my life I have a feeling of belonging somewhere. And some sense of myself. As each day goes by, it becomes clearer to me that there are definite things I want to do when I grow up, and that these hopes are no longer passing fancies. The passing fancy of thinking I wanted to be a nun has long since left me. And the passing fancy of thinking I wanted to be an actress has been put aside in a special niche, since that day when I told Aunt Gertrude and she said to me, An actress! Well—you would have to change your name, wouldn't you, my dear! After all, you *are* a Vanderbilt. Missing, of course, the whole point—but I let it go by without enlightening her. She just wouldn't get it. So these things have slipped away, and into me there comes more and more surely a knowledge of my own existence and what I hope to grow up to be.

First there is, as there has always been, the hope of loving one man and having a family with him in a little home just meant for two, from which I'll never roam—who would, would you? And now running alongside this dream is knowledge that I have a gift for painting. Miss Brown, the art teacher here, encourages me and allows me to work alone in the studio at off-hours. It is huge, this studio at Wheeler, and I can spread out and work there without feeling cramped or that I'm messing up someone else's sense of order. It's so quiet and silent, and I'll be working—and then I'll stop for a minute and see the clock and find that hours and hours have gone by, but in my experience it's only as if ten minutes have passed. Yes, this is joy. And I am discovering that painting is what makes me happiest, and that when I'm working I have the same sense of belonging that I feel when I'm with Big Elephant.

And yet it's not the same, because it comes from myself and depends on no one but me. For a person can leave, and those fatal good-byes must be said, and you are never the same again. But this—no one can take it away, and I need never say good-bye, because to do so would be to say good-bye to myself. And that would never do. It's scary to know, but it's a secret I have no need to share. It's best kept inside myself—yes, it's best that way, glittering and hard as the pear-shaped diamond ring my father gave to my mother, only the paradox is that it's not hard or glittering at all but as shining and tender as love.

60 *Washington Mews*

That December snow kept falling through the night and we would awake to see it piled on our windowsills like freshly baked loaves of bread. There was anticipation in the air, and one morning a message came. From Aunt Gertrude. At Christmas vacation I was to go not to the Castle on Fifth Avenue or to Old Westbury Capital but to Aunt Gertrude's house close to the Whitney Museum—60 Washington Mews—a place I had never been before. As snow fell through the days I thought about this a lot, trying to imagine what it would be like. Then it was good-bye, good-bye to everybody at school, for it was time to go home—home for the holidays. Freddy drove me from Providence on and on through the snow, until we reached the crowds of New York City, inching through the traffic until we came to a cobblestoned street hidden within a city block and closed off by iron gates at either end, for none could enter without a key. A place silent and removed from the city around us as if we had come upon a village somewhere far away in a Russian fairy tale. The numerals on the black door were outlined by snow, and the brass presented itself delicate as lace. A long wait after the first ring and then the door opened. Welcome home, Miss Gloria, Hortense said, and in I stepped to a little foyer and on into a huge living room with a two-story ceiling and a wall of glass looking out onto a garden at the back of the house. On another wall a narrow staircase clung. Up we went to a tiny door at the head of the stairs, and I bent down like Alice in Wonderland to pass through, on into a passageway that led through to the house next door, for despite the enormous living room, space in these former carriage houses was limited, and Aunt Gertrude had acquired several houses side by side, connecting them by this passageway, which took me into a room that now belonged to me. I fell in love with this room and forever after tried to recapture it, but it was hard to

define and has always eluded me. It had, of course, to do with
the time and place, with the coming upon it after climbing the
narrow stairs from the huge living room, becoming Alice to pass
through the door and the narrow passage, to find myself in a
small, exquisite world. It had to do with the two french doors
looking out onto the snow falling on the empty cobblestoned
street below, framed by curtains of taffeta of palest lavender
spilling from the ceiling onto the floor in pools of silk and rustling
across the windows at dusk in a most seductive way. It had to
do with the wisteria vines heavy with snow twining up from the
cobblestones, up around the iron grilles of the token balconies
outside. But most of all it had to do with scale, with the use
made of space, with the silver tea-papered walls, with the day
bed gessoed with water lilies and white butterflies, with the shape
of the Venetian bureau between the windows painted with gilded
winged creatures, and on it resting a crystal flacon of Chanel
No. 5—my first perfume and a present from Aunt Gertrude. It
had to do with the second Alice door flush with the wall, this
time leading down more narrow stairs to Aunt Gertrude's enormous bedroom, high-ceilinged as the living room, her bed facing
another wall of glass and another garden, where everything was
moving and changing with leaves falling or the coming green of
spring. Yes, it had to do with all these things, and of all Aunt
Gertrude's kingdoms, it now became for me the most wondrous
of all.

There were to be dances this Christmas, and I was to pick
out dresses to wear. New dresses. At Bergdorf Goodman there
was gold lamé I craved; but Miss Moore, the vendeuse, talked
me out of it, which was just as well, because I knew Aunt
Gertrude would have a fit and it would have to be returned.
From her point of view, gold lamé would not be appropriate—
no, not at all.

Then I was in Aunt Gertrude's chariot and we were driving
through the night in a city of snow. Sitting in the front seat
beside Freddy was The Constonce. I could see her back as she sat

stiffly, staring ahead. Rats! Was she going to spoil everything? I had just met her, but you can bet I would be seeing a lot of her from now on. She was the maid Aunt Gertrude had engaged to chaperone me, and she was not only going to accompany me to all the dances, she was actually to get out of the chariot and sit in the powder room every single minute until the dance was over and it was time to go home. It was the worst idea Aunt Gertrude had ever had. No one else I knew had this upon her, and I was mortified beyond exasperation.

We were picking up Spencer Stone on the way, and I prayed she wouldn't attach herself to our side as Spencer and I made our entrance into the Plaza Hotel. What a trio we would make, stepping out onto the dance floor in some kind of weird tandem!

There were three feathered white plumes in my hair when I started out for the dance, and the snow had started to fall. It whirled down onto the white of my cape, onto the white bouffant of my skirt, mingling the seed pearls on my dress with crystals of snow. The taffetas had been drawn across the windows of the room above me, and rose light filtered through the night as snow swirled onto the cobblestones and vanished. I stood for a moment looking up, remembering the flacon of perfume on the Venetian bureau in my room. So *much* would have happened by the time I returned—the music ended and the party over—but there, in my room, the flacon would be on the Venetian bureau, exactly where I had placed it as I left for the dance. When I came back, nothing in the room would have changed, even though *I* had . . . Snow touched my lips, and the surprise of it made me tremble.

Maybe we could jump out fast and dart on ahead of her— but she was wiry as a fox terrier, and we would have to leap like frogs to shake her.

Which is just what we did. All she had time to do was call out that she would be waiting in the powder room and not to stay out too late, please, which of course was exactly what we had in mind—not to mention vague fantasies of slipping into the Stork Club again. But the one time we had managed to sneak in, Aunt Gertrude had found out about it and was so enraged she kept me grounded for two weeks, so that we would just have to lay low for a while until she simmered down.

Into the ballroom we ran, under the gilded sky with opaline clouds floating above, into the swirling light and the music. I looked for Johnny Delahanty even though I knew he wasn't going to be there. But then, across the room—my knees got weak, because there he *was—here!*—standing with his back to me. I took a deep breath and held it for as long as I could . . . but then he turned around, and it wasn't Johnny Delahanty at all, just someone who looked like him from the back. . . .

Madeleine Violett tilted her head to one side and looked at Spencer's hands. They were hefty as a mechanic's, but his face wasn't. Spencer—she tapped at his hands flirtatiously—why don't you get your hands to match your face?

How witty she was. And damn it, how tongue-tied *I* was. Why hadn't The Betty arrived yet? She was my bestest friend— when she was around I didn't feel a tongue-tied creature at all but the other half of a crackling, sparkling team—yes, the Redhead and the Brownhead—a team. That's what we were.

But soon I was swept away and boys were cutting in, and one or the other of us would say, Where do you go to school?— words always said to each other to break the ice.

But then another boy cut in, a boy I had never seen before, and there was something about him that was different. It was in the way he moved and in the way he spoke. He knew where he was going. And I knew that he would take me with him.

At the far end of the room—a flash of turquoise blue and crackling red, before swains surrounded her, and I knew The Betty had made her entrance. And a second later she was whirling by us in Frank Birney's arms saying, If you two get any closer, you'll be on the other side of each other.

And we laughed and he held me even tighter.

Soon it would be time to be seated for supper, but he wasn't to be at my table—I was faint at losing him just when I had found him, but what to do? What to do? Well! *He* knew what to do, for when we went to our tables, hocus-pocus had taken place and there he was—sitting right beside me.

I looked at his place card—Winter Austin Smith III.

Taking it from the table, I looked at it again. So that was his name. . . . And I put the place card in my evening bag to keep forever and ever . . . and that is how it began.

Tea Dancing

Next day when I woke up it was very late and the cobblestones were covered with snow and the phone kept ringing and ringing. But *he* hadn't called yet, and every time I got a call I'd say Can't talk now and I'd hang up, because he might call and get busy signals and stop trying.

Just when I'd given up, it rang again.

Can you come tea dancing with me at the Plaza?

When?

Today?

And I almost fainted right there, because if he had said Tomorrow I would have died, and I said quickly, I'll call you right back—I have to ask Aunt Gertrude

Who is this Smith boy? she said when I asked her, and I said I had met him at the dance the night before and that he went to Yale. But that wasn't enough for her and she reached over and picked up the Social Register.

Oh misery!

And I ran out into the snow in my dressing gown and took great gulps of air, swallowing them down until I almost choked.

Then I ran back in again and she said, Gloria, what have you been doing? You're freezing to death!

I'm freezing to life, Auntie Ger, I am I am!

Well, sit down a minute. Now about this tea dancing . . .

Yes—what about it? What about Winter—what about him? Winter Smith?

Well, I'm sure he's a nice young man. His family are listed as absent, which means they must have lived mostly in Europe, but I see they are from New Orleans, and many of them are still there. Where are his family now? Do you know that?

No, I don't I don't I don't know where they are. I just know where *he* is and he's waiting for me to call him back—right now he's sitting by the telephone, and if I don't call him back, he might disappear forever and I'll never never see him again.

Well, Gloria, I don't think it's appropriate for you to be seen alone with him tea dancing. It's not as if it's a private party or even one of the subscription dances like the Metropolitan last night—and you know I have to be very careful so the court will have no reason to criticize what I allow you to do. You must remember the court is always aware of what goes on, and in my position I must be most cautious at all times . . . so I cannot allow you to accept this tea dancing invitation, not even if Constonce went with you—

God, no! Not The Constonce, please! But I tried to keep calm.

Auntie Ger, *when* will I see him, then?

Well, she said, won't he be at the other dance—the Holiday, isn't it? That's coming up soon, isn't it?

Soon, I cried out, *soon!* No—it's three days away.

That's not so far away. But then she relented and said, Why don't you ask him *here* for tea—today—right now. Go and call him back and invite him here for tea—I'd like to meet him.

I ran to my room and dabbed some Chanel No. 5 behind my ears and quickly we were talking on the telephone, and soon he would be arriving for tea—and even though we wouldn't be dancing, I'd be sitting in the same room with him, breathing the same air, and that kept me alive until there he was walking through the door of 60 Washington Mews.

The fire was burning when I brought Winter into the high-ceilinged room whose wall of glass looked out onto the garden. To be in this room among these colors of silk was to be inside a glass ball, the kind children shake to make snow swirl around. Aunt Gertrude sat in her usual place, and my hand shook as into his cup I poured the tea. A drop fell, but no one would notice, and it would be there always, a dot on the patterns of Aunt Gertrude's Persian rug. Why would I remember this long after other things about the day might be forgotten? Outside, the snowflakes swirled around and around and around as I dwelled on this, half listening to Aunt Gertrude and Winter talking of this and that as the day darkened. After a time Aunt Gertrude got up and said she was going to dress for dinner. The fire needs another log, she said, and as the door closed behind her Winter leaned down and placed one on the coals—then he turned to me in the half-light and I put my hand in his.

Viscaya

Viscaya: a place very much like Xanadu, existing only in my mind, for I had never been there. Also existing in my mind was the man who owned Viscaya, a man whose name was James Deering. I knew nothing about him, but he had been my father's best friend, and he was also my godfather.

There was a picture in my mind of the way I imagined this godfather of mine to be. And I got to thinking about him a lot, for when he was not at Viscaya he lived in New York in a house, and one day just before the Christmas vacation was over I looked up his name in the Social Register and there it was—James A. Deering, 45 West Fifty-fourth Street, with the phone number alongside it. Viscaya was far away, but 45 West Fifty-fourth Street wasn't, and just as though it was the most natural thing to do, I dialed the number, because there were things I had to know, things that only he could tell me.

And on the first ring a man's voice answered, just as if he'd been sitting there waiting for my call.

Whooo? he said when I told him it was me.

I talked fast because I had to see him—I *had* to see him. Mr. Deering, can I come to see you? Mr. Deering? Please—anytime you say—*please.* . . .

Well, you see, I'm leaving—you catch me just as I'm leaving for Florida—for Viscaya. Maybe when I come back to New York, maybe then.

No, not then. *Please,* Mr. Deering—I could come over now if you could see me—now, right away?

Oh, no! he said, oh, no!—and I thought he was going to hang up. Not *now*—I'm busy, very busy—very very busy indeed.

I pressed faster. Well, when could I see you? When? Anytime at all, Mr. Deering, anytime you say.

He flubbered around some more, but at least he didn't hang up. And finally the peeved voice said, Oh, all right—all right then—all right—now—today at—at five. But be prompt, will you please, as I have to go someplace at five-thirty.

So of course I got there much too early and walked around and around the block for twenty minutes before it was time to knock on his door.

When I did, it opened immediately and Mr. Deering was standing there. It was one of those New York houses, narrow and dark, with no garden in the back and no way of knowing what time of day it was—a house that comes alive only at night. But I had made it. I was here actually standing inside and shaking hands with my father's best friend. I tried to see his eyes, but he turned away and led me through the shadows through rooms, rooms with white sheets over the furniture as though they covered corpses, on and on, until we came to the living room, where shrouds from two chairs had been removed to make a place for us to sit. Dust had gathered on the table tops, and all at once I knew it was all a big mistake—a mistake to have picked up the phone and dialed Circle 0698, a mistake to be sitting in this dim dusty room with this wooden stranger. But the biggest mistake of all was to have expected he would tell me anything about my father.

My visit with Justice Carew kept coming into my mind—at least I had been able to see his face. But Mr. Deering was faceless and elusive in the dusky light, and there was a long pause as both of us sat there saying nothing at all, until I spoke up and said—

Did my mother love my father?

Well—well—he sputtered. What a question!

It certainly was, but I pursued it.

Why doesn't she ever talk to me about him?

He looked at his watch and I looked at mine. It was ten past five.

Well—well—let me see—what can I say—there were difficulties, you know—

Difficulties? What difficulties?

Well—the mother, you know—Mrs. Morgan—your grandmother—well—she was around all the time, and—

Yesss . . . ?

Well, it was difficult, that's all—as I've said, a difficult situation—very difficult indeed.

In what way?

Well—I don't know, really—it was just—difficult, that's all. Now he was really annoyed and he stood up, expecting me to stand up too and leave, but I held on and didn't move an inch.

Tell me about him, Mr. Deering.

What? What do you want me to tell you?

What was he like?

He still stood, but he hadn't moved to the door. He looked so all of a piece—so grey and cold. And I thought of my father, and I wondered if he had been as grey and cold as this best friend standing here looking away from me and hoping I would walk out of his house and leave him in peace.

Well, I didn't want to know the answer to that, so I stood up too.

Thank you, Mr. Deering, thank you for letting me come to see you.

And we went back through the hall and silently shook hands at the door and he said, Do you ever come to Florida? You must let me know next time you do—you must come to Viscaya—anytime—anytime at all—just give me a ring.

Yes—I'll do that—thank you, Mr. Deering.

And I went out into the street and the door closed behind me and that was the end of that.

Giraffes and Dinosaurs

My sister, Cathleen, was living in Cuba. Why was Larry not with her? What was she doing in Havana all alone? Soon I would find out, because during spring vacation I was to visit her.

In Havana she wore white turbans made of the same silk as the white of her dresses and she had lots of new friends and also a new name, for they all called her Catalina. At night her hair would be gathered into a chignon, and then at Veradero Beach it flowed loose around her while she laughed a lot and talked about someone called Ramón, but still Larry's name never came up.

Then one day Ramón showed up with his almost bald head and I didn't like him one bit. But Cathleen certainly did. And he was around most of the time. Once, driving around Veradero, Cathleen reached over to take Ramón's hand. He pulled away impatiently but then thought better of it, and his hand lay in my sister's hand like a dead bird until we stopped at a café for coconut ice cream.

Everywhere in Havana, in the streets and drifting down from shuttered windows at night, there was music. And at Veradero it was the same. Cathleen and I had our own cottage on the

beach, and every night we sat on the terrace for dinner and there
would be serenades. After a few days Ramón disappeared and my
sister and I were alone together. Maybe she had sent him away
because she wanted this time alone with me to tell me about my
father.

I was on the beach dawdling over a pineapple drink, and she
was swirling ice around over the lime juice she now always drank.
There were no more Coca-Colas because the bitter juice helped
her to lose weight, or so she thought.

What do you and your girl friends talk about? she asked me.

Now there were a lot of ways I could answer that question
. . . but I was trying to think of one that would bring it around
to my father, so I mulled it around for a while without saying
anything.

Clothes? she pursued.

Oh, no, I said, we never talk about clothes—not that much anyway.

Well, what do you talk about then? She smiled in her slow beguiling way and signaled for the waiter to bring her another drink.

Of course I didn't dare tell her that we talked most of the time about boys—boys—boys—boys! I didn't want to shock her, but I had to say something, so I glanced up at the blue sky, and after a while . . . I pounced.

Cathleen, did Auntie Ger pay the Judge to do what he did— you know, about my mother and all the things that happened? All those things about my mother—did Aunt Gertrude pay to have the Judge say they were all true?

My sister said nothing and just sat there twirling the ice around in the empty glass with her coral fingernail.

Time passed and I said, What's the name of that color polish you always wear? It's so pretty, I—

Listen, Gloria, she said, it's a very hard question for me to answer—and I don't know if I should. But I do think you should know that there were things that went on. Money—can be very powerful—and it's possible that certain—well, things—did pass between—I mean go back and forth—but I can't say more than that because I don't really know the details, and even if I did— look, look—

I did—I looked at her face and it filled me with despair. The sand was sucking at us; but I wanted it to—I wanted to be pulled down into the quicksand, yes, sucked down into the sand, to be buried here on the beach at Veradero, buried and have done with it and never be tormented by any of it again.

But instead—a waiter shimmied up with our drinks, and she took the glass and held out her other hand and examined her nails in an absorbed way.

I'll tell you a secret, she said. It doesn't have a name. My manicurist mixes the color especially for me. Soon you'll be old enough to wear nail polish—just think of that!

And I did . . . my mind slid on to other things, and soon it was Winter who occupied my thoughts and I ached with the missing of him, and soon this mixed with the other pain inside me until dusk started settling over the ocean and beach boys gathered the deck chairs around us in preparation for night.

I'm going to take a walk, I said to my sister, and I went to the edge of the sea and walked along the foam of it, far on down the beach away from her. As I walked faster I had the most frightening feeling that I was never going to go back. . . . Faster still, on and on, I followed the curve of the sea until I came to the end of the beach where rocks were piled high against the ocean, and I climbed up and sat looking out over the waves, thinking of nothing at all.

After a time it got dark and I started back along the edge of the sea. Far up on the sand there were animals not seen by day— giraffes perhaps? or dinosaurs? Others with unknown names moved about restlessly as they leaned towards me from the distant darkness. I ran on, my feet skimming the water, but they didn't follow —and soon, far off in the distance at the edge of the sea, I saw a bride, all alone on the beach, and she was walking towards me, and I ran to her—but as I came close I saw that it wasn't a bride at all, it was my sister, who had put on a kaftan of white lace, her hair held back by a white ribbon. . . . And we stared at each other, with no words to say, and soon we were at dinner, sitting at our usual table. There was music and the *guayaba* and cream cheese we always had for dessert. Nothing had changed. And the next day we drove back to Havana.

My sister had planned an evening of dining and dancing the night before I was to go back to New York. I had a blind date called Pancho and we were all going to a nightclub where we would dance to the Cuban rhythms. Pancho was a Pooh Bear, and he led me around the dance floor, undulating in a cuddly manner, with great expertise.

Then Cathleen said she was getting tired, so we dropped Pancho Pooh Bear off at his house, and when we got to Cathleen's she invited Ramón up for a drink. It wasn't all that late, so I sat around with them until conversation lagged and then I said good-night and prepared to go to bed.

Towels were missing from the guest bathroom and there were none to be found, so I went back to the living room, but Ramón had already left, so I went to Cathleen's door and knocked. There was a long wait, and I thought she might be asleep—but how could she be asleep that fast? Suddenly the door opened and there she was in disarray, looking absolutely ravishing.

Is anything wrong? she said in a voice I couldn't recognize.

I wished I had never knocked on that door, because now I could see the Bald-Headed One peeking out from underneath the covers of the bed. Damn the towels. But I had to say something.

I don't have any towels in my bathroom.

Oh! Rosa must have changed them and forgotten to put fresh ones back.

And she ran into her bathroom all flustery on her tippy-toes and came back again on her tippy-toes with an armful of towels.

Here, darling, she said—take these.

And I lickety-split it back to my room. Wow! It gave me a lot to think about.

Next morning not a trace of the Bald One anywhere. But my sister was open as a flower. We had papaya for breakfast and she told me how much she loved Ramón, and that I must promise not to say anything at all about last night—not to Aunt Gertrude or to anyone—because if Larry got wind of it there would be a lot of trouble for her, and the way things were now, she just didn't know what was going to happen.

Did this mean they were going to get a divorce? The idea staggered me, but at the same time it was clear to see she was nuts about Ramón. And I knew how that felt! I must be important to her if she confided these secrets to me, secrets no one else knew about, and all this made me feel close to her, but I was distraught about Larry—and I went back and forth in my mind about this, for it was a serious thing and I wondered what was going to happen in the future.

So with this on my mind I went back to New York. And it was a long time before I thought about my mother and the beauty of her . . . what was going to happen to her, and to me, and whether we would ever really get to know each other . . . or would it always be like this, she somewhere and me somewhere else, walking along in the dark trying to find her . . . ?

The Empress of Austria

Winter's mother and father have a house in New York on Seventy-second Street, and it's right across the street from the house my mother used to live in. This gives much to think on. For all along, while Consuelo-Tamar was standing at the window, looking out across the street and saying *Cuidado, Cuidado,* what she saw was a house—a house that now shelters this boy I love. It makes me trust in the rooms that wait for us . . . rooms we don't know exist yet, but they do. And things will happen in those rooms, and they will happen with people who to us may now be strangers. Terrible things will happen, but great and good things will happen also. Because they *do.* . . . Faith!

I think Winter's parents like me. I keep praying I'm worthy of him because he's so wonderful in every way. His mother certainly talks a lot, but his father is the nicest gentleman, and I love his old-fashioned courtly ways. He must be very old, but that's because Big Elephant said he and Mrs. Smith were married "late" and Winter is an only child. Just like me. Ha, ha! It's quite easy to be with them, because Mrs. Smith chats and chats on and on and on and on. Boy! Would I like to see her and the Little Countess together—*quel compétition!* Naney keeps putting off meeting them, but I could tell right off she hates the idea of me seeing so much of Winter.

Because ever since that first night at the Christmas dance

Winter Smith has been the one for me. And although I still love Johnny Delahanty and always will, as a friend, there will never be anyone for me except Winter Smith, for I know he is the boy I will marry and have children with. (I want six at least, so we'll have to have a big house, I guess.) I wish we could get married right now, today, but there's no chance of that unless we elope to Maryland where you can get married at sixteen without anyone's consent.

Big Elephant doesn't like Winter either. But she *will* when she gets to know him better. She always sides with the Little Countess these days and is fond of saying whenever it can be worked into the conversation, You don't know the world, Gloria! It has an ill-fated ring to it, and nothing I do seems to please either one of them. It was *awful* when Felix of Hapsburg came out to Old Westbury Capital that weekend. Naney drove me wild, going on and on, first about Otto of Hapsburg, talking about him to Aunt Gertrude right in front of me as if I weren't *there*! It was Otto this and Otto that, and then Gertrude this and Gertrude that, until finally she came out with what was really on her mind—Why, Gertrude—Otto would be the *Emperor* of the Austro-Hungarian Empire if there weren't the rumpus going on in Europe—and his wife, well—his wife would be the Empress. *Empress!* And she looked over at me in a significant way, raising her eyebrows to communicate to the powers that be. *Honestly*, Naney! For Pete's sake! But she didn't hear me and went right on—But Gertrude, I do think we ought to forget about Otto—he's too old for her—while the brother Felix is *just* right. Don't you agree, Gertrude?

As for Gertrude, she at least had the grace to change the subject, and said how nice it would be to have Felix of Hapsburg visiting Old Westbury. Some change of subject.

Well, I showed them, all right! Even before I set eyes on him I couldn't stand him. And then I had to be polite for two whole days with Naney and Aunt Gertrude around keeping tabs on me, and Naney saying to Felix, whenever she could wheedle it into the conversation, *Quel dommage* the Empress couldn't have joined us. That's Felix's *mother*! She wanted *her* here too.

It made me sick—and angry!—yes, and not only angry, but *furious*. *Why* don't they like Winter? Naney says the Smiths don't have much money. Which, translated, means they don't have as much money as Aunt Gertrude. But that wasn't the only reason Winter and I could *never never* marry. It was in the Caravan—the worst possible place for this to happen, at the Hotel Fourteen—that the conversation took this turn, and I should have let it pass, but once it had been said, I kept on begging the Little Countess to tell me what it was—this *never never* reason why Winter and I could not marry.

You can't marry Winter—because if you did, why—well—your name would be--*Smith*—wouldn't it? You'd be—MRS. SMITH!

Out of the Caravan into the bathroom I ran—on the floor I lay and sobbed and sobbed—and when I didn't stop, Naney became frightened and patted and patted me, all the while saying, Hush, hush, darling mine—stop now—stop, Little One—and she knelt on the floor and tried to take me in her arms. Listen to me, listen--maybe he could call himself *Smythe*—wouldn't that be a good idea? Yes, yes—or even better, he could hyphenate his two last names, it would be Austin-Smythe—yes, that would be better, much better, wouldn't it, darling mine, wouldn't it? And all the time she kept on crooning to me and trying to lift me to her. But I was too heavy, and over my limbs a paralysis came and I sobbed myself into it until I lay there numb on the floor as though dead.

Time passed, and when I came back into myself the paralysis had gone. But in its place there was a terrible thing. For while I had been asleep, a murder had been committed. But by whom? And who had been killed? For if there is the murderer, there must also be . . . the murderee. But who is to know which is the one and which is the other?

The Baby

Winter Smith and Ray Carswell and Bill Dannat and Harvey Patteson were circling in the hall of Old Westbury Capital, and what they were circling around appeared to be an Angel from the top of a Christmas tree. The Angel was speaking and the Dance List Lads circled, admiring and laughing. This was how I saw her for the first time as I came down the stairs at Old Westbury.

Winter was saying, This is Carol Marcus. Now in talking to me about her they had always called her the Baby, and so I thought her name was Baby, Baby Marcus. But it wasn't—it was a Christmas song, Carol.

We went outside and walked around and I couldn't take my eyes off her. I'd never seen anybody who looked like her before. There were tons of makeup on her porcelain face, even more than on the Martin sisters, and her hair was of course angel in color. Her dress was *very* grown-up too, and she was mesmerizing from every point of view, and I would have given *anything* to be as sure of myself as she was. When she talked it was like quicksilver running in one direction—and then just when you got it, she'd say something that was just the opposite, and it was so unexpected that everyone laughed.

This Angel had the biggest compact ever, even bigger than Cathleen's, and she took it out of her bag every ten minutes or so to search her beauteous face in a most critical way; then she'd take the enormous puff and dab it into the compact, frantically, saturating it with powder white as flour. Then she patted it all around over her face, even though it already was perfect as it was. It was almost as if she didn't *know* how beautiful she was. But how could that be? For she was of such perfection from every point of view, and rested upon each moment so easily, making everything glide into place. *She* wasn't an Impostor, that's for sure, because being that brilliant and that gorgeous meant she must have had a father and a mother right there at her side, not only now but right from the very beginning.

After fooling around outside for a while we went on back to the Egyptian Room, and Bill and Winter and Harvey and Ray started urging her to do her Geraldine Fitzgerald imitation. At first she was hesitant, but we all insisted and sat down on the Egyptian couch expectantly, until finally The Angel, by popular demand, stood in the center of the room and started doing a scene from *Wuthering Heights*—the one where Geraldine Fitzgerald pleads with Laurence Olivier to love her because she is a woman. It came out exactly the way it did in the movie, and as she spoke, even the angel halo waving around her white face didn't distract one bit, because—presto! Carol had turned herself into divine Geraldine Fitzgerald, and it was as if Geraldine were present, right there, standing with us in the Egyptian Room. Now all we needed was one of the boys to be Laurence Olivier. Ha, ha!

But instead Ray put "Moonlight Serenade" on the Victrola and turned it up as loud as it would go, and we took off our shoes and went out onto the lawn in front of the Cottage and danced. Then, in the Egyptian kitchen, I cooked lamb chops for them, peas in butter with lettuce leaves, the way the French do, and baked potatoes with a soupçon of oil brushed over the skin. I cut a little place deep down into the meat of the lamb chop and in it hid a kernel of garlic for flavor, just like a sixpence in a plum pudding. They all said it was a tasty tiffin and later, over Egyptian coffee, Carol asked me where I got the organdy blouse I was wearing. She thinks I'm beautiful! I know because she told me—and I just know we're going to be friends for ever and ever.

Needlepoint

I haven't seen Aunt Consuelo-Tamar in a long time, and it's a surprise to arrive at my mother's house and find her there, the familiar black shape of her, in the living room, sitting with her back to me in the black dress. All thoughts are directed to a round hoop upon which needlepoint has been stretched. She is working the yarn in and out, in and out. From what I can see it's a pattern of bumblebees clustered around a flower—an apple blossom, perhaps? My mother sits in a chair opposite her, also in black. I go immediately to where Aunt Consuelo-Tamar sits, for I know it's expected that I greet Aunt Consuelo-Tamar before greeting my mother. Am I also expected to kiss her? Yes, my mother would expect that, and so I prepare myself. But Aunt Consuelo-Tamar is unaware of my presence as I enter the room, and she continues to remain unaware of me as I walk towards her. She does not look up and no sign comes from her and she continues weaving the yarn in and out, in and out. My mother too is silent, and she watches Aunt Consuelo-Tamar as she bends over the needlepoint.

Aunt Tamar, I say, for now I am standing beside her chair, about to kiss her. Aunt Tamar? Aunt Tamar? But she doesn't hear me, and I look to my mother for guidance. My mother shrugs and gets up to go out the door as if pressing matters were calling her. I now know that it is Aunt Consuelo-Tamar's intention to cut me dead.

I catch my mother as she moves down the stairs. Why? I ask her. Why? My mother turns away, saying, She blames *you* for the Custody Trial. My mother says it quite easily. Is it because she too believes this? If so, how can we ever begin to know each other? I look back at Consuelo-Tamar sitting there in her black with the skeins of colored wool around her and I wonder if my mother or Aunt Consuelo-Tamar or anyone will ever know how

it all came to be . . . or if I would ever be able to tell them.
And if I did, would they understand and forgive me, so that I
in turn could forgive them and no longer be afraid . . . ?

At the edge of dawn I wake and try to remember my mother's
face, for I have been dreaming about her. But she comes to me
not at all. Instead, despair comes like a dark bird and resides in
my soul. Will it be here at daybreak, this silent messenger? Is
it to be here, close to me, always? Will I never be free?

Summer Night at Old Westbury

It is late at night and everyone is asleep except Sharkey. Soon
my bare feet will skim down the stairs along the velvety touch
of carpets, and although it is dark, each step of the way is known
to me, and soon I will be in the room with its dormer windows,
the room I know so well—the room where Winter waits for me.

Last week I ran right into Sharkey on my way back, but he
said Good morning as though there were nothing unusual about
meeting me in this way, in the dawn's light, running through
the halls of the Cottage. And nothing was said to Aunt Gertrude
about this, because if it had been reported, it would have been
the end of things for Winter and me.

How can I ever make them understand about Winter? For
Aunt Gertrude and the Little Countess and, yes, even Big Elephant keep right on paying little attention to the love I have for
him; and the more I love him, the further and further away I
get from the others.

Only my mother seems to understand, and she is all for our
getting married right away, even though I'm only sixteen. She
says there are some states where you can do this if your mother
says it's okay, and I'd do it in a jiffy, but Winter says it isn't
the right way to start our life together. He has a lot of plans for
the future when he will be an ambassador representing our country

in a faraway land and I will be by his side always. How I admire Winter's sense of time about things, because I don't have a sense of time about things at all. He's twenty now and has another year at Yale and he thinks it would ruin our whole future to get married so quickly. I still have two more years at Wheeler, but I'd marry him in a minute, no matter what.

Carol thinks Winter will be President someday. I can see that happening too, but it's hard for me to think ahead like that. What happens *now*—that is what is real to me—and what I long for most is to belong to him. But he says we should wait until we're married. Whenever I get impatient, over and over I sing to myself the song that was playing when Winter and I first danced together:

> *You are the promised kiss of springtime*
> *That makes the lonely winter seem long.*
> *You are the breathless hush of evening*
> *That trembles on the brink of a lovely song.*
> *You are the angel glow that lights a star,*
> *The dearest things I know are what you are.*
> *Some day my happy arms will hold you,*
> *And some day I'll know that moment divine,*
> *When all the things you are, are mine.*

This reassures me. For a day will come, and it will be our wedding day, and on the night of this day—we will belong each to the other forever and ever. . . .

It is raining now, and the sound on the roof of the Cottage pulls me for a moment away from him. But even as I listen to the rain and drift out of this place into the night's dark, I burrow closer. I love you, Pookie, I love you, he says—and in the darkness I know he is smiling. As we are touching the sound of rain sends us deeper into the night until the dark becomes light . . . and never again will I hear the sound of rain on a roof without remembering this.

Do Animals Know?

He's dead. But I don't believe it—all I can do is sit here in the chair I was sitting in before the knock came telling me to go to Miss Van Norman's office right away. Freddy will be arriving soon to drive me to Old Westbury Capital for the funeral—please help me, God. He was such a good driver, and Brünnhilde, even though it was antiquey, never gave him any trouble—he was really crazy about that car.

Winter is going to go with me, but Winter seems so unreal to me now, almost as if he doesn't exist, and he gets edgy about things sometimes, like when he thinks I'm giving too much attention to someone else. Not that I do, but in my mind, as I try to capture him, right now, Winter doesn't seem thrillingly possessive in the way he usually does. He never did like the idea that someone else had meant so much to me, and he won't understand either why now I can't go to Yale for that football game. But how can I go? Inside it's as if I had been with Johnny in Brünnhilde when it happened, but on the outside he'll think it looks as if everything were just the same—and it's not, it's not. How *can* that be? Maybe it's because I haven't been able to cry. When you come right down to it, I wish Winter weren't going to the funeral at all. I'll be worrying about him all the time instead of . . . instead of . . .

I think of death only when I connect it with my father—death was for him, but it isn't for anyone else. The idea I have of death is that it's a beckoning thing, way far off in some future, and it will only happen to people I don't know, and it will certainly never happen to me—no, never. So how could it have happened to him? How, God? How? Do animals know they are going to die? Maybe they're like me and think they will live forever; perhaps they trot along without ever getting the sense of it at all. I'm sure Fritz does.

It was Aunt Gertrude on the phone who told me—she already knew that Miss Van Norman had said I could leave school to go to the funeral. I've never been to a funeral before . . . a funeral . . . Then she said I'd have to get a black dress. I feel so terrible pestering on about that stupid black dress, and now that I'm going to get one it's to wear to Johnny Delahanty's funeral. Why, even when Naney goes on with the Aie-aie-aie!s and the When-I'm-in-my-graves, I never believe she can *really* be in a grave, much less *hers*, for to do that she would have to die first, and the Little Countess *can't* die! So if *she* can't die, how can *he*? None of it makes sense. But I keep going around and around, puzzling over it in that way, and I can't make myself stop. . . .

And then there's that war in Europe. One of us gives a news resumé every morning during breakfast so we hear about what's going on there, but it's all so vague, and then other things come up and we forget about it. Even last week—that blitz in London—I only thought about Aunt Toto for a minute, because she's already left London and she and my mother are going to rent a house in California and live in Beverly Hills. Uncle Harry got out in time too. I don't know where Consuelo-Tamar is, but she'll be all right wherever she is. . . .

What is war like? If we did have one here, Johnny would have had to fight in it, so would Winter and Albert Fox and all the other boys I know. Betty and I never even talk about it, because it couldn't happen here because war is like death—it only happens someplace else, in some other country, and to other people. It could never happen in America—to our country—to our people.

The Prince Friedel—what's he up to these days? And the sister, Baby—what's *she* doing in all this Hitler thing, I wonder? If my mother had married the Prince, why, now we'd be living in Germany and all goose-stepping around saying *Sieg heil!*

On the ground, everywhere, leaves are falling. In a few days he too will have fallen on the ground and into the earth, cold and alone . . . and I'll never ever be able to hold him in my arms again and say to him, I love you Johnny I love you Johnny I love you Johnny . . . Johnny

Seventeen Whole Years Old!

Anne Carter is my roommate this year, and last night she surprised me with a party. Yes! After lights out, from nowhere she whisked out fudge cookies, deliciously gooey, ginger ale too, and we sat on our beds toasting the morrow, my seventeenth birthday. We call our room L'Auberge and make it safe as can be by only bringing best things there, never moaning or groaning to each other about anything. Soon we heard Miss Van Norman on her nightly rounds stopping outside our door in the hall, but she didn't come in although we were *sure* she saw our flashlights from under the door—she must have known it was the eve of my birthday and the mischief we were up to couldn't do much harm. We held our breath to stop from giggling and she lingered outside, without a word, just for a minute and then continued on her way. Oh, we did have fun!

This morning in my mailbox there was a postcard from Aunt Gertrude. It said

Dearest Gloria—just think—today you are seventeen whole years old! Lovingly, Aunt Gertrude.

That's all it says. And I read it over and over again, trying to find some message in the words other than what's written on the card. What she wrote is so simple that it must be a code hiding the real meaning. But I still haven't been able to decipher it. She's really tough to get through to these days, and it's all because she doesn't want me to be in love with Winter. But at least she's invited Mr. and Mrs. Smith to have lunch at Old Westbury Capital. This little event is going to take place during the spring vacation, and—boy! it's going to be some lunch! And last summer Aunt Gertrude did let me visit his parents for the weekend at The Salt Box, their house in Jamestown, so that's an encouraging sign as well.

I really like Winter's father. He sends me books and writes me pages and pages of letters with thousands of sentences all cramped together, written in the blackest ink, but I can't make out his handwriting and it's very frustrating, because when I write back to him it's like trying to answer a letter from someone who's written to you in Chinese. And I worry that his letters are full of queries about my opinions of the books he's sent me—so it's a difficult situation all around.

. The weekend I visited The Salt Box their cook made the best lemon cake, and on top of the pale yellow icing she placed yellow roses from the garden dotted around in a most artful way. It took tons of organization to get so we could spend the night together, but Winter's very good at that, even if he almost fell off the roof doing it. There was no way of getting to the room I was in without going past his parents' room, so he climbed out a window onto a ledge after everybody had gone to sleep and came right over the roof and into my room. At dawn there was a flurry of birds singing—they started up all at the same time and woke us up. We lay there in each other's arms listening for a while, and then, just as suddenly as they had started, they stopped. And Winter dressed quickly and took off, back out the window onto the ledge, and I watched him climb out of sight over the rooftop. . . . Then we met for breakfast and said good-morning to each other just as if we hadn't been together ten minutes ago. Mr. Smith had some of the lemon cake left over from the night before—he really has a sweet tooth—and so do I, so I had some too.

Ever since that weekend, Winter and I have been working on a plan, and now that winter's here, all we need to make it come true is Big Elephant's assistance. And that's going to take some doing.

The Plan

Big Elephant is just like the Nurse in *Romeo and Juliet*. I told her, and I think it pleases her.

Here I am with Winter Austin Smith III in his rented car and we're on our way to.The Salt Box. Yes, it took some doing. We've just ensconced Big Elephant at the Minden Hotel, where she'll reside until Winter and I get back on Sunday. Up until the last minute I thought she would change her mind about going along with all this, because if anything goes wrong she'll be in boiling hot water. I don't want to even think what we'll be in. But *nothing* is going to go wrong. Aunt Gertrude and the Little Countess think Big Elephant and I are spending the weekend together at the Minden, puttering around Providence. And Big Elephant thinks Winter and I are going to spend the weekend with Mr. and Mrs. Smith at The Salt Box. And I think—it's a risky business all around. Of course Big Elephant doesn't know the house is closed up for the winter and that Winter's parents are all cosseted away in their house on Seventy-second Street. None of this is honest, I know, but I'm doing it anyway and telling a lot of lies hither and yon. But so did Romeo and Juliet. (Oh, well—I don't want to dwell on what happened to them.) Anyway, I think that's what got to Big Elephant — the romantic gist of it. Also—she may not be all that crazy about Winter, but Big Elephant does know he's steady and reliable. And he is. He is! He's *perfect*.

The Salt Box

It is silent here—no sound but logs in the fireplace burning through the house as steadily as the sound of rain on a roof of night. Time is this moment only, for the geography of memory has been lost. Dust sheets cover the furniture, but here in the living room they've been thrown aside, and sofa and chairs and this room have become our paradise. When we're hungry, Winter will go into the kitchen and return with a feast prepared with food picked up on our journey here. . . . Then I am alone, abandoned here in front of the fire, and I curl up and allow myself the luxury of missing him. This sofa has become a nest on the topmost branch of a tree where I'm safe and nothing can harm me—and soon he'll return to me.

Maybe later we'll take a walk around the marshes. Everything is frozen and drawn into itself—even the sun dial in the garden is hibernating. The burlap over the rose bushes puckers in the wind. His arm is around me and we will walk on up the road, past houses shuttered against the ice, leaning close to each other without speaking. As it darkens, candles will be lit, and by the fire, blankets will be spread out . . . because we can't stop touching each other. All through the night it will be so, for he will not abandon me again until the flames become coals and more wood is necessary. And while he is gone, I will trace each valley and hill of his face and the memory of his body as I lie here alone in the darkness. . . .

A Three-Act Play

There we were, all sitting in the dining room at Old Westbury Capital. I kept glancing around the table, because if I didn't keep my eyes on them they might all disappear in a puff of the Little Countess's cigarette. Mrs. Smith was close to Aunt Gertrude, the way I had pictured it, and there were the Little Countess and Mrs. Smith babbling away across the table at the same time. Oh, the competition was ferocious. After picturing it for so long, now that it was actually happening I found something unreal about it. Aunt Gertrude wore the usual ropes of pearls, and in her hat of white felt there was a feather of cadmium green, most appropriate for a country lunch in spring. In fact, everything about her manner was most appropriate, but by the time the crème brulée arrived, I knew. Appropriate though it might be, it was not appropriate enough for me. Because although she was friendly as friendly could be, it was not really friendly at all—there was something about us all sitting there that was like a scene in a play, and Aunt Gertrude was giving a real actressy performance.

It filled me with dread, because I knew now that she had absolutely no intention of taking seriously my wish of someday being Mrs. Winter Austin Smith III. Neither did the Little Countess, but I had known that before—before this charade embarked on the moment Mr. and Mrs. Smith and Winter walked through the front door of Old Westbury Capital all dressed up in their spring suits with best feet forward. I wanted to call out to them, Stop! Stop! Let's start over again—go back, back to the beginning, and have the lines different so the words come out right. But it was too late. And it had always been, even before they arrived—from the beginning. Too late! And Winter was sitting there happy as a clam, without a clue that it was all going awry, which made me livid. How could he not know?

Well, he found out soon enough. Here it is a week later and he's coaching me on things I must say to Aunt Gertrude, giving me line readings like It's not a cut-and-dried matter—those kinds of clichés that are all supposed to cleverly persuade her that she *must* give us a definite okay on future marriage plans. If I repeat just what he says, Winter thinks, it will be a cinch to get her to agree to a definite date for the announcement of our engagement. His methods are most professorial, and he teaches me as though I were a precocious infant trying to learn how to spell C-A-T. For one thing, he completely ignores the fact that Aunt Gertrude insists on having a coming-out party for me at The Castle at 871 Fifth after I graduate from Wheeler. Not that I wouldn't much rather marry Winter, but I also want to go to Bennington, because Miss Brown says they have a really good art

department there. But if Winter and I do get married soon—
well, I suppose I could go to the Art Students League in New
York instead.

I wish he'd lay off for a while and stop prompting me on
these hundreds of things to say to Aunt Gertrude. Most of them
I write down, clichés though they be, because Winter says they
have to go in a certain sequence and there are so many of them—
it's now as long as a three-act play, only my part in it is so small
I might as well be the understudy. Winter says I take every word
people say too seriously and that I should stop brooding about
things—yes, *brooding*—his exact word. Well, what I brood about
most is his choosing that word. It has a tingle to it I don't like.
Winter also says that people babble meaninglessly and I shouldn't
pay so much attention to what they say. Certainly his mother
babbles a lot . . . and now I'm beginning to think that maybe
sometimes he does too.

A Party at Meadowlands

My mother's all settled in with Aunt Thelma at 719 North
Maple Drive in Beverly Hills, and I'm going to visit them for
three weeks at the end of June!

Winter is at ROTC Camp in Watertown, but there's a lot
going on at Old Westbury with coming-out parties under tents
on lawns. And dancing that goes on until dawn, when scrambled
eggs with brandied peaches and champagne appear for breakfast,
on flowered tables beneath spreading trees in the fresh morning
light.

Aunt Gertrude let me go to Sandra Davenport's dinner at
Piping Rock. And afterwards Sandra's father made a toast, and
at the end of this toast he raised his glass again and said there
was a P.S. to it, because Mrs. Harriman had asked him to make
certain that everyone present would be sure to continue on to
Nancy Harriman's party at Meadowlands. Almost everybody there

had already been invited, but a few hadn't—certainly not me, as I was considered to be subdeb and subdebs did not go to debutante parties. But it was an opportunity too golden to miss, even if Aunt Gertrude did have a fit.

I camouflaged myself among the merry group and surged through the portals of Meadowlands—but then there was a slight hitch. Almost immediately one of the chaperones spotted me as the Impostor I was and made a beeline towards me, saying, Who are you and what are you doing here? I told her that I'd been at the Piping Rock dinner and Mr. Davenport had said we were all included in the invitation to go on to Meadowlands for Nancy's party. Why did I feel so guilty about it when it was the truth?

Then there was the question of my attire, which caused quite a stir. I had finally taken things into my own hands and had the Egyptian shop whip up a little number from a bolt of red and gold lamé according to my specifications. Lamé was a bit heavy for June, but it had a bare midriff which cooled things off a little. It was the most grown-up dress I had ever had and it had been kept in a box until now, hidden from everyone—especially Aunt Gertrude. All the boys wanted to dance with me, and two of them had the nerve to pinch the skin exposed by the midriff to see if it was real. Ha, ha—some joke! From time to time the chaperones would huddle together in conference, and for a while I had a sense of doom that they were all going to converge towards me en masse and ask me to leave. But it didn't happen. Instead, I met the most divine boy, called Dickie Dickenson—the kind of boy to go on walks over the moors with, and then come home and sit by the fire, drinking hot chocolate and talking about serious things. He goes to Williams and I'm *sure* he's going to call me, and if he does I'm going to see him again.

Once a week I go to Wissy West's house to roll bandages for the war in Europe. Long tables have been especially set up out on the loggia and we sit in rows on spindly gold ballroom chairs facing each other. Dozens of us have volunteered to do this, but no one talks much as we sit there rolling the bandages. It's a monotonous task and I wonder what it all means and then my mind starts to wander. . . .

All my things are ready to be packed for California—except for the red and gold lamé. Of course, everything got back to Aunt Gertrude, and now it's been whisked off the face of the earth. In its place is a white eyelet lace which I pretend to hate, but really it's very pretty. Now there's only one weekend left before I leave, and Aunt Gertrude is letting Freddy drive me up to Watertown to visit Winter—with The Constonce in attendance, naturally. Now that it's time to leave I almost wish I weren't going to California. Things here are starting to be grown-up, sort of, and it would be fun to talk to Dickie Dickenson again.

R.O.T.C.

Ever since I arrived here Winter is acting so strangely—as if he's not glad to see me. Even when he found a way to maneuver around The Constonce so that we could spend the night together, he still acted put out about it all. Maybe it's because he's found out that I'm not worthy of him. It's been a worry all along—a big worry—that he would find me out, and that when he did he would say that I wasn't good enough for him. But here I am— me. And no matter how hard I try, there's nothing I can do to change that. I keep smiling and trying to please him, but he doesn't smile back. Instead, he'll say something sort of sarcastic. If I make believe it's not happening, then maybe the tide will turn. And I do that—but it hasn't. And now he even says sarcastic things to me in front of The Constonce, and I'm still going around like Sweet Alice Ben Bolt. Oh! don't you remember Sweet Alice Ben Bolt? Sweet Alice, whose hair was so brown, who wept with delight when you gave her a smile and trembled with fear at your frown? But I'm not a poem. So what is happening?

I don't know what to think anymore. He said we're going

to play golf, only he knows I don't know how. So he said, I know, Dummy (he calls me that a lot these days), I know you don't know how, but you can at least make yourself useful by carrying my golf clubs—they don't have caddies around here. So here I am following him around the golf course lugging his dippy golf clubs and not doing it too well at that, because he keeps saying, No! not *that* one, Dummy, when I fumble around, not knowing one from the other. He looks like someone I don't know—Rex Harrison in that British movie, perhaps? He always did remind me of Rex in a vague way. Only this is not a movie, it's Winter and it's me, and although I'm here in Watertown on the golf course with him, I might just as well be on the moon. . . .

The Yellow Brick Road

Now that it's getting close to the time I'm going to leave, it all seems much more real to me that I'm going to have my mother all to myself—well, *almost*, because Aunt Thelma will be there. But I'll be staying with her for three whole weeks, day after heavenly day, in a real house instead of in a hotel somewhere, and I won't be a guest the way I usually am—it will be as though I belong there. I do have every right, don't I? To belong there? Because I'm not an Impostor. After all, she *is* my mother.

The more I think about all this, the more thrilling it becomes . . . and I can't wait to get on that yellow brick road leading right through the airport, right up onto the plane that will take me to her, my one and only mother. Yes, I too have a mother, and she will be waiting just for me when the plane lands and I continue on down the yellow brick road straight into her arms. But instead of the magic ruby shoes, I'll be wearing high-heeled black pumps and black fishnet stockings à la Alice Faye in *Rose of Washington Square*. And I don't care what Aunt Gertrude says— nothing, but nothing, is going to stop me from wearing the new black V-neck dress I bought with my own allowance. And even if I have to hold the black layered chiffon hat on my lap for the entire nine hours (imagine—it only takes nine hours from New York to Los Angeles), I'll do it, because I am determined to wear that too. When my mother meets me at the airport, I want to step off the plane and onto the yellow brick road looking really grown-up. Even The Constance, who is going to be glued to my side per usual throughout the entire trip, can't stop me. After all, if it comes to a tussle, I'm taller than she is, and stronger.

I haven't seen my mother since Christmas because she and Aunt Thelma have been getting settled in the house on North Maple Drive. Mummy says the house is divine and she's going to give a party for me soon after I arrive. And I have a date with Phil Kellogg the second night after I get there. I haven't seen him since I was thirteen, which means he hasn't seen me either. Will he be surprised! At least I hope so. I heard he almost married Jane Bryan—I sat through a movie she was in four times, so I really got a look at her, she's very pretty—but they didn't get married. Lucky me. Well—Emerald City, here I come.

No Room at the Inn

Well—Mummy didn't meet me at the airport after all, but she did send a car and chauffeur, and at least I had a chance to unpack and see my room and everything before I saw her, so maybe it was all for the best. She still sleeps late and it was eleven in the morning when we arrived, so considering the distances between places I do understand how she would have had to get up really early. And as it turned out, she was still sleeping when we got to the house on North Maple Drive. So was Aunt Thelma. But Wannsie wasn't, and it was nice to see her there waiting for us. It turns out there's no room in the house for The Constonce—*yippee!* She was unhinged about it, but what can she do. There simply is no room at The Inn, and that's that. So she's scurrying around like a chicken with its head cut off trying to find out which boardinghouse is the closest to 7 1 9 North Maple Drive. Well, I don't care where she goes, just so long as she takes her long list of instructions from Aunt Gertrude with her. Wannsie says everything is at the very least half an hour away from everything else—and that's by car. So it doesn't really matter which one The Constonce decides on, because any way you slice it, it'll take over half an hour to get here.

Wannsie says my mother will be up soon and we'll all have a late lunch on the porch overlooking the garden and the pool. I'm so excited to be here. Should I keep the black outfit on until I see her? Somehow it's not the same effect it would have been had she seen me in it coming on down the steps off the plane. But I'm going to leave it on anyway, even the hat. Why not!

The Invitation List

I've been here quite a few days now, but so far I haven't had the chance to see my mother alone. Whenever I see her, Aunt Thelma is around too, and it's hard to imagine one without the other. But I'll think of a way to get her off to myself, I just need time to maneuver it. The mornings are out, because they both sleep late, and then, once they are up, they come down the stairs together and spend most of the day lolling around in those same robes Wannsie keeps making for them. Aunt Thelma does needlepoint and, for a change of pace, knits. So does my mother, only not so much. Then at some point one of them will shuffle through the *Los Angeles Examiner* to the page where Louella Parsons's column is and whichever one has it in hand will read aloud the gossip, pausing now and then to make comments on this one or that one. Their tresses float down around their shoulders in the same rippling mass, only now they don't look as alike to me as once they did. Perhaps it's that I've seen more of them on this visit. Who's to say?

Aunt Thelma goes out almost every night with Edmond, as she pronounces it, in the French way, although it's really Edmund, Edmund Lowe. He has a mustache and is a very famous actor. He and Aunt Thelma have a lot of giggles together. Mummy doesn't have giggles with anyone but Aunt Thelma and Ketti Keven, but maybe there's a Maurice or a Roberto lurking around somewhere waiting in the wings to make his entrance. Time will tell.

The salad-and-cheese lunches go on for hours and hours, with a basket filled with breads and crackers, and with this there is usually beer from Carlsbad placed on ice in a crystal wine bucket. Wannsie does all the shopping at the Farmers Market and brings back mangoes for dessert whenever she can find them, because they're my mother's favorite.

Right now all of their energies are going towards the list they're putting together for the party they're giving just for me, and I sit listening goggle-eyed as names like Robert Stack are added under

Errol Flynn (I wonder if his Dad is still around?)—

Mr. and Mrs. Ray Milland—

Mr. and Mrs. Charles Boyer—

Mr. and Mrs. Reginald Gardiner—

and so on.

Then there's the Hedda Hopper question, which still remains unresolved. My mother says it doesn't seem right to send her an invitation when their first loyalty is to Louella, and Aunt Thelma will stomp her little pom-pommed foot and say *Shtotacoye!*

That's Russian for *what* is the meaning of this? and the Twins often resort to it when hard pressed. Then they'll both be silent pondering this dilemma, until my mother says, We don't want ruffled feathers, do we now? And they'll fall silent again, giving it more intense consideration. Finally Aunt Thelma, with her usual authority, decides the matter by saying, I think we *must* send her one, because, she adds logically, Hedda's bound to hear

Lolly is coming, and at least Hedda will know she was invited, and this way she'll have a graceful way out. They both stop frowning and my mother pencils Hedda Hopper's name under Louella Parsons's. Then at the same moment they both give a sigh of relief.

Tonight there's to be a party at Mr. and Mrs. Basil Rathbone's and we're going to it. I keep putting off having to wear the white eyelet—it's too babyish to bear. But if I don't wear that, what will I wear? If I get up enough nerve I'll ask my mother to lend me one of her dresses.

The second night I was here I begged my mother not to make me have The Constonce tag along on my date with Phil Kellogg. And guess what? She actually said that the idea of The Constonce going with me on a date was the most *ridiculous*—her exact word—*ridiculous* thing she had ever heard of. And boy, do I feel like a bird let out of a cage. Just watch me fly! Phil is so sweet and he's in love with me and sends me flowers and on one of the cards he wrote—

> *But oh! it was my third love*
> *That gave my soul to me.*

It's from a poem about what a first love gave, and what a second love gave (the second was Jane Bryan, I just *know*), and although he hasn't proposed yet, the third love must be—guess who? I can hardly believe it. But he is such a sincere person, I just have to.

Oh, and don't forget the Baroness Tamara de Lempicka Kuffner, Mummy was saying. She's fun and she does those amusing paintings. And then there's Veneta Oakie—

Is she related to Jack? I say.

Wife, Aunt Thelma says. But he's away a lot.

What a long list it's getting to be. And all those famous people will be coming right here to this house to meet *me*, for my mother has written the invitations out in her own hand:

Mrs. Reginald C. Vanderbilt
requests the pleasure of your company
at a cocktail party Saturday June 21st
in honor of her daughter
Gloria
719 North Maple Drive

It sounds just like a coming-out party. And now it's only a few days away, and I'm in the usual panic about what to wear. The Constonce is no help at all, and she sulks around in the most po-faced way—she even refused flatly to press my black V-neck dress. But who cares? I'll press it myself. Talk about pressed, *her* thin lips are pressed so tight together, all you can see is a lipless face walking around. Well, so what? I don't care what she reports to Aunt Gertrude—I'm having much too much fun to let her spoil things.

Thursday's Child

The most incredible thing happened. Edmond is taking Aunt Thelma to visit Mr. and Mrs. Victor McLaglen for a whole weekend at their ranch in the valley. And that includes Friday. That means my mother and I will be together for three whole days. Now all I can do is pray that Ketti Keven won't be around all the time, because if she is, I'll just never get to see my mother alone.

My mother says she may go and stay with Ketti Keven the weekend that Aunt Thelma is away. Please don't, Mummy, I say to her. My mother answers by saying, Well, maybe Ketti could come here instead and spend the weekend at Maple Drive. Yes—yes—yes! I say quickly—better that than the other.

Now it is Friday and Ketti is not expected to arrive until evening and I am standing here on the porch waiting for Mummy to appear—the table has been set for two, for my mother and I

are to have lunch together, and there will be no other guests. I had hoped to have her to myself for days and days and days, but I *will* have her to myself for hours and hours and hours, until dinner time anyway, so I have nothing to complain about—just this awful heat. Even here under the awning the sun pierces right through it, and it's so hot I want to scream. . . .

I went into the kitchen just now and asked Wannsie, Is she awake yet? Oh, yes, she said, Modom is up and should be down presently. When presently? I asked her. Soon—soon, she said—whatever that means. I walked back out onto the lawn and down to the edge of the pool and waited there with the sun coming down on me like rain.

But here it's still and quiet and it's as though the heat of night surrounds everything in view, for the leaves and the grass have stopped growing and the pool of aquamarine seems empty as we wait, suspended, for the door to open. And when it does it is my mother, far away, as she comes through the door and out onto the porch. She is in white, all white, and the robe around her floats like a gauze cloud. . . .

She pauses and looks out across the lawn but doesn't see me—she doesn't know I've been waiting for her—yes, for a long time. She doesn't know that I become her hand as it holds a fan of rice paper fluttering back and forth, fluttering the tendrils of her hair. She doesn't know that I am the breeze that cools her face. No, she doesn't know this—or anything about me at all. But soon she will, for soon I am going to tell her. I am going to skim across the green of the grass, and in my arms she will be held, but I must be careful not to suffocate her, I must be careful not to frighten her. . . .

She sees me as I run towards her—she waves her fan in greeting—but as I come closer I see that it's not my mother at all—it's Aunt Thelma. And I run past her into the house, but she stops me and says, What's the matter, don't cry, what's the matter? And she frowns and agitates the fan back and forth, as fast as it will go, to cool her face. Where's Mummy, Mummy,

Mummy? Where's Mummy? Oh, your mother . . . There was a change of plans at the last minute—Edmond isn't feeling well— your mother's gone away for the weekend, that's all. Aunt Toto sounded bored and quite put out put out put out. . . . Tell Wannsie we're ready for lunch now, and tell her I don't want the mangoes—to save them for your mother. She should be back Sunday or Monday.

Sunday or Monday or Tuesday or Wednesday, Thursday's child has far to go . . . and if I did see her on Friday or on any of those other days . . . whom would I see? Would my mother be there? Would anybody be there?

Epilogue, July 1941

Phil has driven me to Malibu, inside The Colony, to a house on the beach for a party celebrating the Fourth of July. Olivia de Havilland is here, and Maria Montez, and others I recognize but haven't met until this moment. Inside the house, although the rooms are small, it is cool. The walls are colored like the sea. It's the kind of house I would like to live in with my mother. Alone with her, here on this beach.

Now they are all gathering around a bonfire preparing to steam lobsters in seaweed, and ears of sheathed corn are to be placed on the coals beside them. A man who looks familiar but whose name I can't remember sits and plays a guitar, but no one is listening. Blankets are being carried out from the house to be strewn over the sand. Soon fireworks will be lit.

It is light still on the beach, and I walk away from Phil. I'm walking, but now I start to run. I run faster and faster, without looking back, so I don't know how far away I am from the bonfire and the crowd gathering around it. This is an endless beach and I can keep running, for the sand stretches as far as I can see. Faster I run—faster and faster—for this time I am not going back. This time I'm going to be free.

ILLUSTRATIONS

(All photographs not otherwise credited are from the author's private collection)

Back endpapers courtesy of Diane Wenger Wilson

ACKNOWLEDGMENTS

My loving thanks to Anne Hartwell, Betty Lewis Murray, John Morrison Fraser, Jr., Ellen M. Violett, Philip Kellogg, Anne Carter Grosvenor, Frederick Eberstadt, Nancy Martin Graham, Betsy Drake, and Gertrude V. Whitney Henry Conner for their time, memories, and love; to Isabel Eberstadt for her support and love from the first pages; to Jean Dunn for her devotion and patience in typing through the long hours of each day and often through the night as I wrote my manuscript—my deep appreciation; to Diane Wenger Wilson and Isabel De Silva for sharing their photographs for this book; to Cris Alexander for the inspired work he has done on each and every one. And, last but first, to my editor and publisher, Bob Gottlieb, who was with me every step of the way.

PERMISSIONS ACKNOWLEDGMENTS

A NOTE ON THE TYPE

The text of this book was set on the Linotype in Garamond No. 3, a modern rendering of the type first cut by Claude Garamond (c. 1480–1561). Garamond was a pupil of Geoffroy Tory and is believed to have based his letters on the Venetian models, although he introduced a number of important differences, and it is to him we owe the letter which we know as "old style." He gave to his letters a certain elegance and a feeling of movement that won for their creator an immediate reputation and the patronage of Francis I of France.

Composed by Maryland Linotype Composition Co., Baltimore, Maryland

Printed and bound by Halliday Litho, Inc., West Hanover, Massachusetts